ARISTOTLE AND BEYOND

Written over a period of thirty-five years, these essays explore the topics of causation, time, fate, determinism, natural teleology, different conceptions of the human soul, the idea of the highest good, and the human significance of leisure. While most of the essays take as their starting-point some theme in Ancient Greek philosophy, they are meant not as exegesis but as distinctive and independent contributions to live philosophizing. Written with clarity, precision without technicality, and philosophical imagination, they will engage a wide range of readers, including scholars and students of ancient Greek philosophy and others working on more contemporary analytical concerns.

SARAH BROADIE is Wardlaw Professor of Philosophy at the University of St Andrews.

ARISTOTLE AND BEYOND

Essays on Metaphysics and Ethics

SARAH BROADIE
University of St Andrews

CAMBRIDGE
UNIVERSITY PRESS

CAMBRIDGE UNIVERSITY PRESS
Cambridge, New York, Melbourne, Madrid, Cape Town, Singapore, São Paulo, Delhi

Cambridge University Press
The Edinburgh Building, Cambridge CB2 8RU, UK

Published in the United States of America by Cambridge University Press, New York

www.cambridge.org
Information on this title: www.cambridge.org/9780521870245

First published 2007

Printed in the United Kingdom at the University Press, Cambridge

A catalogue record for this publication is available from the British Library

Library of Congress Cataloguing in Publication data

Broadie, Sarah.
Aristotle and beyond : essays on metaphysics and ethics / Sarah Broadie.
p. cm.
Includes bibliographical references and index.
ISBN-13: 978-0-521-87024-5 (hardback)
ISBN-10: 0-521-87024-0 (hardback)
1. Philosophy. 2. Philosophy, Ancient. I. Title.

B72.B694 2007
190–dc22

2007016476

ISBN 978-0-521-87024-5 hardback

To my father, and to the memory of my mother

Contents

Preface

It is true that over a span of thirty-five years I have spent more time studying the philosophy of Aristotle than the philosophy of anyone, or anything, else. But Aristotle was not the original pull. It was my good fortune, at school and university, to have the chance to learn ancient Greek well enough to read Aristotle eventually; but my first encounter with him, I am not proud to say, was unexciting. It was an encounter, standardly the only one on offer when I read Greats at Oxford, with the *Nicomachean Ethics*. At the time this work seemed pedantic and prosaic by comparison with the Plato I knew from the *Phaedo*, the *Republic*, the *Theaetetus*, and the *Sophist*. However, literary and stylistic comparisons were not at that time the most pressing concern, because I was then discovering philosophy *per se*, and in particular acquiring an abiding fascination with the notion of causality. Hume's *Treatise* (although Hume is mentioned only twice in this volume) was a mighty stimulus. The first paper here, 'Affecting and being affected', responded to a causal question inspired by a passage in Plato's *Sophist* (248a–e): what stands behind the intuition that to know something is not *ipso facto* to affect it? Causal questions have shaped the majority of these papers, if one is allowed to include as expressing such influence the ones that discuss the idea of the *summum bonum* as good-maker (chapters 9, 10, and 11).

The first paper, as will be apparent, manifests the faith, at that time unpunctured, that 'linguistic' philosophy could light our steps. Perhaps because of the reasons why this faith where it still exists has long since been thrown on the defensive, it made sense for me quite early on to jump ship from philosophy as I first conceived it to be to the study, through the medium of an ancient language, of remote great philosophers. It was the interest in causality that led me, at Frederick Broadie's suggestion, to examine the concepts of change and agency in the laboratory of Aristotle's *Physics*. Then came an outside invitation to do work on Aristotle's *Ethics*; and, in short, I was fortunate to live long enough to realise the greatness of this material too. Plato and Aristotle remain perpetual inspirations because of their quest for precision in non-mathematical conceptual thinking, and because of the depth, fullness, vitality, and universal interest of the ideas the precision subserves.

Acknowledgments

Chapters 1–9 have been published elsewhere, and are reprinted here with virtually no alteration. Chapters 1 and 2 appeared in *Mind* (as by Sarah Waterlow): respectively, *Mind* 79 n. s., 1970, 92–108, and 83 n. s., 1974, 372–87; chapter 3 in *The Journal of Ethics* 5, 2001, 21–37 (under the title 'From Necessity to Fate: a Fallacy?'); also in *Perspectives on Greek Philosophy: S. V. Keeling Memorial Lectures in Ancient Philosophy* 1992–2002, ed. R. W. Sharples, Aldershot, 2003, 127–41; chapter 4 in *Philosophical Papers* 31, 2002, 117–43; chapter 5 in *Metaphysics, Soul, and Ethics in Ancient Thought*, ed. R. Salles, Oxford, 2005, 81–93; chapter 6 in *Philosophical Topics* 15, 1987, 35–49 (under the title 'Nature, Craft and Phronesis* in Aristotle'); also in *Biologie, logique et métaphysique chez Aristote*, eds. D. Devereux et P. Pellegrin, Paris, 1990, 389–403; chapter 7 in *Proc. Aristotelian Soc.* 101 n. s., 2001, 295–308; chapter 8 in *The Blackwell Guide to Aristotle's* Nicomachean Ethics, ed. R. Kraut, Oxford, 2006, 342–61; chapter 9 in *Virtue, Norms, and Objectivity*, ed. C. Gill, Oxford, 2005, 41–58. Chapter 11 is adapted from 'Aristotle's Elusive *Summum Bonum*', in *Human Flourishing*, eds. Ellen Frankel Paul, Fred D. Miller, Jr., and Jeffrey Paul, Cambridge, 1999, 233–51.

CHAPTER I

Affecting and being affected ⸱

I INTRODUCTION

What is it for one thing to affect or to act on another? Examples come to mind: bending a bar of iron, moving a ball, melting wax. But there are other relationships one can have with an iron bar: one can also look at it, think about it, want it, approach it. Are not these too kinds of doing to it? We might say: even thinking about something is treating it in a certain way. Yet we should hardly admit that thought, sight, desire, and approaching affect or act on their objects. If we want to say that these are ways of treating things, then we have to say that not all cases of treating things are cases of affecting them.[1] To put it in the formal mode: not every transitive verb 'φ', i.e. not every verb 'φ' with active and passive voices, is such that '$x \varphi s\, y$' entails 'x acts on or affects y'. Let us call the values of 'φ' for which this entailment does hold, affective verbs, and those for which it does not, non-affective. Now the question of this paper is: what are the logical characteristics of affective, as opposed to non-affective, verbs? Or to put it in the material mode, using the term 'operation' neutrally: what are the logical characteristics of affective as opposed to non-affective operations?

The question is not: how do we *know* that thinking about something, or wanting it, does not affect it and that melting it does do so? – as though perhaps we cannot be sure of this. I am going to assume that we are able to distinguish correctly between affective and non-affective operations. The inquiry is simply into the formal features that constitute them one or the other.

---

[1] This is not to deny that, e.g., looking at something might contingently result in affecting it. For instance, looking at someone might cause him to blush, or to freeze immobile. The point is, that looking at, wanting, approaching, etc., carry no (conceptually) necessary implication of affecting their objects. ('Necessity' throughout this paper refers to conceptual or analytic necessity.)

Some more examples of affective verbs: 'to stretch', 'to bruise', 'to shake', 'to heat', 'to cure', 'to calm', 'to compress'. Let us call this list A. Examples of non-affective verbs: 'to remember', 'to mention', 'to learn', 'to understand', 'to love', 'to miss', 'to outgrow', 'to precede'. Let this be list B.

All the affective verbs so far mentioned are verbs of changing: i.e. for these values of 'φ', '$x \varphi s\, y$' entails 'x changes y'. But it is a mistake to identify changing with affecting. To affect a thing is either to change it or to keep it the same, in some respect. For instance, if you hold a hydrogen balloon to the ground, this affects it no less than if you had pulled it to the ground. Hence we should add to list A such verbs as 'to hold back' and 'to keep rigid', which imply prevention from change.

To say that affecting a thing is either to change it or to prevent it from changing does not help much to answer the question we have raised. For now the question rephrases itself as: what are the distinguishing marks of changing and keeping the same, as opposed to other sorts of operations? The answer cannot be in terms of changing and unchanging truth-values. That is, it cannot be right to say: 'φ' is a verb of change if '$x \varphi s\, y$' entails that some proposition is now true of y that was not true before, and 'φ' is a verb of keeping the same if '$x \varphi s\, y$' entails that some proposition is still true of y that was true before. This lets through too much. Notoriously, if Phaedo outgrows Socrates, Socrates need not have changed; yet a new proposition is true of Socrates, namely that he is shorter than Phaedo. Again, if Phaedo keeps his eye on Socrates, it is true of Socrates that Phaedo is looking at him and that Phaedo was looking at him before; yet in doing this, Phaedo does not prevent Socrates from changing in any respect.

In what follows, I have been able to give only necessary, not sufficient conditions for a verb's being affective. These necessary conditions emerge from considering the following questions: (1) What logical characteristics must the object of an affective verb possess? (2) What are the logical features of affections, or the properties that things get through being affected? (3) What is the basis of the relation between an affective verb and the verbs which are its contraries? The meaning of contrariety between transitive verbs is explained later. These questions take up the next three sections of the paper. It will turn out, I think, that none of the verbs in list B fits the resultant conditions. However, there is one distinct class of non-affective verbs which do fit them, thus showing them not to be sufficient conditions. In the last section, I discuss this class of verbs and point, though vaguely, to what it is that marks them off from affective verbs.

II THE OBJECT OF AN AFFECTIVE VERB

(a) Affecting a thing includes changing it in some respect and keeping it the same in some respect. Now one can only keep something the same in a respect in which it could change. For instance, one cannot keep a horse equine. Therefore an object can be affected only insofar as it can change. Now change, and therefore affection, can happen only to things that exist. (So existence itself is not a property with which things can be affected. 'To create', 'to destroy', 'to keep in existence' are therefore not affective verbs, although they are in some ways like them.) We thus have the following argument against some of the verbs in list B above: something can be mentioned, loved, missed, thought of, desired, although it does not exist. Hence to mention, to love, etc. something, is not to affect it, and these verbs are non-affective.

(b) If 'φ' is an affective verb, given the truth of 'x φs a C', it must be possible to answer the question 'Which C?' And if x φs y, where 'φ' is affective, it must be possible to answer questions of the form 'Is y P or not P?' for all applicable values of 'P'. In other words, what is affected must be a particular thing and a fully determinate thing. Indeed both these requirements, I believe, follow from the requirement that what is affected must exist. This condition, like the existence condition, rules out some of the verbs in B, but none of those in A, from being affective. One can want a child, love a good comedy, think of a sunset, without there having to be answers to the question 'Which?'; and without there having to be answers to all possible questions about the nature of what is wanted, loved, thought of. The same is true of mentioning.

(c) Another characteristic of the verbs already ruled out in (a) and (b) is that for these values of 'φ', 'x φs –' is an opaque context. Though all Cs be D and x φs a C, it does not follow, for these values, that x φs a D. Again, if x φs y and $y = z$, it does not follow that x φs z. Now it seems clear that the context 'x affects –' is not opaque; that whether or not a thing is affected does not depend on the aspect under which it is considered. If all Cs are D and x affects a C, then it affects a D. Similarly, 'x affects y and $y = z$' is conclusive grounds for 'x affects z'. None of the verbs in list A gives rise to such opaque contexts as we are considering.[2] And it can be shown that if the schema 'x affects –' is not opaque, any schema that implies it is not opaque either. That is to say, when 'x φs –' implies

---

[2] This statement is qualified in the last paragraph of this section.

'x affects –', i.e. when 'φ' is affective, '$x\,\varphi$s –' is not opaque. For suppose the opposite, that 'φ' is both affective and opaque. If it is affective, then '$x\,\varphi$s y and $y = z$' is conclusive ground for 'x affects y and $y = z$'; and this is conclusive for 'x affects z'. But if it is opaque, '$x\,\varphi$s y and $y = z$' does not imply '$x\,\varphi$s z'. Now it could be that we have no reason to think that x affects z unless we have reason to think that $x\,\varphi$s z. But as '$x\,\varphi$s y and $y = z$' by itself is no reason for the latter, by itself it is no reason for the former. So given '$x\,\varphi$s y and $y = z$', we cannot conclude to 'x affects z'. So this proposition both is and is not conclusive ground for 'x affects z'. Thus, any verb 'φ' such that '$x\,\varphi$s –' is opaque, is not an affective verb.

(d) The conditions above, that the grammatical object of an affective verb must designate an existent, particular and determinate, and that it must be intersubstitutable with extensional equivalents, only rule out about half the verbs mentioned in list B. Another argument is possible, which perhaps rules out more of them but which is weaker in other ways; it is as follows: 'Many of the operations of list B can take as objects abstract entities such as propositions, concepts, rules, the meanings of words. Such things may be known, learnt, understood, etc.; they can even be loved. But abstractions cannot be said to be subject to change, and therefore not to affection. So to know, to learn, to understand, etc. is not to affect. Further, positions in space and time such as point A14 on the grid and midnight 3/11/1941 are a kind of abstraction: yet they can be preceded and approached. Hence these verbs too are not affective.' The main weakness of this argument of course is its reliance on 'abstract entities'. Whether or not there are such things, our ideas of them are not solid enough to build on. Is it right, for instance, to lump together apparently quite different things such as concepts, dates, and legal systems without more ado? And the assertion that abstractions cannot change itself needs as much proof and explanation as the conclusion it is supposed to prove and explain, namely that 'to learn' and so on are not affective verbs. As it stands, this argument is of little use.

Before going further, we should note the fact that the same verb may be affective and non-affective in different contexts. For instance, 'carve' is surely affective in 'he is carving a stone', but not in 'he is carving a statue', for here the carving creates the statue not affects it. 'He threw a grenade' implies that the grenade's position was changed, but 'he threw a lob' does not imply that he affected, rather that he produced a lob. Again, there is 'x cured this man' and 'x calmed this stream', as opposed to 'x cured this man's arthritis' and 'x calmed a storm'. In the two latter, what was cured or calmed was thereby destroyed. A different type of case is 'he is carving a battle-scene', as opposed to 'he is carving a stone'. The former may be true although there is no answer to the question 'Which battle-scene?' or to, say, the question 'Is it set in Germany or not?' Anselm Müller pointed out to me another sort of case: '*x* has swollen the number of cars on the road', '*x* has lowered the price of oil', as opposed to sentences like '*x* has swollen the balloon', '. . . has lowered the bucket', where the verbs are certainly affective. In the first pair of sentences, they are not, by (c) above. For suppose that the price of oil = $35 a barrel (I am assuming that this will pass as an identity statement). 'He lowered the price of oil' does not imply 'he lowered $35 a barrel'. And if the price of oil = the price of tea, the first sentence does not imply 'he lowered the price of tea'. Similar examples are: '*x* changed, or affected, the colour of the walls', '*x* changed the direction of the telescope'. Here even 'change' and 'affect' turn out to be non-affective. If there is any force in the argument of (d) above, it can be applied here too: the verbs in 'he lowered the price', 'he changed the colour' are non-affective because the grammatical objects designate universals, abstractions. (d) would also show that 'twist' is non-affective in 'he twists the meaning of "republic"'; whereas it is affective in 'he twists a bit of putty'.

III AFFECTIONS

If a verb '*φ*' is affective, there corresponds to it a property or set of properties with which things are affected when they are *φ*-ed. Let us call these affections. Examples of affections are: straightness, degrees of curvature, degrees of length, motion, colours. I shall now set out some logical features of affections. In this way we reach a necessary condition for being an affective verb: a verb is affective only if there corresponds to it a property or set of properties with these features.

(i) An affective verb is *necessarily* connected with a certain affection or set of affections. For example, if *x* straightens *y*, necessarily *y* is straight. If *x* heats *y*, necessarily *y* has one of a set of different possible temperatures. If *x* sets *y* in motion, *y* is, necessarily, moving in relation to something. This is not to say, of course, that there is any one referent in relation to which *y* must move, if it is set moving.

(ii) If '*φ*' is affective, and the corresponding affection is *F*-ness, then if *x* *φ*s *y* so that *y* is *F*, *y* would not have been *F* if, under the circumstances, it had not been *φ*-ed. Affecting a thing makes it different in some way: not necessarily different from what it was before, since not all affecting is change, but different from what, under the circumstances, it would have been had it not been affected. If something is changed to being F, it was not-F before and would have remained not-F if it had not been changed. And if it is kept F, that is, prevented from becoming not-F, it follows that it was going to become not-F and would have done so but for being prevented. Just as x must be not-F if it is to be changed to F, so it must be going to be not-F if it is to be kept F.

For instance, when the affective verb corresponds to a single affection, as 'cure' does to health: if x cures y, y is healthy, and would not have been healthy if, under the same circumstances, it had not been cured. If x holds y rigid, then y is rigid and would not have been if not so held. Now for cases where there is a set of several possible affections: if x warms y, y is warm to some degree, and although it might have still been warm if, *ceteris paribus*, nothing had warmed it, it would not have been so to the same degree. Or if it would have been so to the same degree, it would not have been to the same extent: less of it would have been that warm. Again, if x sets y moving, y is moving relatively to something, and would otherwise have been at rest in relation to that thing, although it might still have been in motion relatively to something else.

Let us put (i) and (ii) together. If 'φ' is affective, there is some property F-ness such that necessarily: if x φs y then y is F or is F to some degree or extent or relatively to something, etc.; and if under the same conditions y had not been φ-ed at all, it would have been not-F, or F but not to the same degree, extent or relatively to the same thing, etc. Let us call this proposition SI. It is important that the counterfactual supposition in SI is 'if y had not been φ-ed at all', not 'if y had not been φ-ed by x'. If the latter were the supposition, SI would be false. For suppose that $x \neq z$ and that x and z both simultaneously give y a push, setting it in motion, relatively to m, say. Suppose, as is possible, that the action of each by itself would have been sufficient to move y. Then x sets it moving: but if, *ceteris paribus*, x had not done so, still y would have been moving, relatively to m, through the action of z – not with the same velocity, but still moving. Only if nothing had moved y, would it have been at rest.

Now let us see whether all the affective verbs in list A above meet this requirement SI, and then whether SI is strong enough to rule out non-affective verbs. For 'to stretch', 'to bend', 'to compress' in A, there are degrees of length, curvature, pressure. For 'to move' there are different positions or degrees of place. 'To shake' can be explicated in terms of degrees of vibration. For 'to calm' and 'to melt', there are calmness, softness and liquidity, which admit of rough degrees. There are even degrees of bruises. If y is bruised, it has more or worse bruises than it would have had otherwise. Again, if y is held back, necessarily it is in some position which it would not have been in had it not been held back. To take some more examples of affective verbs: 'erode', 'push', 'cut up', 'cook', 'distort'. The object eroded is a certain shape and size and would not have been that shape and/or size if it had not been eroded. That which is pushed is either in motion or under pressure, and would otherwise have been at rest or under less pressure. That which is cut up is now in more pieces than it would have been: that which is cooked is now less raw than it would have been. There is no positive name for the affection things get through being cooked, apart from the participle 'cooked': however, this affection is a distinguishable, identifiable state, and if we coined a word for it, the word could be defined ostensively. The same is true of 'distort', which is affective in certain contexts;[3] there is no name for the affection, apart from 'distortedness'. But again the affection can be distinguished and pointed out. Doing this involves knowing not only what the object is like now, but also what its natural or original shape was or should be. Distortedness is in this respect unlike health or lengths or degrees of pressure.

But S1 as it stands is also satisfied by non-affective verbs. For instance, if x knows or loves y, then necessarily y is familiar or dear to x, and would not have been if nothing had known or loved it. If x approaches y, y is some distance from x, and if, *ceteris paribus*, nothing, and hence not x, had approached it, it would have been a different distance from x. But if 'being dear to x', 'being three miles from x', etc. are names for *affections* which y gets through being loved or approached, we shall have to conclude that 'love', 'approach', etc. are affective.

Again, for many values of 'φ', affective or not, 'x φs y' necessarily implies 'y is being φ-ed'. For example, if something heats y, it is being heated; if something learns it, it is being learnt. And if nothing had heated or learnt y, y would not have been being heated, learnt.

Again, for many values of 'φ', affective or not, 'x φs y' necessarily implies 'y has been φ-ed'.[4] For example, if something moves y, it has been moved, if something observes or thinks about y, it has been observed, etc. And, it would seem, if nothing had moved or observed it, it would not be something which has been moved, observed: the properties of having been moved, having been observed, would not belong to it.

[3] Cf. 'twist', section 2 ad fin.
[4] Cf. Kenny, 1963, ch. 8, on performance verbs and activity verbs.

Someone may want to say that *being learnt*, or *heated*, *having been moved* or *observed*, *being dear to x*, etc., are not genuine properties: S1, one might say, must be interpreted as referring only to real properties, and then these ones present no difficulty. But of course this is no solution unless we are also told the difference between 'real' properties and others. I am using 'property' to mean anything designated, indicated, denoted, by a predicate expression. In this sense these are perfectly good properties, and show S1 as it stands to be too weak.

I shall answer these difficulties, in the reverse order, by presenting some further logical features of affections.

(iii) An affection, it seems to me, is a property which something can lose once it has it. This of course, says more than that it is a property which something has contingently. For example, it is only contingent that Tom is a war veteran: it is by no logical necessity that he went to the war and survived it. But having done so he is, necessarily, a war veteran for the rest of his days. Affections, on the other hand, can cease to belong. For instance, something is kept rigid say for ten minutes: there is no logical reason why it should not have been kept rigid for only five; in which case it would, *ceteris paribus*, have become bent, thus losing the affection. And a change, I think, can always be repeated; which implies that if y is once changed to being F, it can return to being not-F.

But the property of having been φ-ed, whatever the value of 'φ', is like being a war veteran or being Tom's widow: once something has it, it must stick. If x moves y, then y is, necessarily, something which has been moved, and cannot cease to be so. The property is fixed, just as the past is fixed.

If $x \varphi$s y, y has the property of having been φ-ed. But it is only by an equivocation that we can think that y would not have had this property if nothing had φ-ed it. It is true that if nothing had ever φ-ed it, it would not have had the property. But it might have had the property even if nothing had φ-ed it now. If it had ever been φ-ed before, it would still have the property now, whether or not anything φs it now. But in S1 above, what is meant is of course that (for affective 'φ') if $x \varphi$s y, y has some property now which it would not have had now if nothing had φ-ed it now, i.e. when x does.

Thus, even when 'φ' happens to be affective, the property of having been φ-ed is not an affection. So although, e.g., 'to learn' carries *having been learnt* with it, this does not mean in the least that 'to learn' is affective.

(iv) An affection is not tied to any single operation. For instance, if y is straight, this may be because at that instant something straightens it, or because something is keeping it straight. If it is 30° hot, this could be because it is being kept at 30° or because it is being heated and has just reached that point, or because it is being cooled. In short, if *F*-ness is an affection, there is no single operation φ such that '*Fy*' necessarily implies 'something φs *y*'. It is clear, then, that the property of being φ-ed, whatever 'φ' may be, is not an affection: for if *y* is being φ-ed, necessarily something φs it.

Here I would add that as well as being independent of any one particular operation, affections, or at least some of them, are independent of affective operations altogether. That is, something can have an affection *F* although nothing affects it so that it is *F*. A branch grows curved – do we want to say that something is changing its shape to that curve, or keeping it that way? These phrases are appropriate not when it follows its natural bent, but when, say, a weight pulls it into a distorted shape, or when a rigid frame holds it. Again, a moving body in free space continues its motion, although nothing moves it. Its motion stays the same, although nothing keeps it the same, and its position changes although it is not being changed.

In saying that something may be *F* although nothing makes or keeps it so, I do not mean that it is *F* independently of all conditions. There must be causally related conditions without which the body would not continue to move, etc. But these are not agents that move it. This conflicts with Hume's remark, *Treatise* Book I, part III, sect. XIV, that there is no logical difference between efficient and other causes. For if not, we ought to be willing to say of the free space, without which the body would not move, that it moves or keeps it moving, i.e. is an efficient cause of its motion – in the same sense in which one says that a horse keeps a cart moving.

(v) Finally, if one subject φs *y* so that *y* has a certain affection, *y* would have had the same affection if a different subject had φ-ed it, under the same circumstances, and in the same way. For example, if *x* heats *y* or raises *y* in relation to *A*, *y* has a certain temperature, is a certain distance above *A*. And if *z*, not *x*, had heated and raised *y* in the same way, the same amount in relation to the same thing, *y* would have had exactly the same temperature and position. This principle, that the same affection can arise through the action of different subjects, or agents, is like, or perhaps in the end the same as, the principle that an effect is logically independent of its cause.

But suppose *x* loves or knows *y*, so that *y* is dear or familiar to *x*, or rates *y* high relatively to *A*, so that *y* is worth more to *x* than *A*. If *z*, not *x*, had been the subject and had loved, known y equally much, rated it relatively to the same thing, y not only would not but could not have had the properties it gets when x is the subject. When x is the subject, y is dear to x; when z is, y is dear to z. Again, if x approaches y, y is a certain distance from x, which it would not have been otherwise *ceteris paribus*. But if, *ceteris paribus*, z, not x, had approached y, from the same point, the same amount, etc., y would not have been that same distance from x. Hence, being dear to x, and so on, are not affections of y, although y necessarily gets these properties if it is loved, etc.

It is true of course that whether x or z loves y, y has the property of *being dear to something*. But the point is that it would not be the same something. Contrast this with genuine affections, which can also be described indefinitely. X heats y so that y has some degree of heat, and if z, not x, had done what x does, y would again have had some degree of heat: the *same* one.

If we add these last points to S1, the result is:

If 'φ' is affective, there is some property F-ness, such that:

(1) necessarily, if x φs y then y is F or F to some degree, etc. and would not have been so then if, *ceteris paribus*, nothing had φ-ed it then;

(2) once something is F or F to some degree, etc., it can cease to be so;

(3) 'y is F' or 'y is F to some degree, etc.' does not logically imply 'something φs y';

(4) if y is F or F to some degree, etc. when x φs it, it would have had the same property if z, not x, had φ-ed it as x φs it, conditions being the same.

Let us call this S2.

I think it is clear that each verb in the original list A is associated with a property such as S2 lays down. To take only one example (as most of the cases seem obvious), if x holds y back, necessarily y is in a place which it would not have been in otherwise, *ceteris paribus*; once y is in this place, it can leave it; that y is in it does not entail that anything is holding it back; if z had held it back, not x, *ceteris paribus*, it would have been in the same place. Other intuitively affective verbs such as 'cleanse', 'injure', 'push', 'discolour', 'starve', 'moisten' also satisfy S2. So do the psychological verbs 'depress', 'reassure', 'frighten' when they are so used that the subject refers to the cause of fear, depression, etc., not to its object, as in 'Tom depressed me with remarks about the coming revolution' and not as in 'The coming revolution depressed me'. For we may treat the properties: being in low spirits about A, . . . about B, . . . about C, etc., analogously to the properties: being in motion relatively to A, . . . to B, . . . to C, etc. Just as the latter set is necessarily connected with the verb 'set moving', so the former set is with the verb 'depress'. Now if x depresses y, y is low-spirited about something, and to some degree, and would not have been low about the same thing, to the same degree, if nothing had depressed him then. Once low in this way, y can cease to be so. Y can be thus low although nothing at the moment depresses him, causes the depression: for instance if something has earlier depressed him, and he is still under the effects. Finally, if z, not x, had depressed y about the same thing, to the same extent, y would have been in the same state.

None of the verbs in list B seems to carry with it a property that fits the requirements of S2. They carry properties that fit some but not all the conditions in S2. For example, if x approaches y, necessarily y is in space: if x understands y, necessarily y is intelligible. But y would still have been in space or intelligible even if not approached or understood. Again, if x thinks of y, precedes y, wants y, y is necessarily in x's thoughts, after x, desirable to x, and would not have been so if nothing had thought of it, etc. But y would not have had these properties if z and not x had been the subject instead. I can think of no properties associated with these verbs that fulfil all the conditions. Nor can I find any for other intuitively non-affective ones such as 'study', 'surround', 'contain', 'outdistance', 'own', 'desert', 'lack', 'need', 'despise', 'resemble'.

What about 'frighten', 'depress', 'reassure' when their subject term refers not to the cause but to the object of the emotion? It seems that just as the object of affecting must exist (see section II) so must the subject. 'His poverty depresses me' surely does not imply that *it* affects me, since this statement can be true even if he is not poor. And applying S2 confirms that the verb here is not affective. If his poverty depresses me, the property that applies to me and would not have applied otherwise is: being in low spirits about his poverty. But first: 'I am in low spirits about his poverty' necessarily implies 'his poverty depresses me' (against (3) of S2; compare this with the case when the subject is the cause, not object, of depression). Secondly, I could not and so would not have had *this* property if not his poverty but something else had depressed me (against (4) of S2).

Negations of verbs are not affective, by both S2 and S1. If x does not injure y, y need not be any different from what it would have been if it had not not been injured. If it had not not been injured, it would have been hurt. And it may still be hurt even if x does not injure it – say, if something else does. Hence, 'avoid injuring', 'fail to injure', are not affective either.

So far I have said nothing about verbs that take both a direct and an indirect object, such as 'explain', 'teach', 'sell'. If *x* teaches *z* to *y*, it cannot be that *z* is affected. But it seems reasonable to say that *y* is affected by being taught something. So we need to analyse this in such a way as to exclude *z* from being affected but to allow that *y* is. In different words: we need to show that the verb phrase 'to teach – to someone' is not affective and that the phrase 'to teach something to –' may be. I have not been able to show this properly. The most I can say is this: suppose that '*y* is ψ-ed' entails '*y* is φ-ed'. And suppose that 'φ' is non-affective. Then, unless there are independent considerations, we have no reason to think that 'ψ' is affective. For example, '*y* is taught', in the sense in which French is taught, implies that *y* is learnt, and '*y* is explained' implies that *y* is understood. But (by S2) 'learn' and 'understand' are non-affective. So we have no reason to think that 'teach', in this sense, and 'explain' are anything but non-affective, unless there are further reasons. This leaves it open whether being taught, in the other sense, and being explained to, are ways of being affected. 'Teach' as in 'teach a pupil' certainly satisfies S2; the relevant property is *learning*, and the different objects of learning may be treated as different modifications of the same property. Cf. above on 'being low-spirited'. If *x* teaches *y* something, then *y* learns something, which he would not have learnt then, *ceteris paribus*, if not taught then. He can learn and then cease to learn it. That he learns it does not entail that anyone teaches him. And if *z*, not *x*, had been the teacher, *y* would have learnt it just the same.

I shall end this section by drawing out one consequence of S2. By (1) in S2, affecting something makes a difference to it: changing it makes it different from what it was, keeping it the same makes it different from what it was going to be. And (4) amounts to the assertion that if 'φ' is affective, the property *y* gets through being φ-ed is the same, regardless of the agent. It follows that, for affective 'φ', if *y* is φ-ed by whatever agent, then *y* must have lacked or been going to lack the very same property. Affecting something is like stopping a gap; the gap is the same, no matter what puts in the filling. Whatever heats *y* to 30°, *y* must have lacked that temperature before, and whatever keeps it in place P, *y* must have been going to go elsewhere. But if *x* outgrows *y*, *y* must have lacked one property, viz. being smaller than *x*; while if *z* outgrows it, it must have lacked another, being smaller than *z*. If *x* forgets *y*, *y* must have been familiar to *x*, but *this* does not follow from *z*'s forgetting it. Thus if you coil a rope, a necessary condition is met for you or anyone else to straighten it; whereas if you enter London, this is no guarantee that anyone but yourself is logically in a position to leave it. I might throw a stick in order that you should be able to bring it back, but I cannot learn a date in order that you should be able to forget it.

IV   AFFECTIVE VERBS AND THEIR CONTRARIES

One can find another logical difference between affective and non-affective verbs by using the notion of contrary incompatible verbs. I say that 'φ' and 'ψ' are *incompatible* if and only if:

$$(x)(y)\ x\ \varphi\text{s}\ y \rightarrow\ \sim (x\ \psi\text{s}\ y);$$

and that they are *contrary* if and only if:

(1) $(x)(y)\ x\ \varphi\text{s}\ y \rightarrow\ \sim (x\ \psi\text{s}\ y)$, and:
(2) φ-ing something does not make it such that it cannot be ψ-ed, and vice versa. Thus 'kill' and 'cure' are incompatibles and not contraries, while 'cure' and 'injure' are contraries.

It is easy to think of contraries for the affective verbs in A; the contraries themselves need not be affective: 'heat' / 'cool', 'strengthen' / 'weaken', 'bruise' / 'leave intact', 'stop' / 'keep moving', etc. There are two main ways in which affective verbs have contraries.

Examples of the first are 'stop'/ 'set going', 'cure' / 'injure', 'moisten'/ 'dry'; of the second: 'heat' / 'cool', 'raise' / 'lower', 'slow down' / 'acceler-ate'. All these pairs are such that if a thing suffers one of the operations, this does not make it such that it cannot suffer the other. But the first lot are incompatible because they imply incompatible present predicates for their objects, and the second lot because they imply incompatible past predicates. That is: *x* cannot both moisten and dry *y*, because *y* cannot be both dry and wet. But *x* cannot both heat and cool *y*, because *y* cannot have been both cooler and hotter than it now is, i.e. have been at two temperatures immediately before.

It is obvious that, given an affective verb 'φ' and a verb 'ψ' contrary to it in either of these ways, not only is it impossible for the same thing to φ and ψ the same thing at once: it is also impossible for different things to φ and ψ it at once. For the incompatibility of 'φ' and 'ψ' rests on the incompatibility of the properties which they imply for their objects, and these properties are the same whatever the subjects. Contrast this with a pair of contraries such as 'beget' and 'conceive'. Let us assume that male and female are logically incompatible. The same thing cannot beget and conceive the same thing, not because the same object cannot be begotten and conceived, but because the same subject cannot be both begetter and conceiver.

Now since affections come in sets of contrary properties, we should expect every affective verb, every verb which imports an affection, to have, at least, one contrary verb importing a contrary affection. If such contraries do not always exist in language, we ought to be able to construct them. If the word 'expand' did not exist, then, given the word 'contract', we should have invented it. This means that for every affective verb 'φ' there should be a contrary 'ψ' such that the same thing cannot be both φ-ed and ψ-ed at the same time, whether by the same or different subjects.

The verbs in list B have some obvious contraries, but not ones that fit this condition. X and z can approach and leave, know and forget, hit (= *tuchein* in Greek) and miss, outgrow and fall short of, the same thing at the same time – as long as $x \neq z$.

It may be that 'understand' / 'make unintelligible' and 'see' / 'destroy' are incompatibles like 'moisten' / 'dry': that is, one might claim that nothing can be both seen and destroyed, etc., whether by the same or different subjects. But these are not contraries according to our definition. An object that is destroyed is put out of the running for being seen. I can only think of one case, though perhaps there are plenty, that really works for non-affective verbs: that of 'approach' and 'know to be unapproached' and the like, assuming that the second can count as one verb. If anything knows y to be unapproached, nothing can approach it. These are contraries, although funny ones, by our definition at least.

One might say that the contrariety between 'heat' / 'cool', 'moisten' / 'dry' is adjectival: they imply contrary properties (past or present) for the object. There is also adverbial contrariety, such as that between roasting and boiling, which achieve or can achieve the same result, but by contrary methods. The same object, the same part of it, cannot be roasted and boiled at once by one or several agents. Compare the adverbial contrariety of 'infer' / 'intuit', 'run to' / 'fly to', 'buy' / 'steal'. These non-affective operations again can achieve the same result, by contrary means. But provided that the subjects are different, they can be done to the same thing at the same time. For example, you steal the Hope diamond just as I sign the deed of purchase.

Finally, talking of adverbs, when 'φ' is affective, if anything is φ-ed moderately, nothing can φ it intensely at the same time, unless the agents are acting jointly; and if anything is φ-ed quickly it cannot also be φ-ed slowly. If x exerts intense pressure on y, and z exerts gentle pressure on it, this can only mean that they jointly, though unequally, produce a greater pressure than either does alone. It cannot mean that y is under both intense and moderate pressure, is under two degrees of pressure, at once. When 'φ' is not affective, this is not so, although of course even here the *same* subject cannot φ the same thing intensely and moderately. For instance: x loves y violently, z loves it mildly: it does not follow that y is more loved by the two together than it would have been by only one. Y is not necessarily dearer to both or to either than it would have been to one alone. Again, if 'φ' is an affective process-verb and x and z each begin φ-ing y at the same time, one cannot φ it fast and the other slowly. To say that something is heated both quickly and slowly would imply that it reaches the same degree of heat at an earlier and at a later moment, but without having lost that temperature in the interval. Of course x and z may heat it between them: that is, neither of them alone does what amounts to heating, but each helps to heat. And in that case, x may do its share of the work quickly and z slowly. But this is different. However, when 'φ' is not affective there is no such impossibility. Different subjects can, though the same cannot, outgrow, etc., y fast and slowly, beginning at the same time.

V   AFFECTING AND ALLOWING

I have not given a sufficient condition for affectivity. Here I shall discuss only one set of verbs which are not affective but yet satisfy the conditions that have emerged above. These are verbs of *allowing*, such as 'let fall', 'allow to bend', 'leave at rest'. 'Let fall' satisfies just the same conditions as 'lower', its affective counterpart. First, 'let fall' is not intensional except when 'lower' is and it cannot take an abstract entity for object except when 'lower' can. The verbs in 'x lets the bucket fall' and 'x lowers the bucket' both fulfil the conditions for affectivity in Part II, and in just the same way, and those in 'x lets the price fall', 'x lowers the price', are ruled out by them in just the same way. Secondly, both verbs satisfy S2 in Part III, and with reference to the same necessarily connected set of properties. Finally, 'let fall' has contraries 'let rise', 'raise', etc., such that nothing can let y fall if at the same time anything lets it rise, etc. Yet allowing something to be or become F is not affecting it so that it is F: it is rather the obverse of affecting it.

I think the difference between letting something be F and affecting it with F-ness is that the second is work, but not the first. Only it is rather obscure exactly what *work* is. But this much does seem clear: one can ask of work 'How long does it take, how much force or strength does it take, how much energy or effort does it take to do it?' These questions do not all always apply. The first does not when the work is necessarily something done instantaneously, and the third only applies when the worker is supposed to be a person or at least an animal. The important point is that the answers to all these questions vary with the subject of the work, or the worker. In general, a more powerful or able subject does the same work in less time and/or with less effort than a weaker one. What counts as power of course depends on what sort of work is in question.

The answers to 'How long, how much force, how much effort is needed to heat y a certain amount, to straighten y, to set y moving, etc.?' depend partly on the nature and circumstances of y, but also on the nature and circumstances of whatever the subject is supposed to be. The answers are different for different subjects and objects. And just the same is true for the questions 'How long, how much force, how much effort does it take to learn French, understand this equation, outdistance the runner ahead?' The answers depend on what the subject and the object are like.

I am not sure that one can even ask these questions about allowing: 'How long does it take, how easy is it to allow y to be F?' Allowing something to happen or be is not interfering with it when one might have done so, and not interfering with something is simply being out of its way. What constitutes out of the way depends on the kind of event or situation it is. It may take time, strength and effort to get out of the way, but not to be there. The questions 'How quickly, easily did x let y fall, allow y to get hot?' seem to make sense only if they are slightly twisted to mean: 'How easily, quickly did x get into a position to do so?' or: 'How easily, quickly did y, not prevented by x, fall or get hot?'

In any case, even if these questions can be asked in neither of these twisted senses, but in the same sense as 'How long did it take for x to heat y?', the answers do not depend on the nature of the subject x. No matter how able or strong x may be, y does not fall more quickly, stay still more easily when x allows it to, than when a weaker subject, z, does. Once x is out of the way, the ease and speed depend entirely on y itself and y's *other* circumstances.

There are thus two sides to affecting, only one of which I have treated fully. First, affecting is opposed to operations that make no difference to their objects, such as learning, approaching, etc. But as far as making a difference is concerned, affecting something so that it is F should be grouped with allowing something to be F. In either case, the object is F because of what the subject does: both affecting and allowing have an effect on the object. But secondly, there is the element I call work: affecting something makes a difference to it, but actively as opposed to passively. This distinction between operations involving work and ones that do not cuts across the distinction between having an effect and having no effect on the object. As far as work or non-passivity is concerned, moving something is to be classed along with learning something, and is to be contrasted with allowing the thing to move.

CHAPTER 2

Backwards causation and continuing

Although much attention has been given in recent years[1] to the topic of backwards causation, little if any has been paid to the concept of temporal continuing, which I hope to show is not only relevant to that topic but decisive for its concludings. Michael Dummett, indeed, in his fascinating 1954 paper showed himself aware that 'backwards causation' must square itself with temporal continuing. But little more seems to have been added since then. In this paper I shall argue that the temporal direction of causation is determined by the temporal direction of the continuing of events, and that as long as this is not clear, the argument for backwards causation looks sounder than it otherwise would. If my argument holds, it will follow that should there be no such concept as 'backwards continuing', neither will there be such a concept as 'backwards causation'.

The argument requires us to examine the relation between the temporal direction of continuing and the temporal direction of causation. I shall begin by comparing backwards causation with forwards causation in order to find whether there is something absent in the former and present in the latter that we can identify as what makes forwards causation the viable concept it appears to be and whose absence in backwards causation correspondingly denudes it of meaning. I shall argue that even forwards causation would not make sense as causation at all if the events it relates were not taken as continuing in time; and that it is just this that is missing from backwards causation as philosophers have generally represented it. The question then arises of whether we can make sense of backwards causation by postulating something in it corresponding to the continuing of events in forwards causation, i.e. a continuing of events in a *reverse*

---

[1] Pears (1950–1); Dummett (1954); Flew (1954); Ayer (1956), 170–5; Black (1956); Flew (1956); Scriven (1957); Pears (1957); Flew (1957); Chisholm and Taylor (1960); Dray (1960); Dummett (1960); Gorovitz (1960); Gale (1965); Mackie (1966); Gale (1968); Swinburne (1968); von Wright (1971). (For more recent bibliography, see Le Poidevin and MacBeath (1993), 225–6.)

temporal direction. I shall maintain that such backwards continuing is not a possible feature of the experience of beings like ourselves, and that, accordingly, any definition we can give it is necessarily a schema devoid of content. And given this is true of backwards *continuing*, it is also true of backwards *causation*.

The supporters of backwards causation generally represent it as in all except one respect the same as forwards causation, the exception being its temporal direction. In both cases we have causation holding between an earlier and a later event or state of affairs,[2] and the difference is simply that in forwards causation the cause precedes the effect, in backwards it succeeds it.

Now this alleged parallel between the two kinds of causation aids the case for the possibility of the backwards kind. For the great conceptual stumbling block for backwards causation is its requirement that what has not yet happened should cause events in the present. Since events future from now do not now exist, we cannot easily understand that 'they' could influence anything preceding 'them'. Now the parallel with forwards causation, if valid, can help here, as supporters of the possibility of backwards causation have often noted. For although the parallel does not explain how an event not yet here can be a cause, it encourages us not to mind not understanding. For, it is argued, it is also true that events that are past do not now exist, and yet this does not for a moment seriously shake our belief that 'they' (the nonexistent past events) can determine the present.

However, this parallel cannot help the case of backwards causation unless it genuinely holds, and I shall argue that if it did, backwards causation and forwards causation would be, not equally possible, but equally impossible. Yet forwards causation is *not* impossible, as the supporters of backwards causation must agree, since they base their argument from the parallel on this premiss. Now, what the parallel assumes, is that a past and a future event are in the same way not present. Just as future events have not yet begun, so past ones are now over, and if causal relations can hold across the break between what does not exist and what does, when what does not exist is in the past, why not also when it is in the future?

It is true that statements of the form 'X is now happening' are equally false both when X is over and when X has not yet begun. But it does not follow that the ground of the falsity in each case stands in the same contrast with the present. And there are reasons to suspect a difference.

---

[2] Throughout this paper, 'event' is used to cover both events in the sense of changes, and states of affairs.

In the first place, it is not clear that the 'fact' that X will start happening is a fact in the same sense as the fact that X has finished happening. If, as is arguable, the Law of Excluded Middle does not apply to future contingent statements, this would be a consequence. However, even if (as is also arguable) the Law does apply here, it does not follow that what has happened and what has not yet happened but will, are to be opposed in the same way to what is happening. For if they are, then how is it that we find it possible to conceive of the world stopping now, of there being, in other words, no future, but not of its having started only this moment from nothing before? Whatever we include under the term 'the present' seems to require an immediate past (five minutes would be plenty) to enable it to make sense as a present, whereas it does not in the same way require an immediate future. Thus we are tempted to say that the past is 'in' the present in a way in which even the immediate future is not. Now implicit in the theory that backwards causation is possible is an instruction to ignore this temptation, and what I wish now to consider is whether this instruction is warranted. I shall do so by asking whether, once we obey it, we can still make sense of forwards causation, let alone of backwards.

The question, then, is this: if what preceded a given event in time has no more existence at the time of the event than what will succeed it has, can that event be thought of as the *effect* of anything preceding it?

Now what does it mean to say that an event is caused by something preceding it? Is what is supposed to precede it the total cause (the sum of the causal conditions) taken as a whole, or does the total cause only partially precede it, so that part of the total cause occupies some of the time the effect does? If it totally precedes it, can it be said to be a cause of it at all? But if it partially overlaps the effect, how can any but the overlapping part of it be causally related to the effect? If, however, only this part causes the effect, how can we continue to think of this as forwards causation, i.e. a relation connecting earlier to later events?

To begin with, let us consider what follows if we take forwards causation as entailing that the cause as a whole precedes its effect. One consequence not easy to accept, is that once the cause-event has taken place, then even with all continuing traces of it obliterated, the effect must occur. We shall have to go into the question of whether this consequence is a conceptual absurdity, or merely something strange; at any rate, this is hardly the kind of situation we ordinarily have in mind when we speak of earlier events causing later ones. We would not ordinarily be inclined to deny that an event F was caused by an earlier event E simply for the reason that once E had happened, F could still have been prevented or stopped short by the removal of some contemporaneous causally necessary condition. Thus the common sense view of forwards causation by no means insists that the cause as a whole be earlier. The obvious reply, that it is hardly the business of common sense so to insist, returns us to the question whether, strictly speaking, our concepts permit us to consider an event to be a cause at all, if it wholly precedes its alleged effect.

The problem still facing us is that of making sense of the idea that what does not exist (because over and gone) can have effects. We are not now concerned with the question whether this is any more a difficulty in the case of a later than of an earlier cause. The problem now is whether, even with an earlier cause, it is possible at all. However, it may be thought that there only seems to be a problem if we allow our thinking in this area to be ruled by some scholastic dictum such as that only the actual can cause the actual, or by an animistic picture of all causes as agents acting. It is therefore worth pointing out that the difficulty is not evaded but if anything underlined by the possibly more sophisticated analysis of causation in terms of necessary and sufficient conditions. How can E be sufficient, or sufficient under the circumstances for F, if when E comes about, F does not because F is later than E? How can E be necessary, or under the circumstances necessary, for F if, when F occurs, E is absent because already over?

It might be said that this old paradox proves no more than that it is possible to push the language of sufficient and necessary conditions too far when speaking of causal relations, useful though that language is in some respects. Such a remark would suggest that once we drop that particular terminology, there is no conceptual difficulty about a cause wholly preceding its effect. However, I shall now argue that even if we free ourselves from that terminology, serious problems still arise for the notion of a wholly precedent cause, centring in particular round the question of the temporal continuity of cause and effect. This question I shall now consider in some detail, in view of its general importance for the topic of the temporal continuing of events. The concepts of temporal continuity and temporal continuing are closely related, as will appear.[3]

I shall argue in the first place that if an earlier cause of an event wholly precedes that event, then the cause cannot be held to be continuous in

---

[3] The ensuing discussion of the temporal continuity and continuing of events does not depend on assuming that time itself is continuous in any absolute sense. That question lies outside the scope of this paper.

time with what it causes. I shall then argue that the temporal continuity of cause and effect is something we cannot afford to drop from the concept of causation as a relation between earlier and later events, if that concept is to preserve the implications that the term 'causation' would suggest.

Now, as to the first point, if an earlier cause as a whole precedes its effect, there are, necessarily, stages of the effect (the later ones) with which the cause is not temporally continuous, and there are likewise stages (the earlier) of the cause which are not continuous with the effect. It is no use saying that the cause, though it is cause of the later stages of the effect, is only cause of them by first being cause of the earlier stage; or that the cause in its earlier stages only causes the effect through its own later stage – as though by these moves we could get rid of any direct causal relation between non-continuous stages of events. For even if we hold that not the effect, but only its earlier stage, is continuous with the cause, and not the cause, but only its later stage, with the effect, there still remains a later stage of the effect's earlier stage with which the cause cannot be continuous, and an earlier stage of the cause's later one with which the effect cannot be. For the trouble is that if an event is taken to precede its effect, then some, at least, of what it immediately causes must lie after it, and so at a temporal distance from it. It must, in other words, cause at least some of what occurs on the later side of the temporal boundary between itself and its subsequent effect, since otherwise its effect, if any, is not subsequent. Thus if an earlier cause wholly precedes its effect, it cannot be temporally continuous with all of its immediate effect.

But must a cause and its immediate subsequent effect be temporally continuous? To deny this lands one in no formal contradiction. Moreover, it must be admitted that as we ordinarily use the concept of cause, the question of continuity hardly arises. On the ordinary, and indeed on the scientific level, what primarily interests us about a causal relationship is not the relation itself, but the knowledge it affords of what happens under what conditions. Thus we expect the particular effect we are interested in to follow the cause within a given time, more or less roughly estimated. A time lag only interests us to the extent that something might occur in it to prevent the effect; i.e. to the extent to which it may compel us to modify our expectations. But the general question of whether the effect could follow after a time lag empty of any intermediate link, yet still be fairly termed an 'effect', is not, on this level, a matter of any importance whatever.

However, those aspects of a causal relationship that strike us on this level cannot, without further argument, be taken to be all there is to it: if only because, as I said, from this point of view the relation itself is scarcely considered, let alone examined to see what it involves. The fact that we form our expectations regardless of whether cause and effect are temporally continuous is no evidence that in reality they might just as well be discontinuous. And when we turn to consider what has to be the case for the aforementioned practical and scientific uses of causal relations to be possible, it appears that temporal continuity is by no means a matter of indifference, as I shall now proceed to show.

Suppose that there is a time gap between cause and effect. By 'time gap' I do not mean an interval of empty time, whatever that could be, but an interval in which nothing occurs of any causal relevance to the separated cause and effect. Now if such a gap is possible, it could in principle be of any length, so that the question arises as to what, in any particular case, determines the length it is. Suppose we say that nothing determines it: then in the first place, there can be no ground for expecting the effect to occur at or within any given time (even roughly estimated) after the cause. But if that is so, we lack any rational basis for our procedure of matching up particular cause-events with particular effect-events. The fact is, that ordinarily, in believing that As cause Bs, we take it for granted that for any particular A that occurs, there is some particular B to be assigned to it as its effect rather than the effect of any other A. But if nothing limits the time gap between cause and effect, then given a succession A_1, B_1, A_2, B_2, A_3, B_3, etc. (at whatever intervals), there can be no reason to prefer any one of the Bs as the immediate effect of A_1. Indeed, why on this view should we not suppose that B_1, B_2, and B_3 are all immediate effects of A_1? If nothing limits the interval between cause and effect, then why should A_1 be limited to causing over an interval of a single length? Why should not Bs at different times all fall within its causal scope as non-simultaneous but causally coordinate effects of A_1? In that case, a single A-type cause, A_1 would be doing the 'work' of any number of different, differently dated, A-type causes. It might be objected that this possibility is too absurd to be entertained, since if B_1, B_2, and B_3 are all assigned to A_1 as its effects, then there are no Bs left to assign to A_2 and A_3, which are therefore left without effects, or anyway without B-type effects; and this contradicts the initial hypothesis that As cause Bs. But does it? For if there is no fixed time interval between an A-type cause and a B-type effect, we can always fend off the falsification of that hypothesis by arguing that although A_3 (say) has not yet been followed by the B which is its effect and which must follow it if the hypothesis is not to be disconfirmed, still the B in question is yet to come, since however late it comes, it will not be any less an effect of A_3.

In general, therefore, events of one kind can only be supposed to cause events of another on the assumption that any time gap between them would be of regular length. Otherwise a causal hypothesis could never be falsified, since there would be no time by which the alleged effect must happen if it is to be counted an effect. Moreover, if the time-gap is irregular in length, then those regular event-concomitances which are ordinarily taken to confirm a causal hypothesis, in fact provide no evidence for it. For if there is no reason why *A*s should be supposed to cause those *B*s that succeed them at some regular interval, rather than other *B*s, following at no matter what intervals, then the fact that again and again an *A* is followed at a regular interval by a *B* is no evidence of causation between *A*s and these (the regularly following) *B*s: nor is it evidence (why should it be?) of causation between *A*s, and *B*s following at various arbitrary intervals; so that it is no evidence for the truth of '*A*s cause *B*s' whatever.

Suppose, then, we postulate a time gap between cause and effect, but one that is of regular length, in any given type of case. This too has disturbing implications. For we can hardly help asking why in a given sort of case it is always the length it is; yet we cannot, on the present supposition, fall back on the form of answer we should normally give, i.e. one in terms of the time needed for something in the interval to happen which is causally relevant to the coming about of the effect. For such an explanation presupposes that there are causal conditions *continuing* right up to the moment of the effect. So must we then say that the interval just is the length it is? To let this go as a brute fact might be tolerable if we were dealing with isolated cases; but the supposition we are considering is that the interval is a regular length in all cases of a given kind. And just as, with event regularities, we seem all but inescapably drawn, whether logically or psychologically, to invoke a causal nexus as explanation of the regularity, not merely as another name for it: so in this case too we surely would be, where the regular companions are two events and a time gap. We may find ourselves thinking it is not A_1 but A_1 *succeeded by a certain length of time*, that is cause of B_1. In that case, we would have made a length of time as such into a causal factor. For since, *ex hypothesi*, it is not the content of that time that is causally relevant, it can only be the duration itself that is. Weird though this conclusion is, it is less so than its alternative, which is to see the length of time preceding B_1 as an *effect*, or *part of the effect*, of A_1.

If we draw back from such consequences, the only alternative (apart from altogether abandoning the notion of causation between events of different times) is to recognise the temporal continuity of cause with effect as a necessary condition of causal relations between earlier and later events. If, however, the cause is to be seen as temporally continuous with the whole of its immediate effect, then, as I argued above, the cause cannot as a whole precede the effect. It must continue not merely up to, but during it. For only in this way is each temporal stage of the effect continuous with some stage of the cause.

But can we maintain that this is the temporal relation of cause with effect in forwards causation without getting trapped into saying that what this shows is that really there are no causal relations between earlier and later events, and, therefore, no such thing as forwards causation? The preceding argument presses us towards the conclusion that since the earlier event can only be continuous with all of its later effect in so far as it continues during that effect, and since without continuity of cause and effect there is no causation, it follows that only in so far as the earlier event continues during the effect is it cause of that effect, whereas in so far as it (also) precedes it, it is not its cause. Indeed, this does follow. But it only provides a reason for denying that earlier events can cause later ones if it can be shown that the event that precedes the effect cannot properly be thought of as the *same event as* the event that continues on during it. If it cannot, then we should certainly have to say that what precedes the effect, being a different event from what overlaps with the effect in time and thereby causes it, is other than and therefore is not what causes it. So there would be no causation between earlier and later events. But must we be driven this way? For there is an acceptable sense in which it may be said that an event E that preceded a given event F, also (i.e. the same event) continued during F. In this sense we are able to say that even though E could only have caused F, or had F causally dependent on it, *when* E was contemporaneous with F and 'there' for F to depend on, still the same event E had also been going on before F, so that *what* preceded F was *also* F's cause. The statement that an earlier event caused a later one no more implies that it caused it *when* earlier, than the statement that Jack's mother was alive in the First World War implies she was then Jack's mother. Both these assertions rely for their meaning on a concept of identity through time, in the one case of a human being, in the other of an event. There seems no reason why we should be any more suspicious of the idea of one and the same event continuing to happen than of that of the same object continuing to exist. Indeed, the theoretical consequences of denying endurance to events are quite as awkward as those of denying it to objects. How in practice we identify a present event with one that was occurring earlier, is a question there is not space here to consider, and which anyway deserves attention to itself. The point of importance for the present purpose is that if there is a valid sense in which it can be said that an event that was happening earlier is still happening now, there is also a valid sense in which it can be said that an event that was happening earlier is cause of something now.

Forwards causation, then, has the following temporal structure: the event we call cause begins before that which we call effect, and then continues up to and during the time during which the effect itself continues. In this structure, the temporal continuing of events is thus a necessary element, since on the argument so far, forwards causation can only make sense as a relation of continuing events.

However, before we can bring this result to bear on the problem of backwards causation, we must examine in more detail the precise meaning of 'continuing' in this context. If ordinary modes of speech are anything to go by, the temporal continuing of events has an earlier-to-later direction. For we speak of events as if they continue through time *from* earlier *to* later. Now, if this is in fact their nature, then it follows quite easily that the direction of causation must also be earlier-to-later or forwards. For if forwards causation depends on the continuing of events, and if this must be from earlier to later, then forwards causation would naturally be supposed to take its direction from that of the continuing. But if the direction of forwards causation is determined by that of the continuing events involved, it follows that there could only be *backwards causation* if there were such things as *backwards continuing* events whose direction determined that of the causal relation connecting them. Thus, if temporal continuing is only from earlier to later, there can be no backwards continuing, nor therefore any backwards causation.

The question that arises now, is whether events can only continue in the earlier-to-later direction. This breaks into two questions: must their continuing 'have a direction' at all? and, if so, must it be forwards? As far as the first question is concerned, what has to be determined is whether, when an event is said to continue from an earlier to a later time, anything more is meant than that it extends between these two temporal limits. This would be to say that they mark off the interval during which it takes place and that at any point between them one would find the event occurring. And simply to say that an event extends through a time is not yet to say that it in any sense has a temporal direction. Now if the continuing of an event is no more than its temporal extension, then continuing is no more intrinsically directional than extension. In that case, either causation too has no intrinsic temporal directionality, or if it has, its source must be looked for elsewhere than in the continuing of the causally connected events.

But it can be shown that the continuing of events that is necessary for causation is not merely their non-directional extension in time. For if it were, backwards causation, as its supporters have vigorously claimed, would *be* no more mysterious than forwards; but nor would it even *seem* any more mysterious or for that matter any less commonplace. And this they have never claimed, if only because if it were true the first claim would be pointless. Now, an examination of the temporal structure of forwards causation showed that the cause is an event that begins earlier than the effect and continues up to and during it. The question is, would this structure be adequately represented if, instead, we described the cause-event as *extending* from before the effect, up to it, and overlapping with it? Any adequate account must bring out what it is that enables us to class the relation as one of *forwards causation*, with the earlier event as the cause. Now the analysis showed that we are justified in doing so only because the very same event can be taken as having continued from earlier before it caused the effect, to later when it did so. But would we still be justified in calling this 'forwards causation' if, instead of taking the event to have *continued from* the earlier *to* the later time, we take it to have *extended between* those times? In other words, can we say that the cause is earlier than its effect simply on the ground that, as well as coinciding in time with the effect (since otherwise it could not be its cause), it also extends pastwards beyond it?

If this is indeed adequate ground for asserting a forwards causal relation, then by parity of reasoning, in a case where the cause not only coincides in time with the effect but extends forwards beyond it to a later time, we have equally good ground for asserting that backwards causation holds. If the forwards relation consists only in the fact that the cause-event also precedes the effect, then how can backwards causation be anything more than the fact that it also appears after it, as in the case of the heat-wave that turns the milk and persists after its turning? So what we would be dealing with under the provocative title of 'backwards causation' is just a familiar type of forwards causal relation, that in which the cause does not cease when the effect does. But what puzzles those who puzzle about backwards causation is certainly not the undeniable existence of cases such as these. We should note too, that on this view not only is there no *problem* of backwards causation, but it is even possible that the same event, extending both backwards and forwards beyond its effect, as can happen, would be a forwards *and* a backwards cause. But this suggests that what we are now discussing, and what, in terms of extension alone, is all that there is to discuss, is a temporally *directionless* relation. For to say that a relation has *a* direction, is to exclude the possibility that in any given case, as well as having one particular direction, it also has an opposite direction. But a temporally directionless relation would not be causation as we ordinarily think of it. If it were, no problem about the reversing of its normal direction could arise, firstly because it has no direction, and secondly because having none, it can as well be taken to have either as the other, and even both at once.

There must, then, be more to forwards-directed causation than the fact that the cause-event extends to the pastward side of the effect. But what more can it be than that the extending is itself directional? Thus, if an event F is the effect of an earlier event E, this not only implies that E, as well as taking place during F, also happened earlier, but it also implies that E takes place during F having *continued from* earlier. And the reason it is not so easy to suppose that an event might be caused by a later event, is that the cause would then have to be understood not merely as coming after the effect, but as taking place during it, and as doing so by *continuing to* the time of the earlier event *from* later.

I have argued that an earlier cause is not to be thought of as simply preceding and then overlapping its effect, but as continuing from earlier to the time of the effect. But now, is this temporally directed continuing which has turned out to be essential to causation through time, necessarily from earlier to later? Our problem now is to decide whether events could be intelligibly supposed to continue from later to earlier. If not, backwards causation is unintelligible too, since if it is causation in the same sense in which forwards causation is causation, the difference being only in their temporal directions, backwards causation must involve a temporal continuity of cause and effect which in turn requires that the events concerned should not merely extend but continue through time from later to earlier. This backwards continuing cannot be pronounced impossible on purely logical grounds, any more than backwards causation. Nor can we argue that because all continuing in our experience is from earlier to later, therefore all must be. In fact, it is not clear how it could be demonstrated that there could not be backwards continuing. I shall argue only that it is not something of which we can make sense, the structure of our temporal knowledge and experience being what it is. However, this does not entail that we can give no purely formal account of what it would be for an event to continue backwards. On the contrary, such an account must be possible if we are to nail the subject under discussion. We can trace the outline, so to speak, that the concept of backwards continuing would have if for us there were such a concept, and by means of this schema not only fix what it is that is being talked about, but also show that the 'it' in question cannot make sense for beings like ourselves.

The schema with which I am operating is based on the following logical fact. An ordinary (forwards continuing) event E can at any time between its beginning and its end truly be said to be 'now continuing'. This assertion carries an implication concerning the time prior, but not subsequent, to its utterance. For whereas its being true now that E is continuing implies that for some time before now, E was occurring, it leaves it open whether after now, E will or will not be occurring. It is this fact that enables us to construct a formula for temporal continuing which is neutral as to direction, and which can therefore yield schemata for both forwards and backwards continuing, depending on how it is filled in. For E's continuing now implies E's occurrence before now, not because the time before now is the time before, but because, according to our ordinary way of thinking, this is the direction from which E is continuing. A spatial analogy makes the point. If a body of water is spreading from north to south, then for any given spot that it reaches, the truth that the water is there spreading implies that some water lies to the north of that spot, but not that any does or does not lie to its south. Clearly this implication holds of one direction and not of the other not because north is north and south south, but because the north is, in this case, the direction from which, the south the direction towards which, the water spreads. Thus if, for any place in its path, the proposition that it is there spreading had implied instead that water lies to the south of it, while implying nothing either way about the northward area, this would have shown the direction of spreading to be from south northwards.

Analogously for an event E in time. The temporal direction *from* which E at any given moment is taken to be continuing, may be specified as the direction wherein E's continuing at that moment implies E's occurrence for some time; and the direction *towards* which E at any given moment is taken to be continuing may be specified as that wherein neither E's occurrence nor its non-occurrence is implied. Thus, for example, an event E is taken to be continuing from later to earlier if and only if, for any moment while E continues, the assertion that E is then continuing implies that E will be happening for some time after that moment, while leaving it open whether E happened at all before it.

On this analysis, the sentence 'E is continuing now' (whichever temporal direction be intended) could only be asserted of actual experience by beings who (a) are prepared to assert, and so take themselves to be apprised of, the truth of what it immediately implies, namely that in the time immediately to one 'side' of their now, E has been / will be occurring; and (b) are not prepared in the same way to assert, because not supposing themselves in the same way apprised of it, with reference to the time immediately to the other side of now, that E will be occurring or that it will not / that E has been occurring or that it has not, during that time. This analysis claims no originality in general conception; it follows the insight of those philosophers who have taken the directionality of events in time to be logically inseparable from the asymmetry of our knowledge or certainty at any given time concerning what precedes and what succeeds that time. If past and future were both epistemically open in the way that only the future is for beings such as us, there could be no experience of events as continuing, in *either* direction. If, on the other hand, both were certain in principle as for us only the past is, events would appear, so to speak, to be continuing from both directions, which is to say they would not appear to have any direction, because not any *one*, and so would not be experienced as continuing at all.

The schema of backwards continuing, then, can only be given content in actual application to experienced events by beings whose temporal knowledge of those events is, like ours, asymmetrical, but asymmetrical the opposite way. And since causation through time makes no sense apart from continuing events, the notion of backwards causation is for us as meaningless as that of backwards continuing. They could take on meaning for us if, as well as the temporal knowledge we have, we could also come to have knowledge with the opposite temporal structure. Whether or not this is conceivable, is not a question to be considered *en passant*, and I shall say no more of it here. As far as the debate on backwards causation is concerned, the important point is that this, conceivable or not, is the sort of knowledge we should need in order to make sense of the concept. But if so, much of that debate has been beside the point. For it has centred largely on imaginary cases which, it is claimed on one side and denied on the other, can only be interpreted as cases of backwards causation. But the events in them are all conceptually ordinary, i.e. forwards continuing, events. Otherwise they would hardly be fit subjects for examples, being neither imaginable nor describable by us. What this shows is that disputants on either side have assumed it feasible to study the problem of backwards causation with reference only to the *relation*, taking it for granted that the temporal structure of whatever that relation, if possible, would relate, can present no problems of its own. If the argument of the present paper holds good, then the case for the possibility and conceivability of backwards causation, on whatever else it may take its stand, cannot rest on plausible examples of backwards-causal situations, since such situations could only be properly illustrated by reference to events whose temporal nature makes them incomprehensible in any but a purely schematic fashion to the very beings, ourselves, for whom the illustrations would be intended.

It remains to ask why, in discussions of the direction of causation, the subject of temporal continuing has been so largely neglected, in view of its importance for the problem. One reason, I would suggest, is that one cannot see causation between earlier and later events as essentially a relation of *continuing* events without facing a consequence perhaps not envisaged in most current treatments of causation, viz. the irredeemable dependence of the concept of causation on concepts of McTaggart's A-series. For the experience of events as continuing presupposes an asymmetry of temporal knowledge which is not an asymmetry as regards earlier and later events as such, but as regards the earlier and later than now, i.e. past and future. The directional continuing of an event only comes out, so to speak, for someone who is able to view it as now continuing, knowing of its existence to one side but not the other of now; or as something of which it was or will be true that it is now continuing. Whether this entails, as for McTaggart it would, that continuing, and therefore (if I am right) causation are 'unreal' or 'subjective', is not up for discussion here. But what can be said now is that the precise context in which philosophers have given most thought to causation is one in which, by its very nature, events need not be considered as continuing at all, in either temporal direction. I mean the context of scientific investigation of causal laws in nature. For neither the purpose nor the method of science requires that any official notice be taken of continuing. It is true that we can only know of particular events at first hand by experiencing them, and that we cannot experience them except as continuing, from earlier to later. But it does not follow that the knowledge of events a human scientist values is knowledge of them as experienced. And in fact, this element does not figure in a finished statement of a law and its evidence. Moreover, it does not help the empirical search for regular event-patterns to be thinking of each event as something of which 'it is continuing' is, was or will be true. The temporal direction and indeed directionality of past events is irrelevant when it comes to examining the records for possible regular sequences; and once past events have suggested an hypothesis, the empirical inquirer looks toward present and future events only to check for such similarities or dissimilarities to the past ones as will have a bearing on the hypothesis – which says nothing as to their temporal continuing as such, although it may be specific as to their temporal length or extent.

But what is irrelevant for the scientist cannot be safely relied on to be so for the philosopher. The one, for his purposes, need not think of events as possessing any temporal direction, whereas it may be that the other must, if what he means to have in mind are temporal entities at all. If not, it is only too easy to envisage for them a relation which, like them, lacks any intrinsic temporal direction, and which therefore seems theoretically capable of going either way. Since, however, the entities related are now being considered in abstraction from their temporal continuing, it is not clear that the relation itself can still be thought of as temporal either. In that case, whether its direction be forwards or back, we have no right to look on it as running forwards or backwards in *time*.

CHAPTER 3

From necessity to fate: An inevitable step?

I INTRODUCTION

I begin with the ancient Stoics, end with the Aristotelians, and in between shall draw together some thoughts not ascribed to anyone in particular.

The Stoics were universal determinists. That is, they held that whatever takes place is and always has been inevitable or necessary, given its antecedent causes.[1,2] This doctrine provoked one of the catchier bits of ancient reasoning, the Lazy Argument. Paraphrased for the modern ear, it goes: for any event E, (1) if the world is such that it is inevitable that E will occur, then E will occur no matter what else happens; and if the world is such that it is inevitable that E will not occur, then E will not occur no matter what else happens; but (2) (according to Stoic determinism) either the world is disposed in one of those two ways or it is disposed in the other. So (3) either way, the outcome will be whatever it will be no matter what else happens. Consequently, even if the occurrence of E is preferable to its non-occurrence or *vice versa*, nothing that anyone does with a view to producing the one or blocking the other can make the slightest difference. For example, if you, a sick person, are going to recover from your illness, then you will recover regardless of whether you get medical help. If, on the other hand, you are going to die from your illness, then you will die from it whether or not you get medical help. Either way, it is pointless to try to get medical help.[3]

---

[1] See Long and Sedley (hereafter, L&S), 1987, section 55, J–N, vol. 1, 336–8. The most comprehensive and penetrating study of Stoic determinism is Susanne Bobzien's (1998), of which see especially Chapter 5, 'Fate, Action, and Motivation: the Idle Argument'.

[2] The formulations in this paper take no account of the fact that Chrysippus, the major figure of early Stoicism, defended a sense of 'necessary' such that not everything inevitable (because fated) is necessary; nor of the fact that he seems to have distinguished 'that which is necessary' from 'that which is necessitated' (see Bobzien, 1998, 122–43).

[3] Cicero, *On Fate*, 28–30, L&S, section 55, vol. 1, 339–40; vol. 11, 340–1. My paraphrase substitutes 'it is inevitable that' for Cicero's 'it is your fate that' to reflect the fact that the argument means to

The Stoic Chrysippus (third century BCE) was quick to counter the Lazy Argument.[4] He rejected its first premiss, reasoning that if (for example) your recovery is the inevitable outcome, then determinism entails that such earlier events as are naturally required for this outcome have always been inevitable too because of antecedent causes. If, as would normally be the case, your recovery depends on your receiving medical help, then your receiving it, and therefore your taking whatever action is necessary for getting it (since it is assumed in the example that getting it depends on you), will also have been caused. Perhaps you go for help on impulse, or because reflectively it seems the wisest thing to do, or because you yield to someone else's advice. But whichever of these psychological antecedents obtains, it too has always been inevitable, just as it has always been inevitable that you would take the action you will take, and will recover in consequence. On this account there is no reason at all to think that you will recover regardless of what you do.

The universal determinist, then, does ask us to believe that in this world it has always been inevitable that you would act as you do, and therefore always inevitable that you would decide or otherwise come to act in that way. And this may be a hard belief for common sense to take on board. But there is another proposition which is not merely hard to believe, but is repugnant, intolerable and outrageous, namely that *in general* the outcome of your action would have been just the same even if the world had been such that in it, you acted in the opposite way under the circumstances. However, as Chrysippus showed, the Stoic determinist definitely does not ask us to believe the intolerable proposition. So, since it is the intolerable proposition that yields the lazy conclusion that action in general is pointless, Stoicism is not vulnerable to the Lazy Argument.

We can illustrate Chrysippus's point by an example which Aristotle uses to explain the idea of dependence.[5] It is impossible in Euclidean geometry that the inner angles of a triangle add up to more or less than two right angles. Because of this, the internal angles of a quadrilateral necessarily add up to four right angles, since a quadrilateral is composed of two triangles. It follows that if, *per impossibile*, the internal angles of the

---

derive fatalism in the modern sense (= 'the fated result will occur no matter what else') from determinism. Note that the Lazy Argument need not assume that all events are predetermined. In essence, it is just meant to apply to any that are.

[4] Cicero, *On Fate*, 28–30, L&S, section 55, vol. I, 339–40; vol. II, 340–1.
[5] Aristotle, *Eudemian Ethics* II.6, 1222b31–6.

triangle added up to three right angles, then given the original relation of triangle to quadrilateral the internal angles of the quadrilateral would add up to twice three = six right angles. The fact that it is impossible for the angles of the triangle to add up to three right angles should not, and does not, make it the slightest bit tempting to conclude that if, *per impossibile*, they did, the angles of the quadrilateral would not, so to speak, follow suit but would still add up, as they actually do, to four right angles.

What does contemporary philosophy have to say on this matter? Well, even if not on the sub-atomic level, on the level of human actions and events of immediate practical significance determinist doctrine is as alive and kicking today in some quarters as it was in the age of Chrysippus. Its modern sympathisers, like Chrysippus,[6] find the challenge of reconciling universal determinism with intuitions about human *freedom* and *responsibility* a fruitful source of serious business. However, reconciliation is one of those things that are necessary only when there is some reason to suspect they may be impossible; so the same question continues to stimulate incompatibilist answers too. But on both sides of that debate, no philosopher today of any skill or training sees the *Lazy Argument* as posing a difficulty for determinism. All, it seems, agree that universal determinism is at least consistent with the general efficacy of human action, and that any argument to the contrary is obviously based on a fallacy.

But in taking stock of things alive and kicking, we must also concede that in some quarters the Lazy Argument is still one of them. Which of us introducing a class to the theory of universal determinism has not had to face the student who responds: 'But if that's true, there's no point in doing anything!' Perhaps we remember making just that response ourselves when we first heard about the theory; and perhaps also remember our teachers patiently explaining to us, as we in turn explain to our own students, that the response is a fallacy. From the premiss that something had to happen, given the way things were, it simply does not follow that the same thing would have happened no matter what else had been the case, and that action is therefore pointless. To think otherwise, we may tell our students, is an 'elementary' fallacy.

These students are in rather good company. The Lazy Argument was endorsed by the great Aristotelian commentator, Alexander of Aphrodisias (second–third centuries CE), and something like it had already been

---

[6] L&S, Section 62, vol. I, 386–94.

endorsed by Aristotle himself (fourth century BCE). Writing about a hundred years before Chrysippus, Aristotle declares:

These and others like them are the absurdities that follow if it is necessary for every affirmation and negation (either about universals spoken of universally or about particulars) that one of the opposites be true and the other false, and that nothing of what happens is as chance has it, but *everything is and happens of necessity*. So *there would be no need to deliberate or to take trouble, thinking that if we do this, this will happen, but if we do not, it will not.*[7]

And against determinism Alexander argues:

If . . . we are going to be persuaded that [all things come to be of necessity and] we are not in control of anything, [then] we will leave aside many of the things that ought to be done by us both on account of having deliberated about them and on account of eagerly undertaking the efforts involved in what is done; we will have become lazy with regard to doing anything of our own accord, on account of the belief that what ought to come about *would* come about, even if we did not exert ourselves about what needed to be done.[8]

The fact that Aristotle makes a move resembling the Lazy Argument,[9] and that Alexander follows with the Lazy Argument itself, may simply betoken confusion on the part of these philosophers. But it also prompts one to wonder whether the Lazy Argument, or something like it, might not have genuine force after all. The rest of my discussion will elaborate this suggestion.

First, let us clarify some terms.

Determinism with respect to an actual event E (or non-event, not-E) is the view that it was always necessary that E would/would not occur.

Fatalism with respect to actual E (or not-E) is the view that E would/would not have occurred no matter what else occurred beforehand.

Futilism with respect to E (or not-E) is the view that rational effort on our part regarding E/not-E is pointless. ('Rational effort' covers deliberation on whether to bring about E or not, and efforts to implement the conclusion of deliberation.)

We should distinguish several grounds for being a 'futilist' with regard to E/not-E: that is, for judging it pointless to make a rational effort concerning E/not-E.

---

[7] Aristotle, *De Interpretatione* 9, 18b26–33 (italics added).

[8] Alexander, *On Fate* XXI, 191, 17–24. Since Alexander must have known the Chrysippan rebuttal of the Lazy Argument, his revival of the latter suggests that he does not consider the rebuttal completely effective. As we shall see (section IV, below), the rebuttal cannot be mounted within an Aristotelian framework.

[9] Aristotle moves straight from 'everything is necessary' to 'there is no point in deliberating or taking trouble', whereas in Alexander the inference is mediated by the assumption that if everything is necessary, the same outcome occurs no matter what we do.

(i) Whatever we decide/try to do (or let happen), the empirical result will be the same.
(ii) Whatever we do (or let happen), the value achieved will be the same.
(iii) Epistemically we are in no position to prefer that E occur rather than not, or *vice versa*.

A futilistic attitude towards E/not-E may be adopted for empirical and in principle alterable or avoidable reasons. For example: (i) Once Aida and her lover are entombed, the result will be the same whether or not they reconcile themselves to their premature deaths. (ii) Two identical bowls of soup are equally available to the man driven by hunger. Nothing is gained or lost by his consuming this rather than this, or by consuming them in one order rather than the other. (iii) People often decline to vote because they feel they know too little to judge whether candidate A's victory and candidate B's defeat is preferable, or the reverse. Here, however, I am only concerned with putative cases in which the reason for futilism is in principle unchangeable and inescapable: for short, cases of 'in-principle futilism'.

It is clear from the explanation of the terms that fatalism with regard to E/not-E constitutes a type-(i) ground for the corresponding in-principle futilism. I now want to ask whether determinism with regard to E/not-E entails or logically supports any kind of in-principle futilism with respect to E/not-E.[10]

We have already seen that determinism with regard to E/not-E does not in general imply a corresponding fatalism. The implication fails for Stoic determinism, as Chrysippus showed. And in this respect modern causal determinism is like Stoic determinism. For when we teach about determinism today, we save the doctrine from the charge of entailing fatalism by an argument essentially the same as the one Chrysippus gave. Consequently, it seems fairly clear that neither Stoic nor modern determinism provides a type-(i) ground for in-principle futilism. For it is difficult to see why one would endorse such a ground for futilism with regard to a given E/not-E if not because one is fatalistic about it. So, in general, the determinist as such has no more reason to be a futilist[11] on the first ground than to be a fatalist concerning any event. Nor is there any reason to think that determinism commits one to the second ground for futilism.

---

[10] The present discussion will not be exhaustive. For one thing, the list of grounds for futilism may be incomplete.
[11] I.e., in-principle. This is now to be understood throughout.

However, in what follows I shall argue first[12] that causal determinism, as we understand it today and as the Stoics understood it, entails the third ground for futilism. It follows that this sort of determinism *approximates to* fatalism in so far as it shares the latter's capacity to generate futilism. I shall then argue[13] that a distinctively '*Aristotelian*' determinism with regard to an event E brought about by my action entails fatalism with regard to E. In sum, this essay is a two-way attempt to vindicate the untutored reaction to determinism: 'If that's true there's no point in *doing* anything.'

To pave the way for these arguments, let us first engage with the topic of *fate*.

II FATE

By 'fate' here, I do not mean what the Stoics meant, namely the pre-necessitation of things that we have been calling 'determinism'. I mean the pre-necessitation that is supposed to hold regardless of how one tries to get round it. How might fate in this narrower and seemingly more sinister sense come into anyone's picture? These days, no one respectable believes in fate (do they?) any more than they believe in general that action and choice are pointless. Why would one postulate fate, and what would one be postulating? Let us imagine some situations.

There is a soft-drinks vending machine, and someone wants a Coca-Cola from it. He puts in money, pushes the Coke button, and the machine delivers his order. But somehow or other we who are watching know that even if he had put in a bid for Pepsi or Sprite or ginger ale, he would have been served a Coke. Is this fate? We are not in a hurry to think so, because we can easily hypothesise 'ordinary' explanations for what happened. Perhaps the machine is stocked only with Coke, so you get that whichever button you press. Alternatively, although the machine contains a variety of sodas, the man has an unconscious tropism towards Coke: whichever button he means to press, his hand ends up on the Coke button, whether he means it or not. We could think of explanations for this, neurological or psychological; so no need to invoke fate.

Let us change the example. Let us suppose that someone wants to go to his class reunion. It is held every year, not always in the same place. Every year he plans to go, but something always crops up to prevent it. On one

---

[12] Section III, below.   [13] Section IV, below.

occasion he falls ill just beforehand. Another year, he misses the last flight because of exceptional traffic on the way to the airport. Next time, his plane is hijacked to Cuba. Or it has to land at the wrong destination because of weather. On another occasion, the Post Office loses a letter that announces to him (in timely fashion) a change in the reunion's date, so he turns up when it is over. And so on. He is not in general accident-prone. It is just that the reunion seems to elude him systematically. Here we, and he, might begin to think him 'fated' not to get to it, even if we are aware of hardly knowing how to make sense of the thought. If we do find ourselves thinking in this direction, presumably this is because it makes even less sense to suppose that the person's failure to get to the reunion year after year is simply a string of coincidences. Nothing miraculous has happened. On each occasion, the failure has its own perfectly natural explanation. But if everything is perfectly natural, how is it that such different sequences all wind up in the same outcome – an outcome, moreover, which far from being the sort of thing one might expect to happen again and again, is the sort of thing that tends to happen quite rarely, the world being what it is?

The pattern we have suggests *purpose*. When the same result occurs over and over although what leads up to it is quite different each time, the result begins to seem like an end that is being aimed for. It is the mark of purpose that different methods are used to achieve it, reflecting differences in the circumstances. The person might not unreasonably come to think that even when he does not get the flu or break his leg at the last minute, when nothing makes him miss the plane, when the weather is propitious, when he has checked for a possible change of date or venue, etc., etc., even so, favourable as all these circumstances are, some other 'means' will be 'found' to thwart his endeavour – a perfectly natural means, of course. Not unreasonably, he might wonder whether next year, or the one after, the cause might not be a perfectly natural plane crash; and then he may think: 'I'd better stop trying to go; it will be my fault if engines fail or wings ice up, and a plane full of people falls out of the sky.' This sort of thinking is not irrational, given the facts. But of course these are fictional facts. We are making this story up so as to understand the meaning of 'fate'. If comfort is needed, can we not comfort ourselves with the thought that the likelihood of a situation developing in which a rational, enlightened, person might rationally invoke fate is at least as unlikely as the series of repeated failures to get to the reunion?

However, the repetition is not all that unlikely, if, as the protagonist begins to suspect, his non-appearance at the reunion is consistently purposed. But here we should pause to bring out the fact, implicit in the fictional situation so far, that the hypothesis that a natural or human purposive agent is responsible for the repeated outcomes is, from what we know of the circumstances, as far fetched as the hypothesis of coincidence. For I am assuming that 'the circumstances' include a complete lack of evidence for some single natural or human cause. In this situation, even the hard-headed might find it least unreasonable to resort to talk of 'fate', meaning by this an agency concerning which all we know is that it has a certain purpose concerning the man and his reunion,[14] and is clever and foreknowing and powerful enough to carry out this intention no matter what. It is omnipotent with respect to this purpose, even if its unlimited power is limited just to this goal. Hence we cannot track the fate down as we could a natural or human agent, since then we might be able to hobble it or deflect its reach, or even discover what it is after and persuade it to act differently. Certainly, it would seem that, as far as fate is concerned, the man's not getting to his reunion is a matter of great significance; but there is no way – no natural way – of discovering what that significance is.

We can now pinpoint an important difference between the fatalism illustrated in the story, and determinism in its Stoic and modern forms. Determinism is universalisable, fatalism is not. If the happening of some events is and always has been pre-necessitated (determinism), it does not follow that the same is not true for every other event. But if it is pre-necessitated that a given event E will happen somehow or other no matter what (fatalism), the events which on a given occasion pave the causal path to E are not such that they too would have happened no matter what. It is obvious in the reunion story that each time many things happen which would not have happened if particular conditions had been different. For example, if we imagine the protagonist stopping because of a red light *en route* to the airport, we assume that he would not have stopped at that point had the light been green, *ceteris paribus*; and we need not assume that it would have been red no matter what moment he reached it. And if we allow ourselves to postulate an unpreventable purpose in order to explain the otherwise inexplicable pattern of events, it is because the pattern seems to show us a series of individually dispensable means to the same inevitable end. If we suppose that the events that are means on one occasion would have happened no matter what (for example,

---

[14] The purpose, of course, might be not that he will never get to the reunion, but that he will get to it once in fifteen years, or only when some rare visitor is present.

regardless of whether they led to the so called end), they no longer figure as means, but rather as ends in themselves.[15]

Perhaps we can now let go of the notion of fate. We invoked it to fill an explanatory gap which was only fictional, after all. And even if we ourselves were faced with the fictional events, we might insist, despite the absence of evidence, that the pattern must be due to a naturalistic cause. In that case, of course we would not be thinking of the failure to get to the reunion as something that will happen inevitably, no matter what. For a natural cause, if there is one, can in principle be identified and disabled so that it no longer has its effect. And if there is a natural cause (this includes human agency), we are under no temptation to ascribe mystical significance to the repeated outcome. If the cause is a human agent, then presumably the outcome is significant to him or her, but in ways that we can find out.

So far we have been considering fate as a conceivable explanation of a conceivable pattern of events. But if the latter is only *conceivable*, we can be forgiven for postponing a decision about whether we ourselves would postulate fate until such time as we ourselves are actually faced with such a set of facts. Sufficient unto the day – especially if the day in question is utterly improbable.

But even if we stay within familiar horizons, the idea of fate exercises a certain subliminal appeal. Consider some past event or conjunction of enormous cultural or personal significance. On the personal level, it is not unusual to be literally unable to imagine how one's life would have gone if twenty or however many years ago one had not met the 'significant other', or had never stumbled into one's line of work, or had had or not had children as the case might be. The concrete imagination takes its cue from our life as we have actually lived it, and when no alternatives can be pictured with comparable vivacity, as David Hume might have put it, it is as if for the concrete imagination there *are* no alternatives. So, looking back, it is as if I was bound to meet that person, to go to that place from which so much started. (Something of this mind-set coexists in many of us with the presumably more rational belief that alternatives were possible for the person I was then; I might have been luckier or unluckier. Since the more rational belief assumes the standpoint of me back then, e.g. wondering whether or not to accept what turns out later to have been a life-shaping invitation, it abstracts from the concrete consequential detail

---

[15] It may be correct to say that the means are fated, given that the end is fated; but this is not to view the means *fatalistically*, i.e., apply the Lazy Argument to them too.

of the path actually taken, and so this path, or the initial stretch of it, is as schematic as the alternatives.)

Let us think briefly about history-shaping events and individuals: to each her or his own choice of example. Suppose that the Persians had permanently occupied Greece and Athens at the beginning of the fifth century. Suppose that Plato or Aristotle had died in infancy. We cannot begin to imagine how Western history would have gone – how things would have been *now*, for instance. There is no point in even trying, any more than in trying to formulate a coherent alternative to '2 + 3 = 5' without changing the meanings. There is nothing to hang on to. This well-founded paralysis of the imagination expresses itself in the imaginational thought that there had to be a Plato who did what Plato did, and there had to be an Aristotle. Or, rationality off guard, we catch ourselves thinking that if the actual Plato (or 'Aristocles', as some think his parents actually called him) had died as a child, another giant would have come in his place, to do essentially the same work. The other, we might think, would have been 'sent'; or the climate of the time was ready to bring such a figure forth. One way or another, the outcome would have been in important respects the same.

If, in the sort of context I have just tried to sketch, we fall back on the idea of a fated event or the fated contribution of some great person, it is not in order to explain the otherwise inexplicable. Rather, 'fated' now functions as a modal strengthener ensuring framework-status to the item in question. By fate, this actual, but by naturalistic standards no more than contingent, entity is guaranteed existence under all the alternatives felt by us to be culturally or personally possible.

It is time to turn to the two arguments promised earlier.

III   SHOWING THAT UNIVERSAL DETERMINISM GIVES GROUND FOR FUTILISM

The argument is not complicated. Much of what we do, we do so that things will be better in some way than they would have been if we had not so acted, or so that they are more likely to be better. We base the judgment that things will be, or are more likely to be, better if we do D on a comparison with the way things would go if, *ceteris paribus*, we don't do it. Judgments about the way things would go if *ceteris paribus* we don't do D are based on induction. We can't be certain of them, but we can have good evidence for them, and that is sufficient basis for action. We also generally think that we can in principle make a reasonable judgment on whether things *would* be relevantly equal if we don't do D.

This is important because we measure the actual gain achieved by doing it through comparison with how things would have been otherwise, not merely through comparison with how they are before we do it.

Now if, after doing D on the basis of the kind of comparison I have sketched, we were to become aware in retrospect that we lacked and still lack any grounds for making that comparison, then we should see ourselves as having done D in the dark, and as still not knowing what might have been gained or for that matter lost through our doing it. And if at the time of deciding whether to do D we had realised our ignorance with respect to the difference our doing it would imply, it would have been rational for us to conclude it pointless to deliberate on whether or not to do D: and, if for some reason we had already started to do it, equally pointless to care whether or not we carried it through successfully, since we have no idea what, if anything, would be gained or lost thereby.

Suppose for example that I am driving, and I slow down to avoid hitting a neighbour's dog. I have quickly and, let us assume, by ordinary standards reasonably, judged that it is safe to brake a bit and that my car will hit the dog if I don't. I briefly imagine the yelp of pain and then having to walk towards my neighbour's front door with a dead or injured dog in my arms. It is to forestall such distressing events at no cost that I act so as to avoid the creature. My reasoning assumes that whether I avoid it or not, a great deal in the situation will be the same either way. In both cases I shall be driving this car; the road conditions will be the same; the dog will be crossing the road in the same way; it is my neighbour's adored companion; if I skid on braking I will not run into anything; the dog is not surrounded by a protective force field; and much else. My reasoning is that if I don't brake, I will have harmed the dog gratuitously. This assumes that how things were up to the moment of braking is the same in many significant respects as how things would have been up to that moment had I failed to brake. It is on the basis of these features that I reckon the difference made by action rather than non-action and *vice versa*.

Now most determinists are like ordinary people in the way they reckon the net value, in a case like this, of braking to avoid the dog. They too compare the immediately foreseeable consequences of braking with those of not braking against a background of relevant circumstances the same either way.[16] It may look as if the comparison enables them, just as it

---

[16] Most if not all real-life questions of moral and legal responsibility assume that in general, we can make reasonable judgments about the differences made by actions. When determinists try (as most do) to accommodate ordinary intuitions about responsibility to their doctrine, they show that they share the assumption.

enables the rest of us, to explain afterwards just what one did gain by braking on that occasion. In fact, however, or so I would argue, determinists are rationally disqualified from enjoying or offering any such explanation. They can say what would have been gained by braking *if*, in the absence of this event, other circumstances had been relevantly the same. They can say that braking in the actual situation stands for something better than any not-braking that might be supposed to occur in a relevantly similar hypothetical situation. But this leaves it open whether that is the situation one *would* have been in even if one had not braked. If we have no reason to believe it is, then we have no reason to hold that it *was* a good thing that I braked, and to be pleased that I did.[17] Conversely, if we are confident that the braking *was* a good thing, this is because we do not compare its results with those of non-braking on the mere *supposition* of similar conditions; rather, we consider it on the basis of an *assertion* that such conditions were in place and would have been in place whether there was braking or not. And we take that assertion to be justified. But it is justified only if one is justified in assuming that the common conditions and their causal antecedents were causally independent of the braking and *its* causal antecedents. This justification would be lacking if there were reason to think that things are connected in such a way that the hypothetical scenario in which I didn't brake is one in which a relevant common condition was absent. (For example: I only wouldn't have braked if I had been distraught or in a great hurry. My neighbour, who knows me well, was observing my demeanour as I loaded the car, etc., and she rightly judged that I was calm. But if she had seen reason to judge otherwise, she would not have let her dog out of the house. Here, my braking to avoid the dog and the dog's being there to be avoided are consequences of the same cause, my calm, and are related in such a way that the absence of either entails the prior absence of the cause and therefore the absence of the other.)

Again, one is not justified in assuming that the relevant actual conditions (relevant, that is, to its being a good thing that I braked) would have been in place whether I had braked or not if *one has no reason at all to believe that it is true that they would have been.* Now, in practical life

17 We still have reason to hold that my braking *would have* been a good thing *if*, had I not braked, the rest of the situation had been pretty much as it actually was. But this does not justify my *being* pleased that I did brake, for unless we have reason to believe that the antecedent of the above conditional is true, we have no reason to believe that the actual braking *was* a good thing, and hence to be pleased about it. (This point is brought out more fully in chapter 4, sections VI–VII. It depends on the commonsense assumption that actuality belongs to this actual world absolutely.)

we make this sort of assumption all the time, with a good deal of confidence. But certainly if we are determinists we are not entitled to such confidence. For the determinist, if the braking had not occurred, this would have been because the antecedent situation was different in some way from actuality, and this because of a difference in its antecedent, and so on. And causation being what it is, each of these differences would have bred subsequent effects, branching out into further effects and further differences. Moreover, at each stage there are different ways in which the antecedent might have been different enough to cancel the actual effect, and each of these different ways breeds its own ramifying set of different consequences. Not only can we not keep track of any given set of ramifications, but we cannot know which of them would have been, so to speak, *the* one that would have been realised in the world as it would have been if I had not braked for the dog. In fact that question makes no sense. In many examples one need back-track no more than a year from yesterday to find oneself drowning in ignorance of how the course of events today would have differed from the actual course were it the case that some humdrum event of yesterday had not occurred[18] – never mind back-tracking to the beginning of the world, as we are bound to if we are determinists.

But it is only the determinist who drowns, because of the doctrine that every stage is pre-necessitated by what went before. If and only if we understand the present as not so rigidly connected to the past, we can breathe easier and judge with reasonable confidence that events do make the differences they ordinarily seem to us to make. Determinists, on the other hand, ought to refrain from such judgments, since they have no epistemic right to them if their theory is true. Indeed, if their theory is true it is pointless to care about doing something rather than something else, since the difference it makes for good or ill is a blind guess for all of us.[19,20]

---

[18] This argument has force even without chaos theory and the 'butterfly effect'.

[19] Sometimes, however, we act not so as to get something done, but simply so as to instantiate some form of conduct, such as keeping a promise. This sort of practical attitude may be available to the determinist. It would be an absolutely rigid deontology, since it could never take account of consequences.

[20] In fact, as I argue in chapter 4, section VIII, this should be a welcome conclusion for the ancient Stoics (although, as far as I know, they never drew it), because of their ethic of acceptance. Logically, I cannot regret running over the dog if I am convinced that there is no reason to think that things would have been better if I hadn't.

IV   SHOWING THAT 'ARISTOTELIAN' DETERMINISM WITH
RESPECT TO *E* ENTAILS FATALISM WITH RESPECT TO *E*

The modern causal determinist typically holds that earlier conditions
necessitate and explain the existence of later ones. We have seen that it
is a mistake to infer from this that later ones would have occurred no
matter what went before. But let us now consider determinism as it would
be from an Aristotelian perspective. (Here it is enough to consider the
pre-necessitation of some given event, without assuming that everything is
thus determined.)

The Aristotelian typically holds that explanatory causal necessitation
by one event of another runs from later to earlier. The later is the final
cause, and the necessitation is in most cases hypothetical.[21] If there is
going to be a house, materials for the roof and walls, etc., must be
assembled for the sake of it. If the fruit of a tree is to develop to the
point where it can shed fertile seeds, the fruit must be sheltered from the
sun; hence for the sake of the tree's reproduction there must be leaves
growing in a certain position; and for leaves to grow where needed, leaves
must be made of relatively light material, not heavy matter that settles
round the roots. For Aristotle, teleology is the most scientific approach to
any subject matter that can sustain it. In the natural world, life-forms
obviously provide the most promising subject matter. But, strange as it
may seem to us, Aristotle even applies this scheme of later causally
necessitating earlier to the movements and positions of heavenly bodies.[22]
This is understandable, since for him the heavenly bodies are alive and
instinct with intelligence and presumably purpose.[23] At any rate, causal
necessitation of earlier by later is, for him, the scheme of choice, just as, no
doubt, the reverse is the scheme of choice for us.

In the house and tree examples, an Aristotelian regards it as contingent
whether the end in question actually comes to be.[24] In the first place, the
particular house or plant might not even have got started. Secondly,
the processes of building and growth might have been interrupted before
the end was reached. Buildings and trees are sorts of things that cannot grow
or be produced except in dependence on an environment, which is also,
necessarily, an arena for possible interference. Since builders are intelligent,

---

[21] Aristotle, *Physics* II.8–9.
[22] Aristotle, *On Generation and Corruption* II.11.
[23] Aristotle, *On the Heavens* II.12, 291b19–21.
[24] Cf. Aristotle, *On Generation and Corruption* II.11, 337b30–4.

they take account of this pervasive fact about building. And so, when it comes to growing, does the intelligence-like formative principle in the plant. Each is primed to pursue the end by varying, if necessary, the means in response to environmental challenges that arise. Otherwise, every challenge would bring the process to a halt. It is precisely because experience gives us reason to believe that, within certain necessary constraints, if the subject had not pursued its end in one way, it would have done so in another, that we see the process as purposive at all. In these cases it is the variety of ways of getting to the same result that leads us to postulate intelligence or something like intelligence as the guiding principle.

Compare this with Aristotle's heavenly bodies. We would have to have, as he had, a prior and independent belief that each heavenly body is governed by a distinct intelligence before we felt any inclination to look upon their movements as purposive. This is for two reasons. First, their movements are circular, continuous and everlasting.[25] Hence whatever position[26] we designate as an end led-up-to, the heavenly body does not stop there, but passes on as if that were no more an end-point than those preceding it. Secondly, according to Aristotelian physics, nothing about a heavenly body or its environment represents a possible threat to its single-minded progression. Its matter is such that it cannot decay or falter; its environment is such that it cannot be stopped or knocked off course. Thus its movement does not betray purposiveness by adjusting to potential obstacles, for potential obstacles are impossible up there. Even so, Aristotle applies the schema of purpose, declaring that a chronologically earlier stage must occur because a later one will, the former being a necessary antecedent for the latter.[27] The case is like those of the house and the tree, except that here the necessity is absolute, not hypothetical, since the celestial movement has always been going on, and nothing can upset its continuation. In other words, if the later stage is going to come about, what naturally leads up to it must, for the sake of it, come about first. But (since the movement is necessary and continuous) the later stage will come about, and will come about necessarily; and because of that, what leads up to it will come about necessarily too. And this is not only

---

[25] For Aristotle, this means 'temporally infinite in both directions'. But the present argument is not affected if we understand 'everlasting' as 'enduring for the whole of time' and take the entirety of time to be finite.

[26] E.g., a solstice; Aristotle, *On Generation and Corruption* ii.ii, 337b13–14.

[27] (I have discussed the difficulty of applying Aristotle's teleological account of change to the case of celestial motion in his universe in Waterlow (1982), 249–51.)

true now, but has always been so. That is to say: for as long as the movement has been going on (for ever) it has always been necessary that the particular later stage that we have in mind will come about, and therefore it has always been necessarily being led up to by whatever has to precede it.

Now imagine that someone proposes to the Aristotelian that some sublunary event, such as a particular house's getting finished, or someone's getting over an illness, is like the celestial positions in that its coming to pass is and always has been necessary. So this sublunary event is like the celestial positions in that its coming to pass has always necessarily been being led up to. Now if the completion of the house is an end, then its coming about is and always has been simply necessary, and by the teleological scheme every stage leading up to it has been for the sake of it. If, on the other hand, the completion of the house is and always has been necessary as a means to some further end, then every stage leading up to it has been for the sake of the latter.

But such events are not celestial, and like all events down here they and what leads up to them unfold in an environment of potential obstacles. We would expect to see the leading-up adjusting to what would otherwise be obstacles and taking different forms at different stages so as to succeed. We say of the ordinary purposive agent building a house or trying to stay healthy that within a certain range of possibility the actual means he used were dispensable; if one way had failed, he would have taken a different route.

But now if the end's coming about has always been necessary, and has always depended on suitable antecedent means leading up to it, then the series of means stretches back into the infinite past. And, if the end's coming about has always been necessary, and, as with sublunary ends in general, there are different ways in which it might come about, it has always been necessary that it will come about one way or another. Thus if a particular link in the actual chain of means had failed to materialise, as can happen with events down here, some other chain would have been followed, or some other link come into play instead. But then these are not means controlled or controllable by a human agent, since no human agent has such power over means as to make it true that the end will come about *of necessity*. And if a human agent controlled the means, the means-end series would have started from a particular human action or decision at a particular moment within history. But in that case it would not be true that it has *always* been necessary that the end will come about. We therefore have the pattern of purposive action engaged in by an agent that has been monitoring the stream of events from time everlasting so that from time everlasting they have always been being paid out in a way to side-step or compensate for every obstacle.

This, I submit, is the inevitable result of combining the determinist idea that it has always been predetermined that an event E will occur, with the Aristotelian assumption that earlier events happen because they lead up to an end that comes about later. Thus an Aristotelian faced with the suggestion that E's occurrence has always been predetermined sees it as harbouring the following implications: (1) no *human* agent is responsible for ensuring that E will occur rather than not; and (2) if human decisions and efforts are involved, it is only as links in a chain of means to an end that would have come about in some other way had they been absent. So if the determinist tries to explain to the Aristotelian that, when a human agent A voluntarily takes steps to bring about a state of affairs S (for example, A's recovery from illness), either it has always been necessary that A will recover or it has always been necessary that A will die, the Aristotelian naturally infers that whichever the outcome, it has always been predetermined to occur if not by one chain of events then by another; hence it will come about just the same whatever A does or does not do.

CHAPTER 4

Alternative world-histories

I

There is a more pressing difficulty for determinism than the celebrated one to do with ascribing moral responsibility. It arises because we assume that events and actions usually make a difference to the world where they take place, and that we, at least in the short term, can often tell what the differences are. This double assumption, partly about the effects of actions and events, partly about our knowledge of them, seems threatened by determinism. I shall say presently why, but first a word on the greater urgency of this difficulty by comparison with the other, and more extensively discussed, problem to do with moral responsibility.

Moral responsibility presupposes agency, and agents act to make a difference, whether to themselves, to their environment, or to others. Perhaps there are cases where we reasonably hold someone responsible although her action, and even her choice of action, made no difference since the relevant effect was going to come about anyway independently.[1] But I think such cases are possible only if the agent acts without realising that things are set up in such a way that her action makes the relevant effect not even the slightest bit more likely than it would have been without it. One cannot act with the purpose of making some desired thing happen if one is assured that acting so would be completely ineffectual in that respect.[2] We may, in such a case, welcome the occurrence of what was willy-nilly going to happen. This would be evidence, though certainly not conclusive, that we would have acted to make the thing

---

[1] The argument that such cases exist was thoroughly presented first in Frankfurt, 1969. This paper has generated an immense discussion which shows no sign of running out of steam. For a recent account of the debate, see Fischer, 2002.

[2] Irving Thalberg questions the orthodoxy that we cannot intend what we regard as impossible; Thalberg, 1972, 105–14. But it is not clear that his sympathy with the thought that we can, extends to cases where one sees oneself as *completely ineffectual.*

happen if it hadn't been going to anyway (assuming we had the opportunity). Our welcoming the event we didn't bring about would also ground a character-judgment about us rather like (and perhaps even in some cases identical with) the one we would have earned if we had in fact been agents in the case rather than lucky beneficiaries. No doubt, then, there is greater resemblance between someone who welcomes an event she sees as going to happen anyway, and the agent who intends to make it happen, than there is between either of these subjects and the person whose attitude towards the event is negative or indifferent. But the similarity should not mislead us into thinking it possible *both* to intend to bring about what is going to happen anyway independently of one, *and* to be not in the dark about its going to happen anyway.

Surely it is reasonable to take as paradigm of human agency the case where the agent is not mistaken in assessing her situation as one where her agential input is not pointless. That is: surely it is reasonable to treat as paradigmatic the case where active agency with regard to some desired outcome is an appropriate response to the situation, not one that is vain or superfluous. It was with an eye on this paradigm that I observed above that moral responsibility presupposes difference-making agency.

Hence doubt whether determinism can allow for agency is logically prior to doubt whether it can allow for moral responsibility. And the priority is methodological too. If it turns out that determinism makes nonsense of agency, then there is nothing for moral responsibility to be responsibility *for*, and so questions whether determinism threatens moral responsibility, and how, if so, we should respond to the threat, must lapse for lack of a subject. These, then, are less urgent than questions whether determinism threatens agency, and how, if so, we should respond.

Let us turn now to the main argument. I begin by laying out and comparing two conceptions of alternative possibilities.

II

According to one view, there are contingencies or alternative possibilities in the universe, and then matters come to be settled one way or the other in the course of history.[3] We can suppose, for example, that it is unsettled and contingent now whether a fire will break out at such and such a house

---

[3] 'Settled' is Richmond Thomason's word. J. L. Mackie, 1974, used 'fixed' for the same idea. I apply 'settled' and 'unsettled' to occurrences etc. themselves, rather than to truth-values or to sentences. This paper side-steps questions about the truth-value of sentences conveying what is not yet settled.

at future time *t*. The issue will be settled at *t* itself at latest, otherwise at some future time between now and *t*. For example, if it makes sense to think of an outcome as physically necessitated[4] in advance of its occurrence, then in such a case the outcome is to be thought of as settled before it is present. However, in the kind of contingency we are talking about the outcome may not be settled before being present. In general with this kind of contingency, it must first be indeterminate which way the outcome will be. Then conditions arise which necessitate its subsequent occurrence one way and not the other. Now the outcome is settled, although maybe some time must pass before the actuality of it is present. Or maybe the outcome is not pre-necessitated, and it comes to be settled just when it comes to be present. A world containing this sort of contingency becomes determinate bit by bit through time.[5] For as long as even some small-scale outcome *O* is indeterminate, the entire stage of world-history containing *O*, or alternatively its absence, is likewise indeterminate. The entire stage becomes determinate only when the occurrence of *O*, or its non-occurrence, comes to be settled at a given point in the time series. And at that point, *O*-or-not has ceased to be a contingency. One or other side is no longer possible: from being unsettled it has become excluded.

However, to say that a contingency such as *O*-or-not is settled *within* the course of history is to say something stronger than that its settlement occurs at a location in the time series. As we have just seen, this last point also applies to the entire world stage of which *O* or its absence will be a proper part. The stronger point, which applies only to proper parts such as *O*, is that the change from unsettled to settled, and the specific settled outcome, happen and exist in a specific nest of conditions: conditions which are present and can be counted upon to continue into the short-term future whichever way the contingency goes. Since the conditions vary from case to case, the effect in the sense of what difference a settlement makes depends in part on context. Turning up the heating in freezing weather may make us uncomfortably hot, but if the context includes someone's just having opened a window, it merely stops us from becoming uncomfortably cold. This is not, of course, a point just about

---

[4] I.e. necessitated given some state of the natural universe plus the laws of nature. I am not presupposing that nature is as physicalism represents it.

[5] Throughout this paper I am assuming (a) that coming to be settled is necessarily from earlier to later (there is no backwards coming to be), and (b) that nothing can come to be unsettled or contingent from being settled.

the effects of actions. Whether an uncontrollable downpour will help the crop or destroy it depends on conditions which are present whether there is going to be a downpour or not. The conditions (which in this example include the existence of the crop and all that this presupposes) function as constraints on what can happen or arise within or under them. According to this way of modal thinking, the possible is possible-at-a-given-time, because it is the conditions prevailing at a time that define the range of alternatives possible then. What is possible is what is physically possible under those conditions. This is why the conditions that help determine the effect of the downpour will be present whether the downpour happens or not: as constraints on possibility they exist in both alternative possible worlds, the one in which it happens and the one in which it does not. And retrospectively we see the very conditions under which the actual alternative came about as those under which the other would have come about if so it had.

III

Prospectively, our prediction of the effect of each alternative depends on our picture of the conditions, and is well founded only if that picture is. And so with our counterfactual retrodiction of the effect of the unactualised alternative. There is a difference, though, and it is to retrodiction's advantage. Retrodiction, whether factual or counterfactual, is epistemically more secure. In predicting what conditions will be common to both alternatives we can only go by what we observe and what experience has taught us follows or generally follows; but we cannot be sure that what we observe, or the general pattern that what we observe is part of, will not be disrupted, overridden, or cancelled by unexpected interference. Thus we can predict that if it rains tomorrow or the next day the crop will be ruined, and that if it stays dry there will be a decent harvest for the farmer; but whichever rain-alternative turns out actual, the corresponding prediction will be falsified if later on today, unbeknownst to us who make the predictions, thieves will carefully transplant the crop to a far away favourable location. Nor can we be sure in advance that if this does not happen, nothing else will interfere. So the predictions are conditional on a *ceteris paribus* clause whose truth-value is unknown. But retrospectively we know whether there *was* interference or not, and if we know there was none we know that the general pattern (assuming we correctly identified it in the first place) was not upset. So we have the same unconditional assurance in retrodicting what *would have* happened to the crop if the rain (which fell) hadn't fallen, as we have in stating what actually *did* happen to it given the actual rain.[6] We have better knowledge of the counterfactual world retrospectively than of the actual one prospectively.

(A qualification is necessary. The point just made does not, I think, hold when 'If it rains at *t* the crop will be ruined', and the corresponding retrospective counterfactual (given that it did not rain at *t*) are meant to spell out a dispositional property, say the tendency to bruise very easily. That the crop has/had this property is so even if thieves transported it away before the rainfall. Hence the conditionals are not falsified by such a circumstance. To be true for them is to be true under normal conditions – which may not be the actual ones. In this sort of case, retrospection seems to have no epistemic advantage over prediction.[7])

To return to the main argument. I have just watched my companion light a pipe, and am virtually certain that if he had not struck the match, applied the flame, and drawn on the pipe, he would be sitting where he is now (perhaps finishing an actually broken off sentence), holding an intact match in one hand and an unlit pipe and a matchbox in the other. On what is this virtual certainty based? On one level the answer has been given in the previous paragraph. I have extracted a pattern from experience and applied it to the case in front of me, and I am in the best possible position to know that nothing previously unexpected came up to break the pattern. But suppose a philosopher pressed me as follows: 'In a way I do not question the epistemic credentials of your counterfactual belief; it is justified according to standards by which we judge some such beliefs to be more reasonable, given the evidence of experience, than others. But your acceptance of any such belief depends on the assumption that conditions which existed in the actual situation, e.g. the man's being there with pipe and matchbox, would have existed in the counterfactual one too. And surely it is momentous to assume that! For you assume in effect that you as good as know not only what is surely perfectly obvious – namely, that if something which actually happened had not (for example, if he had not lit his pipe), then some other possible world would have been actual instead of this one – but something else as well which is surely not obvious at all: namely, that whatever world it is that would have been

---

[6] (This is not quite accurate. It would be true if unexpected interferences were all such as to block both the actual and the counterfactual (what had otherwise been going to be actual) outcomes. In such cases, the unimpeded occurrence of the actual one is our assurance of counterfactual unimpeded occurrence of the alternative. But there can be interferences that would have thwarted only the counterfactual situation.)

[7] This point arose out of discussion with Lars Gundersen and Agustin Rayo.

actual instead of this one is a world that resembles this one in all sorts of highly specific and not at all to be taken for granted respects. Leibniz has provided a picturesque way for me to put my question. On what basis do you assume that if God had not created this actual world in which the man lit the pipe etc., God would have created instead a world that is *so* similar?[8] Of course God *might* have created, instead of the actual world, one that is very similar to it; but you are implying that God not just might have done this, but *would* have.'[9]

To this I reply in four parts. (1) I do not object to the talk of possible worlds. Even if it is rather thrilling to think that if the person had not lit his pipe on the occasion in question, some (in fact) merely possible world would have been actual instead of this (in fact) actual one, the thrill is not grounds for rejecting this way of conceiving of things. What is exciting need not be faulty or treacherous. However, (2) please do not invoke the Leibnizian Creator in this context. I ask this not from aversion to theism or to using God as a model, but because the Leibnizian Creator suggests a wrong model for the modal concepts I have been using. For according to Leibniz, this, the best of all possible worlds, the one uniquely actualised by the Leibnizian Creator, is a completely deterministic system: for any particular stage of its history, only one subsequent stage is possible. But (3) I by contrast have been operating with a sense of 'contingent' in which it means 'possible either way given our laws of nature plus all mundane particulars that are already settled'.[10] On this basis it is unsurprising that the world of the unactualised possibility is so similar to that of the actualised one. For, self-evidently, constraints on possibility, however one interprets them, obtain in all worlds not excluded by the constraints; hence if the constraints partly consist in the obtaining of some particular set of circumstances, it follows trivially that these circumstances obtain across the entire range of possibilities. (4) Your remarks suggest that I do not know, although I operate as if I know, that the counterfactual world would have been very like the actual world in the ways indicated. I agree with both suggestions. Operating as if I knew this

---

[8] By 'world' ('possible world') in the Leibnizian context I mean not 'possible way things are', since this applies to God's willing that this or that universe should exist, but 'possible creatum', which applies only to *what* an omnipotent God wills to exist or obtain. For the most part in this paper 'world' and 'world-history' are used of the kind of thing a universe-transcending creator is supposed to create, while leaving it open whether any such thing exists through being thus divinely created.

[9] Leibniz would surely have held that if God had not created this, the best possible, world (in the sense of n. 8), God would have willed that there exist nothing besides himself.

[10] This of course entails the unsettledness of what is contingent (as long as it is contingent).

assumption to be true is part and parcel of my interpreting possibility in the way just sketched. Or, more fully: the ease with which I operate as if I knew this assumption to be true shows that the above way of interpreting possibility is the natural way for me to adopt when counterfactual conditionals are in the offing. I am willing, though (at least for present purposes), to go along with someone who tells me I do not *know* the assumption to be true, for I certainly cannot demonstrate that the conception of possibility with which it is bound up is one we *must*, in the context of counterfactual conditions, employ if we are not to count as irrational. Even so, I think it can be shown that rejecting this conception in favour of its rival (I shall consider just one rival) carries a significant cost.

IV

Now for the other conception of alternative possibilities. This incorporates what I shall call the 'Everything Settled' view (ES).[11] According to this, everything in history, from beginning to end or infinitely in either or both temporal directions, is settled at all times in history, or is timelessly settled. Or one can say that history is settled as a whole. Events *occur* at times within history, but there are no times within history when the occurrence or non-occurrence of an event at a given time *becomes settled* (*or excluded*) *after being unsettled*. By the same token, the causes of events occur at times, and if they are deterministic causes they (given the laws of nature) can be said to necessitate their effects; but this necessitating is not a rendering settled of what was not so before the cause occurred. Again, most, if not all, events in history 'make a difference' in that they have effects which would not have occurred if they had not. But no event in history makes a difference *when it occurs*, by making be settled, as of then, consequences different from what would have come to be in place as of then if the first event had not occurred. This is just as true of events for which people are held responsible, and of ones that seem to be strokes of good or bad luck, as it is of events having no personal significance for anyone. It may be conceptually coherent, on this view of things, to blame a nanny's negligence or a driver's recklessness when a child runs out and is

---

[11] ES has obvious affinities with the 'block' view of the universe, according to which all states of affairs are real, whether present, past or future. No doubt 'blockism' entails ES, but (as Stephen Lawrence and Stephen Makin pointed out) one could hold that only the present is real while also seeing the past and the future as completely settled.

hit by a car at *t*. But it is clearly a mistake to wonder if the difference between a future in which the child grows up paralysed and one in which, so far as one knows, it grows up able-bodied, was made *forty-five seconds before*, when the telephone call distracted the nanny, or, rather: *two hours before*, when the postman left open the gate that should have been closed, or, rather: *fifteen minutes before*, when the car's passengers were taunting the driver with being slow and timid. If the difference between those futures is indeed to be considered 'made', in the sense that one of them from being merely possible comes to be settled, whereas the other, from being possible comes to be excluded, it is not made when they are future in the ordinary sense in which things are future by comparison with present events and past events belonging to the same history. For then the difference would be made within history. Any difference made, given the ES view, must have been due to someone or something that acts 'before' history, or perhaps even 'outside' time, so as to realise one entire history rather than another.[12]

An absolutely deterministic history is obviously an ES one. (By 'absolutely deterministic' I mean a system such that (a) miracles and sheer anomic freaks are out of the question, so everything in it happens only according to natural law,[13] and (b) all laws are such that for every subsequent state there is an antecedent one which physically necessitates it.[14] An indeterministic system is one for which either (a) fails or (b) does.) And it is equally obvious, I think, that a history that comes to be settled bit by bit is indeterministic, whether through failure of (a) or of (b). However – and this is perhaps marginally less obvious – an indeterministic history might in fact be an ES one. That a history is such that not every stage of it is necessitated by the preceding stage according to the laws of nature does not entail that the contents of all the stages were not all settled from the start.

Given ES, what can it mean to say that a particular occurrence *O* and its absence are each possible, so that *O*-or-not is contingent? It cannot mean that each is compatible with the laws of nature plus all particulars

---

[12] It would be too quick to conclude at once that the notion of human agency is not compatible with the ES view of history. For a thorough investigation based on the assumption that it is not, see Belnap, Perloff, and Xu, 2001.

[13] Clause (a) is often left out when determinism is specified in the debate on whether we can be morally responsible if the theory is true, because allowing in freaks and miracles does not provide the 'elbowroom' which everyone agrees is necessary for moral responsibility and which some see as incompatible with determinism.

[14] The determination, in this sense, of earlier states by later ones is not examined in this paper.

that are already settled. On that account, either *O* is impossible or its absence is. Given determinism, 'each possible' (in a non-epistemic sense) can mean no more than that each is compatible with natural law. Given ES and indeterminism, 'each possible' is most naturally taken to mean that each is compatible with natural law plus certain boundary conditions, either the boundary conditions at the beginning of the universe or those obtaining just before *O* or its absence. In an ES universe, whether deterministic or indeterministic, nothing ceases to be contingent in the relevant sense; if *O*-or-not is contingent, then if *O* fails to occur, its occurrence is just as possible after the time in question as it was before.

v

Almost everyone, including almost every determinist, believes that we can often be sure that (say) someone has killed somebody, which implies 'has brought it about that somebody is dead sooner than they would have been otherwise (i.e., in the absence of the particular event *E* that constitutes the killing)'. Now, determinists believe that there has never been a stage of history such that given the way things were at that stage, it was possible then that *E* would not take place with the consequences it has. For example, they believe that given that each of the persons involved had simply been born, it was inevitable, given everything else that was so, that they would meet and the killing occur. Yet when determinists think about what the alternative actuality would have been like if, instead of *E*'s happening at *t*, *E* had not happened at *t*, they usually think, like everyone else, that the victim would have been alive at least for a while after *t*, he would have come home for dinner that night, his wife and children would not have been widow and orphans. What singles out determinists is that they do not believe this alternative scenario was ever a possibility, given actual history. But why, and with what right, out of all the alternative and similarly impossible scenarios, including ones in which the man never existed, or was wifeless and childless, or in which the human race never evolved, does a determinist pick just the one everyone else picks as answer to the question: 'How would things have been at *t* and on for a while from then if, instead of happening as it actually did, *E* hadn't happened?'

It is easier to say why than with what right. One wants to be able, sometimes at least, to give a definite answer to that sort of counterfactual question. Let us distinguish between simply asking a counterfactual question, and asking a counterfactual question on the basis of a supposition. Sometimes we wonder: 'Suppose *p* at *t*: how in that case would things have been if E hadn't happened at t?' If E is a downpour, we give different answers depending on whether p says that there has been an ongoing drought in which the seeds haven't started to germinate, or that a splendid crop of fragile fruit was just reaching its peak. Not only are the descriptive conclusions different, but the meaning of p also determines whether the counterfactual non-occurrence of the downpour (supposing p) would have been a bad thing or a good one – say for the farmer on the one hand, and for his non-farming enemy on the other. Sometimes, however, and more basically, we wonder without supposition: 'How *would* things have been if the downpour hadn't happened?' And here we work out our answer against not merely a supposed or imagined background of circumstances which may or may not be the actual ones of the downpour, but against the background of the actual ones, which, far from just supposing to obtain in the counterfactual situation, we categorically assume *would* have obtained in it. The counterfactual conditionals that are central to the argument of this paper are ones delivered as non-suppositional answers to non-suppositional counterfactual questions about particular events.

I shall view such a question as one of a retrospective pair:

(1) If E (which occurred) had not occurred, how *would* things have been? and:

(2) If E (which did not occur) had occurred, how *would* things have been?

corresponding to the prospective pair:

(1*) If E occurs (i.e. will occur), how *will* things be? and:

(2*) If E does not (i.e. will not) occur, how *will* things be?

I shall assume that the paradigm context for the prospective questions is that of *comparative evaluation of alternative near-future outcomes. E* is an event the questioner sees as worth bringing about or worth preventing or not worth trouble either way, or one whose uncontrollable occurrence or non-occurrence is desirable, undesirable or indifferent. It follows from the nature of the context that the two single-starred questions are asked at the same time, hence under the same set of conditions C, and that some of those conditions are seen by the questioner as stretching forward into the imminent future in which E or its non-occurrence will appear. It also follows from the context that the questioner will build into the alternative question-scenarios whatever parts of C are relevant to the evaluation being made. Thus both the scenarios include parts of or expectable developments from C consisting in the existence of persons who are objects of concern for the questioner and likely recipients of weal or woe in consequence of E or not-E. Both scenarios include parts of or expectable developments from C that consist in the good state of things which E will damage or not-E will save; or alternatively (depending on the actual contents of C), each includes parts of C that stand in that relation to the bad state of things which E will improve or not-E will fail to alleviate. Both scenarios include causal laws and any unmentioned circumstances in C that are causally relevant to the predictions that support the comparative evaluation. Now once the event falls due, either happening or failing to happen, one of the two retrospective counter-factual questions (1) and (2) is *born* (arises, becomes applicable), while the other is *aborted* – because its antecedent is true of actuality. The aborted counterfactual is replaced, so to speak, by a different sort of retrospective question, one of the form: 'How *were* things, given that . . .?' Thus we have the non-counterfactual retrospective pair:

(1**) Given that E occurred, how *were* things?
    and:
(2**) Given that E did not occur, how *were* things?

Unlike (1*) and (2*), (1**) and (2**) cannot be asked together. Nor of course can (1) and (2). But (1**) and (2**) are like their counterfactual counterparts in that one is born when and only when the other is aborted. Thus the earlier pairing of (1*) with (2*) is replaced by a subsequent pairing of simultaneously askable questions: either by the pair (1**) and (1) or by the pair (2**) and (2), depending on whether E did or didn't occur. These are sets of twins, necessarily born together or aborted together.

Enough, I hope, has been said to explain why, whichever way the event falls, we seem to know as much as we do about how things *would have been* – not merely how they would have been on some supposition – if the event had fallen the other way. Given the way in which,[15] and the logical company in which, this kind of counterfactual question gets born, it is unsurprising that the world invoked by its antecedent has so much in common with the easily observable actual world.

Here I have tried to give a sort of explanation for why beings such as we, essentially geared to see particular events as bringing weal or woe, operate as if it is quite obvious to us how, in many respects, things would

---

[15] I.e. by transformation from one of a prospective pair.

have been in some counterfactual situation. But, as in other cases, for instance theistic belief, explaining does not make an attitude epistemically respectable. I shall now argue that our assumption that we can form reasonably grounded pictures of counterfactual situations is open to serious challenge. But first let me briefly consider what could be gained by proposing such an argument, even if it is not defective. For it may be said that our seeming to possess the counterfactual knowledge with which I am concerned is so fundamental to our whole way of being that we cannot genuinely question this appearance or subject it to rational criticism. And (it may be said) there is no point in challenging a view unless one is prepared to reject it or at least suspend judgment in the absence of counterargument. The reply to this is twofold. Firstly, if a belief or attitude is rationally wanting, it is worth finding this out even if we are built so that we cannot give it up. Secondly, by studying the conditions under which undiscardable belief *B* would be false or very unlikely to be true, we can increase the chances of holding it in an epistemically respectable way. For example, if *D* is a belief whose truth entails that *B* is false or very unlikely to be true, then if we have been harbouring *D* we can give *D* up and thereby render our adherence to *B* more respectable – unless, of course, we are so unlucky that *D* grips us as strongly as does *B*. Even so, the first part of the reply still holds.

VI

The possible world invoked by the counterfactual antecedent of question (1) above is the non-*E* world picked out as most similar to the actual world, where 'most similar' is given a sufficiently definite meaning by what the late David Lewis called 'the standard resolution' of the vagueness of counterfactual conditionals.[16] (Likewise, *mutatis mutandis*, for the possible world invoked by the antecedent of (2).) The constraints informing the standard resolution are articulated by considering which real-life counterfactual conditionals we normally treat as acceptable candidates for truth or falsity, and observing the differences-from-actuality that are common to the possible worlds of the antecedents.[17] Specifically,

---

[16] 'Counterfactual Dependence and Time's Arrow'. This paper, which first appeared in *Nous* 13 (1979), 455–76, has been reprinted with postscripts by the author in Lewis, 1986 and in Jackson, 1991.

[17] '. . . we must use what we know about the truth and falsity of counterfactuals to see if we can find some sort of similarity relation that . . . [yields] the proper truth conditions . . . we must use what we know about counterfactuals to find out about the appropriate similarity relation – not the other way around.' Lewis, in Jackson (1991), 58.

the world singled out in each case is one where (a) the laws of nature, and (b) earlier history up to just before the event or non-event portrayed in the counterfactual antecedent, are the same as in actuality.[18] It follows that either both worlds, the actual and the counterfactual one most similar to it,[19] are indeterministic in the sense that not all their laws are deterministic, or the laws in both are deterministic, but a 'miracle' occurs in one, in that its deterministic laws suffer an exception.

Now consider these two propositions:

(P)   The most similar non-E world is the one we invoke when considering how things would have been if E had not occurred.

(Q)   If E had not occurred, the most similar non-E world would have been actual instead of this (the actually actual) world.

P is trivially true, since our understanding of 'most similar' has been tailored to reflect the assumptions governing real-life answers to such questions as 'How would things have been if E had not occurred?' But Q is not trivially true. We can see this from the fact that, although laypersons may feel at home with Q, some theorists would reject it. This is because Q presupposes 'absolute actualism', which some theorists reject. Absolute actualism understands actuality as a logically simple attribute that can belong to only one of a set of alternative possible worlds. This is by contrast with the indexical theory, according to which 'the actual world' means 'this world', so that every possible world is actual from its own point of view, and none is actual in an absolute way that privileges it above others. If we think of actuality as a property that (a) belongs to a world or a situation, and (b) would have belonged *instead* to some different world or situation if (for example) E, which happened at t, had not, then we are thinking of actuality as absolute. For on the indexical account no world can be actual *instead* of another: each is actual just 'at' itself.

Let us now raise a problem for absolute actualists who hold the ES view of world history. This problem is the same whether these thinkers are determinists or indeterminists.[20] We may think of a world-history as corresponding to a huge conjunction of propositions representing events

---

[18]   It should be added that the standard resolution is what applies to a certain very important type of counterfactual conditionals, viz. those implying dependence of a later event/non-event on an earlier.

[19]   By the standard resolution. From now on this qualification is taken for granted.

[20]   It makes no difference whether the latter are indeterminists about natural law or allow miraculous exceptions to deterministic laws.

and states of affairs at different times. To suppose false a conjunct of actual-world history, say the proposition that *E* occurs at *t*, is to suppose the whole conjunction false: that this whole history had not been. Given actualism, the question now for the ES theorist is: what conjunction would have been true *instead*? For human beings there is absolutely no way of telling! Even if science can show that actual-world history is the only history consistent with the actual laws of nature, this is no constraint. True, if we assume the actual laws limit what would have been actual instead, we can infer the alternative actuality is the null history; but there is no particular reason for the assumption. True, reflecting on the way we assign truth-values to counterfactual conditionals enables us to sketch some of the big conjunction that corresponds to the most similar non-*E*-at-*t* world. But there is nothing to guarantee or even render it metaphysically likely, so to speak, that this most similar world is the one that *would have been actual instead.*

As long as we operate our standard-resolution rule for counterfactual conditionals, we can determine with reasonable assurance which are true and which are false. Thus the rule enables us to specify, often with considerable certainty, how things would have been if *E* had not happened at *t*. For (a) *in* applying the rule we posit a background similar (in the ways explained) to that of the actual *E* at *t*; and (b) *by* applying it we can infer the consequence of not-*E*-at-*t*. Putting this together gives us quite a full picture of how things would have been. Now if we are also absolute actualists, we nurture the belief that some other possible history *would have been actual instead of* this one in which *E* did occur at *t*. If, however, we are ES theorists too, we are not justified in equating that alternative actuality with the way our rule implies things would have been if *E* had not happened at *t*. For in raising the counterfactual supposition we suppose the never-having-been-actual of all actual-world history. This is what follows from being ES theorists and absolute actualists simultaneously.

Absolute actualists, in other words, do not simply move their thoughts to some possible world different from the actual one but actual from its own point of view. If one simply does this latter thing, then of course one is perfectly entitled to take one's thoughts to a possible world with just the characteristics necessary to make it the proper test case, according to standard human practice, for the truth-value of a conditional such as 'If *E* had not happened at *t*, *G* would not have happened just after *t*'. In similar fashion, if someone says 'Suppose *E* had not happened at *t*. . .' we are entitled to take our thoughts to a possible world with characteristics necessary to make it hilariously funny that E did not happen at t. If we want to laugh or write jokes for comedians, this is the kind of world that being presented with the supposition would prompt us to summon up. If, instead, we want to know what the causal consequences would have been of E's not having happened at t, we take our thoughts to a world that is similar according to the standard resolution. (Yes, there is a huge difference between these two kinds of thought-trip. Ready interest in the causal bearing of events is with us almost every moment, its results shape the content of almost every kind of attitude; whereas readiness to laugh or make laugh is rather restricted even in a dedicated humourist. But I do not see this as telling against the parallel just drawn.)

The absolute actualist, then, does not simply consider the most similar non-E-at-t world, and check what else obtains in it. The absolute actualist also asserts that the world in question would have been actual instead, if E had not occurred at t. Now suppose we have a thinker who, as well as being an absolute actualist, is an ES theorist. (An example is Leibniz, who combined determinism with the view that God conferred absolute actuality on just one possible world.[21]) For such a thinker, I suggest, to raise a counterfactual supposition is to suppose the never-having-been-actual of all world-history. Who can say what sort of world-history would have been actual instead? But it may seem fallacious to interpret this in the way I do, i.e. as an unanswerable question. Surely, one might say, we can consider actual history as an ES reality, and still imagine a small piece E removed from its time t and replaced by a piece that has a contrary nature, and then ask what further difference(s) we ought to imagine as obtaining soon afterwards, given actual laws of nature. And surely if one can do this one *can* say how things would actually have been instead, at the later moment, given the difference at t: things would actually have been just as they are represented in the consequent of a true counterfactual conditional whose antecedent is 'E didn't happen at t' and whose vagueness is resolved by the standard method. In reply: we can imagine a set of sentences 'p', 'q', 'r', etc. arranged so as to constitute a chronicle of what there is through time, and then we can imagine, say, 'q' removed from its place in the chronicle[22] and replaced by '$\sim q$' or by some contrary sentence. We then imagine some related replacement at a later point. But the fact that we can do this, plus the fact that the original chronicle was the story of the actual world, does not make it reasonable to assume

---

[21] See note 8 on the terminology.

[22] 'Chronicle' implies that the order of narration is the same as the temporal order of events narrated.

that the new chronicle is one that portrays the history[23] that would have been actual if E had happened at t instead of not. Suppose, though, one says: 'I am not talking about imagining replacing the actually true story with another story like it in lots of ways. I am talking about imagining replacing one bit of the extra-story reality portrayed in the actually true story with a different extra-story bit.' I reply: 'You cannot mean that you imagine the actually true story first being true and then becoming false because one of the bits that makes it true is removed and replaced with a bit not matched in that story. Nor can you mean that you imagine a story that is actually false – though it resembles the actually true one in ways explained under "standard resolution" – becoming actually true because a demon replaces the extra-story bits that make the first story false with bits taken from corresponding positions in the series of bits that makes the actually true story true. From such incoherent imaginings no conclusion can be drawn. What I think you imagine is something like a space at t in actual history; and then you imagine history as it is if E's occurrence is in that space (which of course is how history actually is); and then for comparison you imagine history as it is if E's non-occurrence is in that space. But any point of view from which it makes sense to imagine the space that can be filled either way (unless it just corresponds to a blank in our knowledge, which is not the issue here) will be somewhere in the time-line before t; and from such a point of view the space is simply a contingency not yet actualised one way or the other. Thus your imagining makes sense only because what you imagine is a bit-by-bit history.'

It is not difficult to see that if determinists embrace absolute actualism by naïvely wondering what would have been *actual instead* if E had not occurred at t, they are committed to asking the unanswerable question: which entire world-history would have been actual instead? But indeterminists too face this problem if they are of the ES persuasion and engage in the same naïve wondering, although in their case the difficulty is less obvious. It is tempting to think that if the occurrence of E at t was not necessitated by previous conditions given the laws of nature, then we can securely infer from the counterfactual supposition that E did not happen to the conclusion that the world that would have been actual instead would have been just like the actual one up to, at and after t, except for the differences made at and after t by E and its effects. But the security is an illusion fed from two sources. Once these are set aside, the inference is

[23] I use 'chronicle' and 'story' for the representation, 'history' for the train of events etc. represented.

revealed as groundless. The first source is the fact that in considering how things would have been in the counterfactual situation, we rightly consider a possible world exactly like the one the inference claims would have been actual instead. But, as we have seen, the rightfulness of that considering does not entail or license talk of what *would* have been actual instead. The second source is the thought that the state of things up to *t* plus any necessary consequences of that state considered in abstraction from the occurrence of *E* and *its* consequences is somehow a settled given, so that the only variation we are entitled to consider is that represented by our mentally replacing the occurrence of *E* with its non-occurrence, or *vice versa*. However, this would be justified only if we were prepared to assert that those elements were in reality settled at a time when, or in a way in which, the issue of *E*-or-not was not. But then we would have abandoned the ES view.

Let us leave the would-be ES absolute actualists, and return to the view of history as becoming settled bit by bit (section II above). Perhaps one who takes this view is not theoretically obliged to be an absolute actualist; but, more important for the present purpose, she is not precluded from it. The thought that if so and so had not happened, such and such would have happened *instead*, is an extremely natural one. Its natural root, very likely, is our use of the pairs of prospective questions such as 1* and 2* (see section V). The members of such a pair not only are asked but also are answered together, since identical features of the context are invoked in answering both. It is this identical-whichever-way-it-goes context that figures as the place or 'stead' 'in' which one and only one of the two outcomes can occur. The bit-by-bit view allows us to take this picture seriously without embarrassment. It allows us to think of the single identical context (and its antecedents) as settled even when it is not yet settled whether *E* will occur or not. This contrast and combination of the settled and the as yet unsettled is exactly what we need in order to sustain the thought that something is actual instead of something else. For a place that is to be filled by this or by that is necessarily fixed by comparison with an indeterminate filling that can take either of the two forms. It is clear, then, that as long as we conceive of the 'stead' as a set of circumstances existing at a time within history, the very question 'What would have been actual then instead, if so and so?' ensures that we draw our answer from features within history, and that we therefore do so by ordinary empirical reasoning. In other words, the question so conceived blocks any passage to the hopeless standpoint that demands to know which entire world-history, if *E* hadn't happened at *t*, would have been actual instead: i.e. in some transcendent 'stead' or lap of the gods outside all history or even outside time.

VII

I have suggested that, for the ES absolute actualist, counterfactually supposing that E did not happen at t implies counterfactually supposing the never-having-been-actual of the whole of actual-world history. If that is correct, the question 'How would things have been instead?' is unanswerable for this type of thinker. But someone may reject my suggestion by saying: 'ES absolute actualists, like everyone else, are entitled – indeed, they ought – to answer that question in the regular way, by invoking the world most similar to the actual. Then their answer, like everyone else's, will be something like "The crop would have been safe at t", "The child would not have been knocked down by the car at t". Of course they gloss this with: "I mean, the world that would have been actual instead is one in which that child wouldn't have been knocked down etc. at t." But the main point is that you have shown no reason why, because they are ES theorists, they should not answer mundane counter-factual questions in the ordinary way, and trust those answers as much as everyone else does.'

I answer firstly that it still remains true that as ES theorists these actualists must understand the counterfactual supposition as supposing the never-having-been of entire actual history. Thus if they are right to be confident, as the objector encourages them to be, that the usual method gives them acceptable answers to ordinary counterfactual questions, they must by implication be right to be confident that the usual method tells them with reasonable assurance what alternative history would have been actual from the very beginning if entire actual history never had been. But it is incomprehensible how the usual method should be so powerful a source of reasonable assurance. Even though it *is* the usual method, how can they be entitled to it on the same basis as everyone else if, in their hands, it is so much more powerful than it is for everyone else?

Secondly, there is a special difficulty about determinism. If absolute actualists hold that determinism is true, presumably they hold it true of the actual world. Now according to traditional determinism, I believe, either it is predetermined that E would happen at t or it is predetermined that E would not happen at t. Thus the counterfactual outcome would have been predetermined no less than the actual one. In the light of modern technical understanding of counterfactual conditionals we now see that this part of traditional determinism must be given up. The possible world invoked under standard resolution shares the past and the laws of nature with this world, Alpha, the one in which we are currently working out how things would have been if *E* had not happened. So if absolute determinism is true of Alpha, the counterfactual world must be one containing a jot or tittle of indeterminism, enough to ensure that in it *E* fails to happen at *t* even though the laws and the past are the same as in Alpha. The jot or tittle consists in a freak or miracle whereby one or another deterministic law fails to hold at or just before *t*.[24] This may seem not unreasonable as long as one stays retrospective. But let us go back in time (in both worlds) to the moment when someone was asking the prospective questions, (1*) and (2*) above. He does not yet know which of the two corresponding worlds will turn out to be the one that is actual instead of (or 'rather than') the other. He does not yet know whether, after *t*, he will be thinking *E*-worldly thoughts about how things would have been if *E* had not occurred, or not-*E*-worldly thoughts about how things would have been if it had. But if he is a determinist and has followed our argument so far, he is supposed to think to himself 'Whichever way it goes, it will be the counterfactual world that is inde-terministic.' And so on for every such pair of prospective questions. But what an incredible coincidence, and a lucky one for determinists, that it is always the counterfactual member of the corresponding retrospective question-pair that invokes an indeterministic world!

It is absurd to be a determinist on these terms, but one can avoid this absurdity by giving up a way of thinking that may be natural but is presumably not indispensable: i.e. thinking of prospective question-pairs as being about *actual* and *alternatively actual* worlds, whichever is which. And the ES theorist, whether determinist or not, can avoid the previous absurdity by rejecting talk of world-history that would have been actual instead of this one, or of this one as actual instead of others. Stripped of absolute actualism, one sees the possible world invoked in answering the question 'How would things have gone if E had not occurred at *t*?' as no more and no less than the appropriate *donné* for the thought-experiment we undertake when we ask the question.

Philosophical debate on the pros and cons of absolute actualism and the various alternative positions has been waged extensively and on a variety of fronts. This paper has adduced a fairly narrow set of considerations.

---

[24] Cf. Lewis, 1986.

They raise amongst others the question (not to be pursued here) whether if we abandon absolute actualism it still makes sense to speak, think, and feel as we do about being better or worse off. I am relieved that I succeeded in bringing about E, or disappointed that G has occurred, because it seems to me that someone I am concerned about is better or worse off than would otherwise have been the case. Is what grounds my relief sufficiently captured by the thought, say, that in the most similar non-E world – let it be a world in which someone failed to start the car – the person is stranded late at night in a dangerous part of town, whereas in actuality the person is travelling home normally, in warmth and security? Has something essential for relief evaporated if I am not allowed additionally to think that most similar non-E world is what would have been actual instead?

VIII

To return to the opening claim of this paper: determinism presents a problem for agency because it presents a more general problem concerning knowledge of, or reasonable grounds for affirming, counterfactual conditionals. The intelligent agent acts so as to make a specific difference – most commonly, to make things better in some specific way than they would have been without this action. Hence the agent takes herself to have a reasonably founded belief that things would have been a certain way. It is very natural to interpret this belief as a picture of what, but for the action, would have been actual instead. But that is what harbours the problem. For according to the argument of this paper, if determinism is true, no counterfactual belief so interpreted (whether it is the belief of an initiating agent or of someone gearing up to respond to an event initiated elsewhere) can be well founded: we can have no idea how things would have been.

What creates the problem is not determinism alone, but determinism combined with absolute actualism. And in this combination what causes the trouble is not determinism as such but the Everything Settled view of the world, of which determinism is just one form. Must one, then, choose between ES and absolute actualism? Yes, if one is a typical contemporary analytic philosopher. By this I mean a philosopher who, among other things, endorses the commonsense assumption that we can sensibly evaluate counterfactual conditionals for truth or falsity, and who explains the evaluation in the terms of possible-worlds theory. Such a philosopher must either deny ES or reject expressions portraying this world as actual *uniquely* – so that any alternative would have been actual *instead.*

But this choice facing the typical contemporary analytic philosopher does not exhaust the possibilities. The ancient Stoics would certainly have declared for absolute (rather than indexical) actualism,[25] and of course they were absolute determinists. To be consistent, they would need to let go of our human sense that we *really can tell* that things would have gone this way or that if *X* or *Y* hadn't happened. Working to weaken our sense of acquaintanceship with mundane counterfactual alternatives, to undermine the feeling of practically jostling up against them, would be a fine exercise for anyone pursuing the Stoic ideal of complete acceptance of all that there is. But literally divesting ourselves of that sense is not a project in which human animals could get far at all, if, as I assume, our every controlled movement is charged with innumerable subliminal counterfactual conditionals. (The thought is that controlled movement is guided by an ever-changing series of subliminal (unarticulated) prospective conditionals which smoothly and often almost instantaneously transmute, as a side effect, into factual/counterfactual combinations such as 'I didn't put my full weight on the branch and it didn't break under me / If I had landed more heavily, it would have started to give way'.[26]) Consider also our sense that physical objects are *there*, with *lives or careers of their own.* I walk back into the room and everything is as I left it, except that the fire has burnt down. I look out of the window to see what is there. That is: the fire has gone on burning just as it would have done had I stayed beside it (no one tending it); what I open the shutters to see is what would have been there even if I hadn't looked. To scrape away at our trust in this sort of counterfactual conditional[27] is to unpick the sense, necessary to human animals, of an objectively real environment.

It might, however, be a humanly viable Stoic-style project to learn to distance oneself from, while still suffering, the intimations of alternative actualities that inform our every step. (It would be like withholding rational assent from superstitious beliefs even though one cannot help seeing any Room 13 as a sinister place for spending the night.) This might result in a supine attitude similar to what is supposedly engendered by

---

[25] It is not clear whether they could allow that any alternative world is in any sense possible. If they could not, then the absolute actuality of this world is in a way less dramatic for them than it is for most absolute actualists.

[26] If the point holds, it surely holds for animals in general.

[27] Whereas we have been mainly concerned with the type used to assert dependence of something on something, the kind just considered is used to assert *in*dependence.

the ancient Lazy Argument.[28] After all, our pre-reflective pictures of alternatives are full of gaps, and often by ordinary epistemic standards they are inaccurate. As things presently are, people investigate an accident because they are not sure they see straight off what would have had to be different for it not to have happened. They deliberate because they don't seem to see straight off what difference in terms of consequences would be 'made' by doing *A* rather than not-*A*. They want to get clear about the difference so as to bring about the better course. But if the thought took hold that such inquiries at best yield empirically coherent *illusions* of reasonable belief about alternative actualities, then in some minds the motivation for inquiring might wither. Yet this is not rationally inevitable. It would be more in keeping with actual Stoic thought and practice to be vigorous in building up those ultimately illusory pictures of alternative actualities in accordance with the ordinary epistemic norms. For the pictures still give us choice. The ethical and intellectual quality of a choice does not depend on what difference it contributes to the world. No doubt we cannot *intend* to bring about *E* and relegate its inferior alternative to counterfactuality if we consider we have no grounds at all for believing that the course of things by comparison with which the *E*-course is preferable is what would have been actual instead. But even in such an epistemic state one can *prefer* one set of things to another. The preference declares what we would intend if we thought we might make the corresponding difference.

---

[28] 'If *p* will be the case, it will be the case whether you try to prevent it/make it happen or not, and the same for ∼*p*; but either *p* will be the case or ∼*p* will; therefore . . .'

CHAPTER 5

A contemporary look at
Aristotle's changing Now

The aim of this paper is to bring two ideas together for mutual illumination. One is Aristotle's conception of the now as 'always different and different' (*Physics* IV.10, 218a10; 11, 219b12–23); the other is the modern dichotomy of time into the two aspects of *order* and *passage*. This dichotomy was first formulated in 1908 by the Cambridge philosopher, J. M. E. McTaggart, who made it the basis of a brilliant and controversial proof of the unreality of time.[1] From then on McTaggart's distinction has dominated discussion of time among analytic philosophers; hence it provides a contemporary perspective from which to think about Aristotle's contribution.[2]

On one side of the distinction, events are considered as past, present, and future, and their occurrence is expressed by sentences with tensed verbs. The most striking thing about this approach is that the attributes of being future, present, and past, and the corresponding tenses, *take it in turns* to belong to each successive set of events. Consequently, what lies (as we say) in the future, in the present, and in the past, is changing from moment to moment. The occasion for which this paper was first written was once future, later on was present, and in a few more days was completely in the past, even if long to be remembered. We can think of each event as passing from the future through the present to the past. Alternatively, we can think of the future, the present, and the past as temporal locations whose contents are always changing in a regular way.

According to the other side of the distinction, events are considered as standing to each other in the relations of *before* and *after* and *at the same position as*, which in its temporal interpretation means *simultaneous with*.

---

[1] McTaggart, 1908, 457–74 (reprinted in his *Philosophical Studies*, (London, 1934)); a revised version of the argument is given in McTaggart, 1927, vol. II, ch. 33.
[2] In adopting this perspective on Aristotle, I follow the example of Richard Sorabji in chs. 3 and 4 of his 1983 study.

The most striking feature of *this* approach, when we compare it with the previous one, is the fact that the essential relationships are immutable throughout time. The deaths of Julius Caesar and Christopher Columbus were once both in the future, are now both in the past, while for many centuries one was past and the other future. But the order of these events is not affected by the time at which we consider them. Hence, although colloquially we use the past tense to express their temporal order – we say 'The death of Caesar preced*ed* that of Columbus' – this is logically quite unnecessary. For it is not as if the death of Caesar once preceded that of Columbus, but tomorrow, perhaps, might be simultaneous with it. Thus we are justified in using tenseless language to express these relationships, and likewise justified in regarding these relationships as 'timeless'.

If we distinguish this second approach by the *immutability* of the relations defining it, then it is natural to expand the repertoire of relevant concepts so as to include *metric* ones. The death of Julius Caesar precedes that of Christopher Columbus *by so much*, an interval which we can specify in years, months, or days. And the size of the interval is as unchanging as the order of the events that determine it. But although the order of the events and the size of the interval between them are immutable and timeless in the same way, there is an important difference. The order is more fundamental. Measurable intervals of time presuppose events in temporal order, but we can surely conceive of a world where events occur in temporal order at no definitely quantifiable intervals.

Given the radical difference between these two aspects of time, order and passage, it is natural to wonder how they relate together in a coherent unity. They are, perhaps, not merely aspects, but *the* aspects of time, since other attributes, such as time's unidirectionality, may be derivable from one or other of the above, or from the pair of them. They may, of course, turn out to be connected only externally, so to speak, so that time is simply their conjunction. If so, then while time itself is all-pervasive and inescapable, time's *nature* would be a sort of metaphysical happenstance: an amalgam of elements each making sense on its own somehow, and neither pointing to the other. From a theoretical point of view such a 'temporal dualism', as one might call it, would be very unsatisfactory, something we should try to resist.[3]

---

[3] The dualism problem clearly arises if the passage-attributes of pastness and futurity are understood (like presentness) simply as monadic properties. However, if we add the understanding that for any two non-simultaneous items that are past/future, one is further past/future than the other, it is

McTaggart, in effect, dispatches this threat of dualism by means of his argument for the unreality of time, on which a few words of explanation are now due. According to McTaggart, time consists of two disparate elements, one the shifting system of the attributes *pastness, presentness,* and *futurity,* the other a timeless series of timeless noumenal items ordered as prior and posterior in a non-temporal sense of 'prior/posterior'. Events considered as becoming past, becoming and ceasing to be present, and ceasing to be future were labelled by McTaggart the 'A-series'. The timeless order of timeless items he called the 'C-series'. Now, according to him, the *temporal* order of events is the product of the C-series and the A-attributes of futurity, presentness and pastness. By 'the temporal order of events' is meant the order in which events, themselves temporal items, stand to each other as earlier and later in time, and in which the intervals between events are temporal rather than more purely formal. What makes this order *temporal,* according to McTaggart, is the fact that its members exhibit change in respect of their A-determinations: each becomes present, having been future, and then becomes past. Thus the system of A-determinations, since it is necessary for *temporal* order, is necessary for time. McTaggart called temporal order the 'B-series'.

Having premised that temporal order, or the B-series, is the product of the system of A-determinations and the C-series, McTaggart then finds logical fault with the A-determinations. He argues that this system harbours either a self-contradiction or a vicious infinite regress. He concludes that no such thing can be real, and from this concludes that time or the temporal order is unreal. For, according to his analysis, time or the temporal order consists of something real, the C-series, and something else, the A-system, which is provably (he thinks) unreal.

In effect, then, McTaggart eliminates dualism between the two aspects of time by relegating one aspect to the status of an illusion. However,

---

possible to convey that *E* stands to *G* in the ordering relation *before* by means of the disjunction: 'Either *E* is past and *G* is present or *E* is past and *G* is future or *E* is present and *G* is future or *E* is more past than *G* or *G* is more future than *E*'. But this hardly allays worries about dualism. Worriers who share McTaggart's assumption that temporal order is metaphysically grounded elsewhere than in the A-determinations (i.e., the shifting system of *pastness, presentness,* and *futurity*) are going to retort: 'That *E* and *G* stand to each other in relations of *more* or *less* futurity/pastness is due to a combination of two more fundamental facts: (1) the fact that *E* is before *G*, and (2) the fact that monadic or absolute futurity and pastness duly accrue to these ordered items. But "duly accrue" in (2) is exactly what we worriers about dualism find unintelligible.' (For a thorough discussion of the point, see Gale, 1968, ch. vi.) One would avoid dualism without denying the reality of one or other side of the contrast, if one either exhibited A-determinations as grounded in temporal seriality (the B-series), or exhibited the converse. An example of the converse would be the Aristotelian theory presented later in this paper.

I should make it clear that he is not, so far as I know, interested in proving the unreality of the A-system because this would save us from an objectionable dualism. No, McTaggart is interested in the unreality of the A-system because of what, in his view, this implies concerning the unreality of time. And discussion by later philosophers has mainly continued to focus on the two matters to which McTaggart himself gave most attention: (1) his argument purporting to prove the logical impossibility of the A-system, which represents the passage of time; and (2) his claim that time, i.e. the temporal order of temporal items known as the B-series, is impossible unless the A-system, or the passage of time, is possible. These are the problems that have tended to absorb philosophical energy, by contrast with the much less talked about question of how, *if* the basic[4] passage-aspect of time is possible and real, it is integrated with the order-aspect, whose logical respectability has not been called into question. There has been rather little puzzlement over the fact that, once the two aspects are distinguished as McTaggart distinguished them, it is difficult to see what there is about either that unites it with the other.

Among moderns, the broadest division is into two camps each of which accepts part and rejects part of McTaggart's theory. Both continue to use the labels 'A-series' and 'B-series' in accordance with McTaggart's practice. Neither, however, has any time for his purely noumenal C-series; hence neither camp thinks of the B-series as in part constituted from it. The camps are united in holding, as against McTaggart, that time is real. However, one camp agrees with him that the A-system is a necessary aspect of time, while rejecting his denial that the A-system is logically coherent and real. The other camp follows him in denying the reality of the A-system, but rejects his claim that it is a necessary aspect of time. Time, to this camp, is the B-series cleansed of A-type determinations.[5]

The first camp have their hands so full defending the coherence and reality of the A-system that they hardly consider the dualistic difficulty that would have to be faced if they win this battle. And consequently they hardly think of taking the kind of step back that in general seems clearly right in this sort of philosophical situation. It is a situation in which a certain analysis of a whole into conceptually independent parts or aspects is initially attractive or even compelling, since it brings real clarification, but then is found problematic for failing to explain why

---

[4] I.e. monadic; see note 3.
[5] This is an ontological position. Its contemporary exponents do not, of course, claim that tensed sentences can be adequately translated into tenseless ones.

the parts or aspects are together in the first place. The right move, once this is seen, is to question the initial analysis – in this instance, the dichotomy we have been discussing. Compare the response of philosophers to the Cartesian mind–body problem. It is very far from being the case that all who find Cartesian dualism repugnant have tried to cancel the problem by, so to speak, first accepting the dichotomy and then arguing that one side of it is unreal. On the contrary, the alternative strategy of questioning the entire divisive approach is well practised and has generated a great deal of positive theorising.

If, to return to the case of time, the A-believers were to mount an initiative showing that McTaggart's seminal dichotomy is misguided, or – a more modest aim – that it is not mandatory, they would deprive the A-disbelievers of one possible source of their disbelief, namely the sense that simply treating time as order plus passage with nothing to be said about why they are together is unworthy of philosophers except as a last resort. For clearly it is more promising (or would be were it the only alternative approach) to think of one of the aspects – for example, the A-system[6] – as an illusion. This holds promise because even if some things may be or must be uncaused or inexplicable, anyone who claims that some X usually considered real is an illusion incurs the burden of suggesting some kind of explanation for the illusion of X: a burden so obvious that to make the claim at all is virtually to imply that in principle an explanation is available.[7] And when the presumed illusion is (as in the present case) an appearance of something which everyone in the contemporary debate agrees is real (namely, in this case, the *temporal order* of events), any explanation is bound to make reference to the nature of that reality even if other factors enter into the explanation as well. Hence to propose that the A-system is an illusion is automatically to adopt a position in which, firstly, there is no A-system to explain, and, secondly, what there is instead, namely a sort of similitude of a real A-system, is firmly presented as *not* arising by brute happenstance alongside of or in the context of the very differently natured reality that is the temporal

---

[6] In theory it might be suggested that the serial aspect is an illusion, but no one seems to have sponsored this alternative.

[7] This is not quite true. If there is a knock-down argument, one on whose soundness everyone agrees, showing that X, which we thought was real, is in fact unreal, then the claim that X is only illusory need not be supported by the promise of an explanation. But it is not clear that such a dialectical situation can occur. In any event, it has not occurred in the case in which we are interested. McTaggart's proof of the unreality of the A-system leaves 50 per cent (I would say) of its readers unconvinced, and no other argument has been produced that is more compelling.

series of events. Even if the explanatory details are not immediately forthcoming, this stance may well seem more rationally respectable than that of an A-believer who ignores the need to explain how the real A-system fits in with the rest of the reality that is time.

I have been speaking in a general way about the problem of integrating the two aspects of time, if one assumes that both are real. Let us now look at the kind of image that commonly suggests itself when we try to bring them together in a single frame. It is a kind of image in which one factor appears as a moving object, the other as an object at rest. We can picture presentness, or the now, as passing like the edge of a wave along the fixed series of events: the part of the series ahead of it is the future, the part behind is the past. Alternatively, we can think of the now as fixed while the events in their order file past it like soldiers past a monument.

Such pictures provoke the annoying question 'At what speed does the now glide along the successive events, or the events march past the now?' But perhaps this question can be legitimately dismissed. The pictured situation is rather like a universe in which just one object is moving from here to there, the positions being marked somehow. There is no answer to the question 'How fast is it moving?', since *ex hypothesi* there is no other movement by which to measure its rate of change. This seems a possible situation, and I shall assume that its possibility allows us in the analogous case of temporal passage to treat 'How fast?' as a question to which it is reasonable not to attempt an answer.[8]

But even granted this leniency, those images of temporal passage demonstrate the problem of integrating the two aspects of time. At first, of course, they seem to solve the problem, since the utter familiarity of seeing something move past something else that is fixed, or of standing still oneself while something moves past one, or moving ahead oneself over a stable ground, lends a comforting glow of what for a moment feels like intelligibility to the temporal case. But this is to mistake the most primitive kind of 'feeling at home with' a subject for the kind that is only attained when the critical intellect has prised out every problem and solved them all to its own complete satisfaction. On reflection, the images actually proclaim the absence of any explanation of the togetherness of the two aspects of time. If a column of soldiers marches past a monument, or the edge of a tidal wave passes trees in a row lining the bank of the estuary,

---

[8] The 'at what speed?' question is raised by C. D. Broad, 1938, vol. II, part I. Broad would probably reject my dismissal of the question, since his wording suggests the view that a movement has a speed even where measurement of it is completely ruled out.

the one element's fixity by contrast with the other's movement strongly suggests that the first would have been fixed whether or not the second was moving, and whether or not it was even present. For the empirical causal conditions for the fixity of something that happens for a while to be spatially fixed are usually independent of the conditions for the motion of something that moves past it or over it. In general, the fixity of what is fixed neither requires nor gives rise to the motion of what moves.

Keeping in mind the modern analysis of time into changeless order plus ever-changing A-determinations, let us turn now to Aristotle. He seems to endorse with enthusiasm precisely the problematic kind of image that we have just been discussing. One of the *aporiai* he raises at the beginning of his discussion of time is 'Does the now remain always one and the same or is it always other and other?' (*Physics* IV.10, 218a10). Later, he answers that the now, and for that matter time itself (*chronos*), is both: always the same and always different and different (*Physics* IV.11, 219b9–33). He explains this by means of analogies, between extended time (*chronos*) and a process of locomotion, and between the now and the moving object:

> The now in a way is the same, in a way is not the same. For insofar as it is in another and another (*en allôi kai allôi*), it is different (which is just what its being now was supposed to mean). But whatever the now is whereby it is the now, is the same. For motion, as was said, goes with magnitude, and time, as we maintain, with motion. Similarly, then, there corresponds to the point the body in locomotion, by which we are aware of the motion and the before and after in it. This is the same thing that it is (a point or stone or something else like that), but it is other in definition – as the sophists assume being Coriscus – in the Lyceum – is other than being Coriscus – in the agora. So this too is other through being at one place and at another place. The now corresponds to the body in locomotion, as time corresponds to the motion. (*Physics* IV.11, 219b12–23, my translation, Ross's text)

This explanation seems to be carefully worked out, but we may well wonder whether it was worth the trouble.[9] For the reasons we have been considering, the analogy between the now and the moving object is surely a potential embarrassment, to say the least; so that Aristotle seems unusually insensitive in pushing ahead with it oblivious of the problems.[10]

But let us look at this further. When Aristotle offers the analogy, we naturally first see in it what *we* expect to see; and then are surprised that he

---

[9] Including the trouble to us of following his exposition, which is very obscure in detail.

[10] Thus Richard Sorabji in fact found Aristotle's discussion quite disappointing: '. . . he makes no less than four comparisons between the now and a moving body, but surprisingly never manages to articulate the sense in which the now is moving' (Sorabji, 1983, 49).

is not disturbed by some of the implications of what we see. In his image of the moving object *we* see also the ground traversed. We see a fixed series of positions stretching ahead of the moving object and stretching back behind it. But a closer look at the text should warn us not to assume that Aristotle here conceptualises the moving object's successive positions in the way that seems natural to us, i.e. as locations on an independently existing ground such as the surface of the earth.

In fact, he compares the now which is always different and different with Coriscus-in-the-Lyceum and Coriscus-in-the-agora. The point about Coriscus, he says, gave rise to a sophistical paradox (219b20), which presumably consisted in the claim that it is a different Coriscus in each place. (The paradox lends itself to a variety of uses: it might be adduced to show that nothing persists through change, or that it is unjust to arrest Coriscus in the agora for a crime 'he' committed in the Lyceum, since as long as Coriscus stays away from the Lyceum the perpetrator does not exist.) The thing to notice for our present purpose is that the paradox treats locomotion as if it were a sort of alteration, and Aristotle here goes along with this. That is to say: his, and the paradox's, walking Coriscus is different and different not for the reason a modern analyst would give, namely that Coriscus stands in the same dyadic relation of *occupancy* to this and then this different spatial locations – but because Coriscus first has the attribute of being-in-the-Lyceum, and then the attribute of being-in-the-agora. The Greek name of each location appears in the dative inside a distinct complex monadic predicate formed with the preposition *en*. Construed in this way, the statement 'Coriscus was in the Lyceum, Coriscus is now in the agora' does not sustain an immediate inference to the existence, independent of Coriscus's occupancy, of an agora, a Lyceum, and places in between. In the same way, the statement 'Coriscus was asleep, now he is awake' does not license the inference that the conditions of sleep and wakefulness exist independently of Coriscus so that he 'leaves' one and 'arrives in' the other.

Of course we all know, and so does Aristotle, that in fact the agora, the Lyceum, and the path between them exist independently of Coriscus's transient occupancy. But we must remember what this claim of independent existence means for an Aristotelian. It means that a place currently occupied by one thing will be or can be occupied by something else.[11] There is no such thing as space or a system of places laid down in

---

[11] 'Will be' for Aristotle, because he rejects the possibility of a vacuum anywhere. However, the main point does not depend on this: 'can be' is enough.

advance of all occupants. A given thing's place exists independently of its current occupant just insofar as the occupant is replaceable there by something else moving in.[12] And as with places, so with paths between places. The path along which Coriscus travels between the Lyceum and the agora exists independently of him just insofar as it is available for others to travel along.

In this respect the 'passing' now is quite different from an object in locomotion. It resembles an object in locomotion in that different and different predicates are true of it. (That will be the case if we treat 'now' as a subject and invent predicates to apply to it whose contents correspond to now-true-now-false present-tensed sentences.) But unlike an object in locomotion, the now is not one of possibly many similar items that can occupy the same positions as it, and traverse the same intervals. In the light of this, let us consider the fact that events become present successively. It is perfectly natural to put this by saying 'the now is always other and other', because different and different things are going on in the present. It is also perfectly natural to liken this different-and-different-ness to the way an object in locomotion is always differently and differently positioned. But from an Aristotelian point of view, this natural comparison lends no plausibility to the thought that the successively present events constitute an order of *before and after* that is independent, both for its existence and for its intelligibility, of the now that 'passes' along it. For this thought to have a basis, it must be true not only that the now is different and different, e.g. is aligned first with my having breakfast, then with my sitting down at the computer, on a certain day – but also that some *other* now is potentially on the scene (in the same perspective[13]) to take its turn at being aligned with the identical successive events.[14] And this is inconceivable.[15]

---

[12] Cf. *Physics* IV.4, on place.

[13] The analogy requires that the scene is the common context for a possible plurality of nows, like a place with different occupants; thus the argument is not upset by the possibility that the identical events are successively aligned with different nows corresponding to different frames of reference.

[14] The common accessibility of a place or a path to different occupants or travellers implies 'where X now is, Y can be, but at a different time'. Thus to the extent that picturing the passage of the now involves picturing it passing along a path accessible to another subject like itself, it assumes a common time in which different now-subjects are possible and can take turns to make the same journey.

[15] For completeness, a further word is necessary about 'Coriscus was asleep, and is now awake'. Either conditions of being asleep are individuated so that that of Coriscus and that of Callias are automatically numerically distinct, or not. If so, then Callias cannot replace Coriscus by 'going to' the same sleepy condition. If not, then perhaps Callias takes on the identical sleepy condition, but this is not replacement, since Coriscus can continue to be 'in it' too. Still, on this view the

Let us see where we are as a result of this part of the argument. Three observations can be made. Firstly: it is natural to liken the change of now *vis à vis* successive events to an object in locomotion. Secondly: this comparison, given an Aristotelian understanding of what it means for a place or series of places to exist independently of any particular occupant or passer-through, generates no temptation to treat successive events as analogous to a series of independently existing places, places which in some sense are 'there' independently of the now's 'visits' to each one. It is, of course, the belief in this independent order that gives rise to the problem of temporal dualism which I discussed earlier. The third observation begins by conceding that, on some non-Aristotelian understanding of the independence of a place from its occupant, the natural comparison between the changing now and a moving object may, for all we know, pave the way to a coherent notion of the order of events as existing independently of the activity of the now. This would be a matter for further investigation. But one can say right away (this is the main point of the third observation) that even if such a notion is available, to embrace it is to incur the problem of temporal dualism (and the consequent temptation to explain away one side of the split as illusory). It might therefore make sense not to rush into that embrace if there is an alternative way of viewing the relation between the now and the order of events.

An alternative is to be found in Aristotle, as I shall now explain. The point at which to begin is his account of temporal before and after. Now the concept of temporal before and after figures in two quite different ways in Aristotle's discussion of time. The first way is more famous, and seems to carry more of the weight of his theory; but the second is the one that will concern us here. In the first way, 'before and after' is part of Aristotle's definition of time (*chronos*) as 'number of motion in respect of before and after' (*Physics* IV.11, 219b1–2). I take this to mean: 'Time is the countable aspect of motion, in which the countable items are distinguished as before and after'.[16] Here Aristotle is not explaining 'before and after', but is using that idea to explain something else, namely time. But quite a bit later on, in Ch. 14, he explains how the expressions 'before'

---

condition exists independently of any particular participant, not as a place but as a real universal. Even so, it would yield a model for a temporal order independent of the now only on the inconceivable assumption that the order could be shared with another now.

[16] For a penetrating exposition see Coope, 2005, parts II and III.

and 'after' are applied to events in time.[17] This is the passage that concerns us. Aristotle writes:

> . . . we say 'before' and 'after' with reference to the distance from the 'now', and the 'now' is the boundary of the past and the future . . . But 'before' is used contrariwise with reference to past and to future time; for in the past we call 'before' what is farther from the 'now', and 'after' what is nearer, but in the future we call the nearer 'before' and the farther 'after'. (223a5–13)[18]

On this account, to say that the death of Julius Caesar precedes that of Christopher Columbus is to say the following: if both events are future, the death of Caesar is the one closer to the present; if both are past, it is the one further from the present. To the modern eye, this way of looking at things is rather strange. In the first place, the present or the now is the reference point for the relative proximities of events to it, and these different proximities to it in turn determine which event is before which. It follows that the now itself cannot be conceived of as preceding or succeeding any event. I think it equally follows that present events, considered as present, cannot be conceived of as succeeding past events or preceding future ones. The present as such is outside the temporal series, since it constitutes the reference point determining the positions of items in the series *vis à vis* one another. Equally strangely, this way of determining the relative positions breaks down when applied to a mixed set of events in which some are past, some future. Thus on this way of looking at things, a past event and a future event stand to each other in no relations of before and after (and obviously they are not simultaneous either). Yet clearly they are in time, and in some sense they are in the same time, since it is by reference to the same now that the future event is before and after others in the future, and the past one before and after

[17] He gives this explanation not for its own sake, but as part of an argument showing that 'what is before is in time' (this is deduced from (1) 'Now is in time' together with (2) 'what is before something else is at a distance from the now', by means of (3) 'if the now is in X, distance from the now is likewise in X'). The fact that the explanation appears thus incidentally in the *Physics* may be thought to imply that it is only a casual remark about the way we use temporal 'before' and 'after'. If this is true, it may be a mistake to call any theory developed from it 'Aristotelian'. (The mistake would be in suggesting, not that the theory is implicitly there, but that it has Aristotle's endorsement.) But the explanation also occurs at *Metaphysics* v.11, which is his main discussion of 'prior and posterior' including the temporal type; hence, far from being casual, the explanation would seem to have been carefully considered by him. See especially 1018b9–29. (The discussion in *Categories* 12 is quite different. The most he finds to say there about temporal priority (although he says it is priority in the strictest sense) is that for A to be prior to B is for A to be older or more ancient than B (14a26–b23).)

[18] *Revised Oxford Translation.*

others in the past. But there is no single temporal *series* embracing both past events and future ones. On the contrary, the now as reference point establishes the past and the future as two mutually exclusive series.

In the passage just quoted, Aristotle says that the now is the boundary of the past and the future.[19] At this point in the discussion, the now seems to be a boundary that divides, not one that unites. For how can the past be united with the future except insofar as events falling on the opposite sides of the now can be exhibited as belonging to a single historical order? But if the now is the principle (*archê*) of two distinct orders in the way we have seen, then the now, by bounding the past and the future and dividing one from the other, ensures that *no* seriality is common to past and future events.

But, of course, the now is not *only* the boundary of past and future. If that were its one attribute, we should have the situation just envisaged. Salvation lies in the further fact that the now is 'always different and different'. The boundary moves, what was future comes to be past. No two non-simultaneous events are permanently cut off from standing in before and after relations with each other. The passage of the now breaks the serial relation between two future events when one becomes present, then past, while the other is still future. But the same passage of the now restores them to the same relation by eventually making both past. If, as Aristotle holds, time is infinite in both directions, there never is or was or will be a moment when all non-simultaneous events constitute a single temporal series. But for any sub-set of non-simultaneous events, at every moment either all its members *are* in a single series (i.e. all are future or all are past) or they *have been* (when all were future) and *will be again* (when all are past).

Let me now go back to the modern dichotomy between temporal order and temporal passage. In that perspective, the comparison of passage with locomotion made it irresistible to think of the now as moving along the series of events as if along an already constituted path, or the series of events moving, like a regiment on parade, as a single block past the now. The thought was: the now's movement presupposes a unitary path laid out for it to move along – as if the now is like us, and can't go anywhere new except along pre-existing lines that link new places to old ones. Or if it was the now we preferred to think of as fixed, then the thought was: events file past the now in the temporal order in which they have already,

---

[19] See also *Physics* IV.13, 222a10–12; 33–b2.

so to speak, been drawn up – an order that is theirs, one and the same, as they approach the now, as they pass it, and as they recede from it into the past. On the Aristotelian view, by contrast, for any sub-set of non-simultaneous events,[20] the changing now takes their seriality away for a time, and then gives it back for ever. For any such sub-set, there has passed, or is passing, or will pass, a finite time during which they fail to form a single series because the now is somewhere in the middle of them. But there has come or will come a moment after which their common seriality is assured for infinite time, because the changing now will have edged them all into the past.

This Aristotelian approach may seem too strange to be taken seriously (although the strangeness might wear off with use). According to it, before/after relations derive from the events' comparative distances from the now in either of the two directions. To us, on the other hand, it may seem intuitively obvious that the dependence lies the other way round: that E's being further into the past, or less far into the future, than G derives from E's being before G. But strange or not, no one can complain that the Aristotelian approach fails to integrate temporal order with temporal passage.

---

[20] I am assuming that between them they span a finite time.

CHAPTER 6

Nature and craft in Aristotelian teleology

PART A: INTRODUCTION

(1) It used quite commonly to be argued against Aristotelian teleology that this type of explanation founders for lack of a suitable psychological basis in most of the phenomena for which it was invoked. The objection was that it does not make sense to attempt to explain X as happening or existing in order that Y should happen or exist unless one assumes that the production of X and Y is guided by thoughts, desires or conscious purposes relating Y as end to X as means. Yet Aristotle himself makes it clear that the domain in which, as he believes, teleological explanation is not merely illuminating but mandatory if we are to have any adequate scientific explanations at all, extends well beyond the domain of entities to which beliefs, desires and conscious purposes can be reasonably ascribed.[1] Nor, on the other hand, does Aristotle protect himself against the objection by introducing a supernatural being who produces or shapes phenomena in accordance with divine intent. Thus if the application of teleology does depend on the presence of psychological factors such as those mentioned, it is a dependence which Aristotle fails outright to notice. Alternatively, there is no such failure because the claimed dependence does not hold.

(2) This poses the question: Is a non-psychological teleology as intelligible as Aristotle evidently takes it to be? We may be tempted to turn a deaf ear to this question if it seems to us that in other respects Aristotelian teleological explanations are effective or at any rate more effective than alternatives given the state of knowledge. But embarrassing though it may be for Aristotelians, the question is *prima facie* a pressing one precisely for them. What makes it so is Aristotle's characteristic appeal to the notion of craft (*technê*) as analogue for his conception of nature (*physis*). Nature, in this context, is not Nature in general, or the cosmos, but the specific

---

[1] See *Physics* II.8, 199a20–1; b26–8.

essential nature of an individual substance, the inner principle of its behaviour and organisation. It is nature in this sense that Aristotle likens to craft – that is, to one or another specific craft; for the crafts are principles of activity vested in particular individuals who live, move, and have their being within the physical world. Craft in its active exercise is evidently end-directed, and to Aristotle the same is true of nature, although less evidently so. Thus it is craft that provides the model for nature, not the reverse. That the comparison goes in this direction might seem too obvious for mention, except that just at this point we confront what seems the most vulnerable spot in Aristotle's position. *If* one were to establish independently the idea of the nature of a thing as end-directed, and were then to use this conception of nature to explain what should be meant by the end-directedness of craft, one might well achieve the interesting result of having developed a notion of craft (that is, the exercise of craft) in which psychological concepts play no essential part. For generally speaking, natures are not psychological, and in this backwards analogy craft would be likened to nature. I shall return later to this possible way of conceiving of craft. Meanwhile, in Aristotle's actual account craft is the model, and the nature of a thing the *explanandum*: which is not surprising, since we have a better pre-reflective grasp of the idea of craft than we have of the idea of a thing's nature. But now the vulnerable side: isn't it also part of that familiar pre-reflective notion of craft that craftsmen are human beings operating from beliefs, desires and conscious purposes – and that without all this, craft would not be possible? But if that is so, are we not right to mistrust Aristotle's confidence that nature can be coherently treated as teleological like craft, even though the operations of nature, unlike those of craft, mostly do not depend on psychological attitudes?

(3) There are a number of problems here. I shall indicate two, with the aim of focusing on the second. First there is the traditional objection to natural teleology: 'How can a state of affairs that is at best future and at worst never occurs at all (since the end may not be realised) exert an influence in the present? Only something now can cause something now: for example, a present desire causes a movement. But nothing future can cause a present movement otherwise than as the object of something present; in which case what really causes the movement is the present item, of which the future one is only the object. So take away such present items as desire, will and conscious design, and you take away the basis for applying any explanation that refers to what is not yet.' It is some-times commented that this argument crudely mistakes final for efficient

causes: efficient causes cannot operate unless as already existent, but the whole point about final causes is that they can (not that this 'can' attributes some extraordinary capacity); thus surprise here simply betrays failure to grasp the idea of final causality. But this response is itself inadequate insofar as it suggests not only that a final cause is not an efficient cause but that a final cause can function on its own without an efficient cause. No doubt that would make sense if one could indeed intelligibly think of a final cause as a surrogate efficient, something planted there in the future and backhandedly stirring things up in the present. That is what the objection rightly finds to be nonsensical. But in Aristotle, final and efficient causality are complementary: the end is an end of or for an agent, and the agent as such is bent on an end. And this comple-mentarity is general, applying where will or desire is present, but also where they are not. Thus it is not as if the absence in a given case of empirical psychological factors forces us into the following choice: *either* (a) there is only a final cause functioning in a vacuum (which is absurd), *or* (b) final causality does not obtain at all, *or* (c) final causality does obtain, but only through the medium of a specially postulated empiric-ally unidentifiable desire or the like. These options are not exhaustive unless one assumes that it is only in virtue of a desire or conscious purpose that an agent can be an end-oriented efficient cause of some objective which in turn functions as final cause of that active efficiency. In other words, the assumption is that intentionality – or more pre-cisely, end-wardness – must be mental or grounded in the mental, in the sense of requiring a mental representation of the end.

(4) However, Aristotelian teleology clearly dispenses with this assump-tion. That brings me to the second problem: does non-psychological end-directedness make sense? This paper is not an attempt at a general answer to this question; it has the narrower purpose of examining for coherence one example of the view at issue – a surely paradigm example, though, since Aristotle is the greatest historical exponent of this way of thinking. A verdict on coherence requires consideration of the relation between Aristotle's doctrine of natural teleology and his use of the craft analogy. That is my concern in what follows. I shall mainly consider two questions: (i) Does the doctrine depend on the craft analogy? (ii) Does the craft analogy import undesirable psychological elements into the doctrine? If the answer to the first question is No, then it does not matter if the answer to the second is Yes. I shall, however, argue that the answer to the first is Yes, and to the second No (respectively in Parts B and C). I shall then (Part D) consider further problems arising from the craft analogy.

PART B: IS THE CRAFT ANALOGY NECESSARY?

(5) In what sense might Aristotle's teleology be said to depend on the craft analogy? Does he, for instance, need the analogy in order to prove that the operations of nature, as of craft, must be explained by reference to the end; or is it in order to illustrate the meaning of this claim, the truth of which is assumed? In one passage[2] he uses the analogy by way of proof, arguing that since nature resembles craft in ways that are not in question, it also resembles it in being teleological. For the most part, however, he seems to employ the analogy with purely illustrative intent. This is the use which I am mainly concerned to justify in the present section (and to question in Part D below). An excellent starting point is at hand in John Cooper's paper 'Aristotle on Natural Teleology'.[3] By a very clear and thorough argument Cooper shows a way in which we may understand Aristotelian teleology without tacit appeal to psychological factors. The argument rests on Aristotle's view that the species are eternal. Cooper presents it as a fundamental fact of the Aristotelian universe that the organic forms realised at any given time should never not be realised through individuals of the relevant kinds. This fact, on Cooper's account, is what we would probably call an ultimate law of nature. That it obtains is not something that can be explained. In particular, it cannot be explained as due to the movements and properties of the inorganic materials to be found in the universe. Cooper stresses, as others have done,[4] that given the evidence available to Aristotle it would be entirely reasonable to conclude that the behaviour of inorganic materials could not account for the formation, preservation, and propagation *in saecula saeculorum* according to kind, of those highly organised self-maintaining systems we call living creatures. On the other hand, to put this down to sheer accident is simply absurd. Moreover, even if (as is assumed not to be the case) organic phenomena could be explained materialistically in terms of the coming together of inorganic elements each pursuing its own natural course, the biological *viability* of the resultant wholes would still be an accidental by-product of the workings of those simpler natures. For what would be explained would only be the individual positionings of the elements which, positioned as each is, happen to compose viable organic

---

[2] *Physics* II.8, 199a8–20.
[3] In Schofield and Nussbaum, 1982, 197–222, reprinted in Cooper, 2004, 107–29. Page references are to the reprint.
[4] E.g. Gotthelf, 1976; Waterlow, 1982, ch. 2.

unities. The unities as such would not be explained. And that, for Aristotle, is no less absurd, given that these supposed 'by-products' are, in his view, *eternally* reinstantiated. But the only alternative to treating the eternal reinstantiation as a brute fact unencompassed by any explanation, is to treat it, itself, as a basic principle *of* explanation. So instead of thinking of it as belonging on the level of what it makes sense to try to explain in terms of matter and to bemoan it as inexplicable if such explanation fails to fit, we should rather think of the behaviour of matter as explicable in terms of *it*. Thus we move to saying that it is *because* there are, and eternally are to be, such organised living systems, that the materials which form their bodies, food, and environment arrange themselves in ways that make it true that those systems are and will be. In other words: since they are and are to be, and since this cannot happen unless the materials behave in certain ways, the materials must behave in those ways – in *order that* the forms be realised.

(6) This analysis is broadly in the spirit of the texts,[5] and, as Cooper points out,[6] it has the merit of showing how a rational teleology need owe nothing to psychological assumptions. Granted that under certain intellectual conditions it is only reasonable to apply teleological explanation to organic phenomena, then *not* to apply it, given such conditions, would be (one might argue) so unacceptable that even if the psychological assumptions were legitimately available their addition could hardly strengthen the already adequate case for *teleology*. But now how does Aristotle's craft analogy fare in the light of all this? On Cooper's account it seems inessential. Thus Cooper writes: '. . . one must reject the suggestion that is sometimes made that this analogy is central and fundamental to Aristotelian teleology.'[7] The dismissal is surprising. For surely it is Aristotle's own texts that cumulatively make the suggestion, through frequent emphatic occurrences of the analogy. Cooper correctly points out that at least one of Aristotle's arguments for natural teleology does not rely on the analogy.[8] However, it does not follow that Aristotle's full view can be properly represented without it. It is possible, of course, that he gives the analogy more prominence than it deserves for the amount of good it does; but why should one suspect this? One motive, if not reason, that might weigh with an apologist for Aristotelian teleology would be the thought that the craft analogy carries unwanted psychological implications.

---

[5] But for an important qualification, see paras. 8–9 and note 9.
[6] Cooper, 2004, 128–9.
[7] Cooper, 2004, 107–8, footnote 2. [8] *Physics* II.8, 198b32–199a8.

(7) Unwanted implications or not, I shall now argue that the craft analogy, though possibly dispensable to some versions of natural teleology, makes an essential contribution to the Aristotelian version. This contribution is, however, of metaphysical rather than scientific significance. Hence it may well be overlooked in the context of the debate on the scientific merits of teleological as opposed to, say, mechanistic explanation. Aristotelian teleology, as clarified by Cooper, rests on two presumptions whose reasonableness depends on empirical evidence together with certain extrapolations from this. One is that the living forms are never not instantiated; the other that this fact cannot be explained in terms of the material components. There is also the consideration that in biology, teleological explanations are found to work well; for example, they generate predictions, and the predictions are often confirmed. Now the empirical facts (or presumed facts) that make teleology scientifically attractive do not in themselves dictate any underlying metaphysic. Indeed, there is no reason why the teleologising scientist, any more than his mechanicising counterpart in some other age (or other field of phenomena), should embrace any particular metaphysics at all. To give a non-teleological example: the reactions of a compound at various temperatures are explained in terms of molecular theory. That explanation is consistent with distinct metaphysical positions regarding the ground of what are empirically identified as causal connections. Thus one may suppose a non-empirical bond or tie by which a molecular re-arrangement is directly 'powered' by a change in temperature; or that the sequent phenomena are 'powered' to occur in the sequence by the will of God alone; or that the sequence reflects a relation between universals; or that nothing whatever is the case beyond the fact that, this time too, an event of the first type is followed by one of the second.

(8) Natural teleology is likewise open to a variety of metaphysical interpretations. For example, one might hold that it is inherent in the nature of something called 'the Universe' that certain forms be always realised. On that view, the form-realising behaviour of materials has a single metaphysical ground, namely the nature of the Universe. If the realising of some specific form is to be considered a goal, then it is a goal for the Universe, an imperative incumbent upon the cosmos.[9] It is not a

---

[9] Cooper's language often leans in this direction; e.g., (my emphasis): '. . . it is an inherent, non-derivative fact *about the natural world* that it consists in part of natural kinds and *works to maintain them* permanently in existence . . . it is a fundamental fact *about the world* . . . that *it* maintains forever these good life forms' (121). But strictly speaking Aristotle's metaphysical pluralism implies

goal for the circumscribed physical entity whose behaviour and development are teleologically explained as being necessary for the realisation of the form. For if the goal is the Universe's goal, the physical entity and its behaviour are means or instruments employed by the Universe; and instruments do not 'have' a goal in the sense in which what uses them has. To make the point we need not imagine the Universe to be a thinking being with conscious purposes, any more than we need suppose a transcendent God who intends that the forms be realised and consequently wills that matter falls into the necessary patterns. The point is threefold: firstly, that the conditions under which it is appropriate to apply teleological explanation as analysed by Cooper may be satisfied even on the assumption that it belongs to *the* nature of *the* Universe that organic forms be always realised; secondly, that such an assumption is thoroughly un-Aristotelian; thirdly, that it fails to be Aristotelian not because the Universe is conceived of as a conscious being (this is not necessary to the assumption), but because there is no place here for Aristotelian natural substances. According to the picture just sketched, the realisation of some given form is a goal served by, but not grounded in, the natures of whatever physical objects behave in the appropriate ways. Are we now even entitled to think of these as having *natures* at all, in Aristotle's sense? For what he means by a 'nature' is not merely a set of dispositions to behave in certain ways, but the inner source of such behaviour.[10] In particular, a nature is the source of the changes by which relatively undifferentiated matter develops into a given form. To speak of the physical thing as the source of its changes in this way is to say more than that it exhibits change that cannot be accounted for by external physical factors. That is an empirical matter, and is compatible with the metaphysical view that all changes are grounded in the nature of the Universe. The Universe thereby becomes the one substance, according to Aristotle's equation of *being a substance* with *being a source of change.*[11] Ordinary physical objects, on this view, must be construed as modes of that substance, they being merely subjects of change, not metaphysically independent sources.

(9) The difference between this and the metaphysical teleology of Aristotle may be illustrated by reference to the logical difference between two ways of representing goals, one predicative, one propositional.

---

that there are as many fundamental facts as there are distinctive organic kinds: for each kind the fact that *it* is always instantiated.

[10] *Physics* II.I, 192b13–23. [11] *Physics* II.I, 192b33; cf. 193a9–10 and 20.

Within a general Aristotelian perspective, it is common ground that (let us suppose) relatively undistinguished blobs of matter (e.g., frog-spawn) change and develop in ways which one cannot begin to explain in terms solely of what is present – the shape, weight, viscosity, temperature, etc. – but which fall into place in the light of our knowledge that what each blob will eventually have become is a frog. Should we then say that the goal is *that there should be (or have become) a frog*; or is it rather *to be (or: have become) one*? The former represents an end logically appropriate for the Universe as agent; the latter for an Aristotelian natural substance, which in this example is precisely that potential frog on the way to becoming what it is *its* goal to become, namely an actual one: which actuality, if achieved, is achieved not merely *for* it but *by* it. Now this is the conception that the craft analogy is surely intended to hammer home: the conception, namely, of particular physical things as themselves meta-physical centres or agents of their development towards form. For the craftsman too is a source of change operating as one of many within the order of nature. The difference is that his goal is not to have become a so and so, but to have made something into a so and so by the practice of his art. So far as natural objects are concerned, one might easily suppose them to be mere subjects of change, who knows what the source of it? But with craft, the functions of *source* and *subject* are clearly partitioned, since in general the development for which craft is responsible is located in an object external to the craftsman.[12] By taking craft as model for the specific natures of particular physical objects, Aristotle unambiguously declares their status as metaphysical centres of activity. Without the craft analogy we should still have teleological explanation, but not the Aristotelian concept of natural substances.

PART C: A NON-PROBLEM OF THE CRAFT ANALOGY

(10) It would be unfortunate if the craft analogy, necessary as I have argued it to be, should finally prove dependent on psychological assumptions alien to Aristotelian teleology. This is now the question. Let us start with the consideration that this analogy is a complex package containing very much more than the elements of belief and desire sometimes deemed necessary for teleology to make sense. If these are what have to be invoked to support the notion of goal-directed natural processes, why say more

---

[12] *Physics* II.1, 192b15–20; *Metaphysics* XII.3, 1070a7.

than that such processes are like the operations of a consciously purposeful agent? Why confine attention to craft, when so many of our deliberate ends and means owe nothing to special expertise? Why not take going to a neighbour's house in order to find out the latest news? Here are some reasons. (a) The world of craft is divided into craftsmen of *various kinds*, each *qua* craftsman seriously dedicated to his own speciality. So it is with the world of natural substances. For each individual there is the circumscribed end proper to its specific definable essence, and for each an equivalently circumscribed range of means. There are no amateurs here, or dilettanti. (b) The matchless professionalism of healthy natural substances is shown in the *regularity* of their behaviour. Craft, with its rules and repeatable applications, echoes this, even though a realistic view of human history must allow that crafts develop, discovering not only new methods but new horizons. (c) Nature makes *correct* moves, and so does craft. That is to say: while a craftsman may make mistakes, his claim to the title, as Thrasymachus pointed out in the *Republic*,[13] depends on knowledge, not on misjudgment. Those who think that teleological explanation needs psychological assumptions are concerned with beliefs (as well as with desires, intentions, conscious purposes). But to play the desired explanatory role, the beliefs need not be correct. It can hardly be that the image of the craftsman is invoked mainly to supply the element of belief; for it is of the essence of beliefs that they can be false, whereas it is of the (normative) essence of craft that it is not mistaken. (d) The metaphysical *unity* of an Aristotelian nature is mirrored by the teleological unity of craft-cognition with craft-goal. By this I mean that the knowledge exercised in craft is normally developed precisely with a view to the craftsman's purpose. This is true not only of the necessary causal generalisations, but also of the particular observations required for applying these in an actual situation. The cognitive system exists and operates only as called upon for the end. Idealised, this concept approximates to the concept of an Aristotelian nature, where the end and the capacity to realise it are perfectly integrated. It is not as if the capacity, in any given case, could have been used to some other end, or is more than is needed for this. Contrast, in this respect, both nature and craft with what we may call 'ordinary' human purposive action, where, as likely as not, the relevant desire or interest and the relevant beliefs or cognitive states, were developed independently and come together by an external synthesis.

---

[13] 340c–e 1. Cf. *Nicomachean Ethics* VI.2, 1139b15–16, where craft is said to be one of the states 'in which the soul grasps *truth* through affirmation or denial' (my emphasis).

(e) 'Ordinary' purposive actions are usually explained by saying that the agent desired so and so or had a reason for pursuing so and so. Such statements do not as a rule appear in explanations of the activities of natural substances, since in general we do not think that these operations express desires or reflective concerns. But the same is true of the operations of craft, considered simply as such. There is a sense in which the craftsman as such is *too* practical to be animated by desire or reasoned concern for the end. To say of someone that he operates as a builder is already to have implied that he pursues the builder's typifying end (not merely that he exercises the special skills). The builder as such cannot *want* to build houses in any sense in which wanting to build houses could *explain* building by *the builder*. As such, the builder has no motive for building, but either simply builds or is simply a potential builder with the skill to build. Nor is it his business, *qua* builder, to have reasons for building. The builder here is, of course, an abstraction, and it is only to this abstraction that these remarks apply. They are not meant to suggest that a human individual might not engage in builder-activity for some reason, or because he wanted to do this work or have its product. Yet even a tree would have to be more than a tree if it were a tree because it desired to be a tree. This is not because trees are incapable of psychological attitudes such as desire, but because even the desires of such organisms, were they to have them, would already be expressions of their perfect tree-form-seeking tendency, hence not explanatory of it.

(11) Point (e) above is the direct claim that the craftsman as such cannot be said to have the psychological attitude of desire for the craftsman's goal. Some of the previous points should help to construct a similar case regarding other psychological attitudes. Aristotle says that craft does not deliberate.[14] He might have added that in paradigm cases the craftsman in action does not even have thoughts about whatever it is he does that constitutes his exercise of skill, except under two circumstances: one, where he is still learning, and the other, where he is demonstrating so as to teach the art. But in the first case he is less than a craftsman, and in the second case more. With regard to the ascription of belief, two features should cause us to hesitate. No doubt we are concerned with an idealised case of craft but it is in terms of such that imperfect cases are to be understood. First, there are no mistakes; secondly, there is perfect fit between the cognitive system and the end to be achieved. But now where

---

[14] *Physics* II.8, 199b26–8.

the question of error does not arise, is there need or room for the notion of belief (at any rate so far as this involves the idea of a true-or-false mental representation)? And where the cognitive material is wholly at the service of a given end, is there room for ascribing a factual (or proposition-asserting) attitude such as the word 'belief' commonly implies? To answer 'Yes' with confidence one would have to be sure that our distinction between belief and, say, desire (which distinction plays a significant part in determining the meaning of 'belief') could still be drawn in the case mentioned. But would that be possible if the alleged belief had no life or history of its own independent of that one conative context?

(12) These remarks are only pointers, but pointers in a direction which for the present limited purpose is perhaps sufficiently clear. We have at any rate shifted the burden of proof to those who would deny what is here suggested: namely, that craft is non-psychological in precisely those respects in which craft is most suited to provide the model for an Aristotelian nature.

PART D: FURTHER CONSIDERATIONS

(13) I have argued that Aristotle's craft-analogy for nature does not introduce the psychologism sometimes feared. But his use of the analogy is by no means all plain sailing. Here I shall examine some problematic ramifications. In the first place, the concept of craft is supported by presuppositions which on reflection might lead one to question the propriety of using it to further our understanding of nature. One such presupposition of course is that a natural order is already there, providing conditions for the growth and exercise of human skill. Even if craft is itself an expression of *human* nature, craft is a rationally organised attempt to control objects and forces already at work independently. Thus craft is a fitting analogy for the nature of a non-human natural substance only to the extent that we can conceive of such a substance as depending for its orderly development on natural qualities and relations of natural objects other than itself: which objects, in this context, are regarded as materials for the realisation of the natural form in question. Aristotle finds no trouble in understanding the world of nature in this way. Nor, I think, should he, so far as method is concerned. Someone might object that if non-human natures in general are to be conceived on the model of the craftsman, then the presupposition just mentioned will force us round in a circle when we come to analyse craft. But the objection is superficial: although we cannot make sense of craft without presupposing natures

which craft has not touched, there is no incoherence in treating the latter as also craft-like in turn. For it is not in the same conceptual breath that we both oppose and liken them to craft. Even if natures are craft-like, it is not on account of this resemblance that nature is a precondition for craft. The dependence here considered of craft upon what is not craft can be grasped without circularity as well by Aristotelians as by those philosophers who claim to find nothing craftsmanlike in nature.

(14) But there is another presupposition which gives rise to doubts less easy to weigh. Just as craft depends on a world of non-human substances confronted as independently there, so craft assumes non-craft on the human side as well. Craftsmen must know what nature makes possible given the human will to guide and divert natural processes towards human objectives. But the objectives themselves ultimately rest on principles belonging to no special craft. The craftsman, whatever his kind, aims at some good; but to say this is to say more than that the craftsman aims at the end that defines the craft. For the end aimed at is not good because in that craft it is the end aimed at; rather, it is aimed at because it is of value as answering to some human need, passion or interest. No doubt if the carpenter were nothing but a carpenter, the good as conceived by him would be nothing other than the production of cabinet work; but the same would be true, *mutatis mutandis*, of the craftsman, if such there were, whose *métier* was to blow curious arrangements of soap-bubbles. In fact, however, it is good or useful that certain articles are produced, because these articles are regularly wanted for reasons having nothing to do with the craft of their production. This is by contrast with the hypothetical case where one can say no more than that the defining end of some conceivable craft *would* be good if its products *were* of any importance. Now the real carpenter, an intelligent human being, operates as such: that is, with an eye to the needs that called forth the exercise of his craft in the first place. While expertise may be necessary to convert, say, the need for shelter and for various utensils into practicable objectives, one does not have to be an expert to appreciate the desirability of such products. This rests with the judgment of those who are not carpenters, or not merely carpenters. Aristotle, as everyone knows, takes such judgments to be grounded in a conception of human happiness or the good of man *qua* man. The lowly carpenter may not give this much thought in the sense of concerning himself with some all-round definition; but he responds to market forces, or ignores them at his peril, both with respect to what he makes, and to its timing and quantity. Thus it is only in a highly abstract sense that a given type of craftsman always produces the

same. There are times when he produces nothing even though awake and physically capable, and so far as he does produce, the character of his objective is constantly subject to re-interpretation such as never occurs in the non-human world according to Aristotle's view.

(15) In short, the specific crafts are not autonomous but operate within limits set by what Aristotle calls '*phronêsis*': wisdom about the whole of practical life. It is true that Aristotle sometimes follows Plato in a schematic division of labour: the carpenter is one entity, and the being who dictates the when, where, and how much of the carpenter's activity is another – the *politikos*, whose concern is for the good in all its aspects.[15] But that is for the purpose of analysis only. The actual carpenter has to be something of a *politikos*: not necessarily a 'statesman' in some high sense, but a social being. His excellence in his particular trade depends in part on this, for who would employ a carpenter who understood nothing but carpentry? More to the point, such a notion is hardly intelligible. Craft is essentially practical, or (to speak more abstractly) a source of orderly change. That is the basis of the analogy with nature. But from craft alone nothing comes about.[16] For even if *what* the craftsman does in making what he makes can be explained by the principles of his craft, *that* these principles operate at all, and when and to what degree, depends on ulterior values. This is by contrast with the nature of a natural substance, which is not merely an inner principle of change, but, as Aristotle says, an innate *impulse* (*hormê*) of change,[17] so that the characteristic developments must occur in the absence of physical impediment. When, as in *Metaphysics* Z.7,[18] Aristotle compares the active essence of a natural thing with 'the form in the soul of the craftsman', he speaks as if the craft-form itself holds all that it needs to function as efficient cause of the product. In effect, then, Aristotle here treats craft as conceptually isolable from those non-technical factors that set its objective. But this is to distort the notion of craft, if (as I argue) we cannot make sense of craft otherwise than as practical, and further cannot make sense of craft as actively practical without noting its dependence on something other than itself, namely general practical wisdom. This is not to say that this isolated notion of craft may not illustrate something of what Aristotle understands

---

[15] See, e.g., *NE* I.2, 1094a26ff.

[16] Cf. *NE* VI.2, 1139a35–7: 'Thought by itself sets nothing in motion; thought that sets in motion is for the sake of something and practical [sc. in the narrow sense in which *praxis* is concerned with the good of man as man]. For this also controls productive thought [i.e. craft] . . .'. (trans. C. Rowe).

[17] *Physics* II.1, 192b18–19.   [18] 1032a32–b1.

by 'nature'; but it does mean that he cannot safely *model* nature on craft, since if we take one thing as model for another, we expect the latter's structure to exhibit all that is essential in the former. If the natures of things really paralleled human crafts, then (as has already been indicated) nature would not behave with the massive constancy that is its hallmark. And the parallel also undermines that metaphysical pluralism which, as I suggested in the second section, the craftsman analogy helps to sustain. We now see that this help is afforded only by a notion of craft plucked out of the system of conceptual connections that give it life. For considered in the round, a craft is more like an organ than it is like an independent substantial principle. With an organ there must be a user who rationally coordinates the use of it with the use of others. The user of a craft is the social individual, who stands in this relation to many crafts, although his involvement with them takes different forms depending on which are practised by him and which by others. Once this line of thought is applied to nature, it becomes tempting to postulate a single universal natural principle directed towards some one end to which each part of the physical world must be understood as subordinate. In a few passages Aristotle seems to move in this direction.[19] We need not wonder, considering that the craft-analogy, unguarded, is bound to lead this way.

(16) I have attended so far to one point at which the concept of craft must be circumscribed if it is to play its expected part in the analogy: this was at the interface of craft with practical wisdom. But there are further necessary restrictions, of which some have to do with the specialist aspect of craft. Crafts are learnt, and they are passed on by teaching: in which respect the species of craft differ essentially from the species of nature. For it is surely of the essence of craft to be transmitted by cultural as distinct from genetic inheritance. Here, perhaps, is the ground for that special dimension of rationality that makes craft so intensely significant to the Greek philosophers. It is the dimension in which functioning in accordance with rational principles is integrated with the reflective knowledge of those principles and with the power to communicate them. Now if, as Aristotle believes, non-human natures act unawares for the sake of ends, and regularly achieve those ends by natural strategies of astounding ingenuity, then what purpose is served by reflection? It cannot be that in general reflection is necessary or even useful for accomplishing ends, since performance is faultless in countless cases where reflection never

---

[19] E.g., *Metaphysics* XII.10, 1075a11–25.

enters. On the other hand, human beings have a nature too; for example, it is natural to them to act reflectively. But nature does nothing in vain. We must therefore suppose that human beings are distinguished by having ends that can only be achieved through reflection, and through the giving and taking of reasons. One such end that concerns us here is the transmission of forms of activity that are saved from dying with the individual only by being taught. *Reflective* rationality, according to this approach, is the means by which human nature compensates for its own failure to provide genetically all that it needs in order to flourish and continue. Non-human natures, on the other hand, are genetically adequate for their own needs, including the need to reproduce in kind. In comparing such natures to craft, Aristotle must prescind from just the feature of craft that so impressed Socrates and Plato: the craftsman's command of reasons for doing as he does.

(17) The crafts develop; and even when the principles of a craft are well worked out, further intelligence is often needed to apply them effectively; there is room for thoughtfulness, inventiveness, and an exploratory attitude to facts and objectives. With nature, by contrast, it is as if the objective has never not been finally formulated and the means completely known. Thus when Aristotle likens nature to the craftsman, he has in mind the craftsman as *already effectively in action*, and leaves out of sight the processes, with all their doubtfulness, trial and error, by which someone sets himself up so as to be thus effective: whether by learning a skill, or by analysing the objective, or by taking closer stock of the facts. It is perhaps at this stage that distinctively *mental* activity is most apparent. We wonder and deliberate, not yet being ready to act with the assurance of those whose knowledge is totally immanent in their action. The thinking in action of the utterly accomplished performer is not alongside, above, beyond, or even about his performance: it is that performance. It is the exercise of *achieved* craft that Aristotle has in mind when he compares craft with nature. The danger of the analogy is not that it will psychologise the concept of nature, but that it will de-psychologise the concept of craft.[20] For there is no distinguishable psychological dimension to the self-contained perfection of craft that figures in the analogy. This ideal efficiency essentially (if it is the efficiency of *craft*) rests on a great deal

---

[20] However, this remark should be balanced by the fact that in the *Ethics*, craft is often said to deliberate, and is used to illustrate ethical deliberation. It is only in the *Physics* that craft does not deliberate.

that is not itself; but to acknowledge these other aspects would be to destroy the analogy.

(18) I began this paper by considering the old-fashioned objection that Aristotelian teleology entails the psychologising of nature. Recent work in philosophy has brought about a more sympathetic attitude to teleological explanation in general; and recent scholarship has given us a more accurate understanding of Aristotle's teleology in particular, and of the place in it of the craft-analogy. But these developments generate a new question for Aristotelians, which I raise by way of conclusion. Can we really give meaning to the notion of craft that figures in his analogy? In this section I have argued in effect that the notion is a false abstraction. In that case it is not clear that we are dealing with a familiar concept at all. These considerations may set us wondering further whether the true direction of the analogy is not the reverse of what it appears. For 'craft' in this artificially truncated version is surely no easier to understand than the teleological 'nature' for which it is supposed to provide the model. Even the term is a misnomer, since the true referent is not craft as we actually find it in human craftsmen, but end-directed automation. For Aristotle, examples of this were fantasy, not fact (although he is not above using his imagination in this connection when it makes a point[21]). What paradigm of automation could he show from the real world more perspicuous or more telling than the natural activity, itself, of organisms? Thus when nature is compared to craft, it is the first that prescribes what the second must mean in this alignment. Taken in the direction in which Aristotle intended it, the analogy fails. But perhaps this argument shows that it was not needed in the first place. For could we make sense at all of what passes for craft in this context if we did not already possess the idea of a type of teleological functioning that needs no roots in reflection?

---

[21] *Politics* I.4, 1253b33–1254a1.

CHAPTER 7

Soul and body in Plato and Descartes

When philosophy teachers present the '-ism's' pertinent to mind–body relations, and are still at the broad-brush stage, quite often one finds them pairing Plato and Descartes as the two most eminent dualists of our Western tradition. As Plato to the through-and-through materialist Democritus, so Descartes to Gassendi, it is often suggested – reasonably, perhaps. As the modern non-reductive materialist to his Cartesian *bête noire*, so Aristotle to Plato on soul–body relations, we are sometimes told – a misleading analogy, some think. For the purpose of contrast with various non-dualist views it may seem useful to group Plato's dualism and that of Descartes together, and in many contexts their differences may not matter. But if one simply compares the theories with each other, not with any third system, the differences are fascinating and seem important.

Of course there are similarities to sustain the initial pairing. Both philosophers argue that we consist of something incorporeal, whether one calls it 'mind' or 'soul', which for the time being is somehow united with a body that is part of the physical world. Both identify the self, the 'I', with the incorporeal member of this alliance. Both hold that my mind or soul will survive the demise of the body by means of which I set down these words for others by means of their bodies to access. Both may be understood as holding that the mind or soul can exist altogether independently of body, though Plato may have changed position on this point.[1] Both are concerned with the immortality of the soul.

Here I shall focus on separability of mind or soul from body in Plato's *Phaedo* and Descartes's *Meditations*. But first a word about terms. Several times already I have said 'mind or soul' as if the words meant the same, which of course they do not. Plato consistently speaks of the soul (*psuchê*), but not so Descartes. In his preface addressed to the theologians at the

---

[1] In the *Timaeus* it is taken for granted that the [highly intellectual] world-soul must have a body; and purified human intellects return to spatial locations in the stars (34a8 ff.; 41d4–42d2).

Sorbonne, Descartes claims that he will prove the immortality of the soul. He is using the Church's label for the doctrine, but it is doubtful that what he thought he could prove is what the Church means by the phrase. Roughly, I suppose, the Church's meaning spotlights the human individual minus a biological body. It is this that can sin and be forgiven, is summoned to the Last Judgment, has prayers said for its salvation. But what Descartes believed he could show is the immortality of the mind or intellect, and although the mind, as he was forever stressing, is prone to error and should be expected to conduct itself according to an intellectual code of conduct, its errors are not sins or offences against morality. In more philosophical contexts Descartes explicitly distinguishes mind from soul, reserving 'soul' for that which animates the body. In this sense of 'soul' he either denies that any such principle exists or reduces it to a physical configuration. The biological difference between a living body and a corpse is the purely physical difference between a machine in working order and one that is broken or worn out.

So what Descartes is left with, in addition to his machine-body – *if* this or any other body even exists, which at the beginning of the *Meditations* he calls into doubt – is a mind whose business is to think and imagine, but not to animate any corporeal system. And since it is himself that he finds thinking, and since he is unable, no matter how hard he tries, to doubt his own existence as this currently thinking thing, Descartes identifies himself with this mind. But at first he is not in a position to assert that he, or the mind that is he, can exist without the body, because *prima facie* it is possible that the mind's existence or its essential activity of thinking depends on body in some way. For even though the mind does not require body in the way in which an animating principle presumably requires a body if it is to do its thing of animating something, the mind may depend on the body in some other way, a way in which, so to speak, it is the body that gives life to the mind, much as an arrangement of particles gives rise to a magnetic field. Later on, however, Descartes maintains that according to his clear and distinct ideas of mind and body, neither of these natures contains or refers to the other. And meanwhile he takes himself to have established that everything he clearly and distinctly perceives is true. Hence he can conclude that mind, and perhaps soul in the theological sense, is separable from body, which is the basis for proving the mind or soul immortal.

Or, more precisely, Descartes can conclude that mind and body are separable from each other once he is free of his initial wholesale doubt concerning the real existence of body. For obviously if the physical world is only his finite mind's dream object, neither it nor any of its parts can exist independently of that dreaming. And in that case it may not be easy to show that the finite mind that dreams such a dream – a dream in which it is embodied and its body is part of a physical world – can be free of dreaming this or other dreams like it. But if we take the opposite hypothesis, that the physical world exists independently, then this world, especially the part of it that is Descartes' body, can reasonably be held responsible for the appearances of the physical that are present to Descartes' mind. In that case it is reasonable to assume these appearances will cease when body and mind actually separate. The mind will then be phenomenally unembodied as well as really so. But as long as it is uncertain whether the physical is real independently of the finite mind, one can suppose that either this mind generates the appearances from itself, or they are caused in it by God. But since the finite mind cannot be separated from God any more than it can be separated from itself, on either of these hypotheses the cause of the appearances is necessarily always with that finite mind – so why should it ever be without the appearances? It is true that in *Meditation* VI Descartes says he can clearly and distinctly understand himself to be a complete being even without his faculty of sensory and imaginational appearances. From this he concludes that he or his mind can exist without that faculty and its objects. It follows from this that those objects, the empirical appearances, arise neither from his own intellectual nature nor directly from God who is always present to, or even in, his mind. Thus Descartes is only one step away from concluding that the immediate source of these appearances must be something altogether different from mind, both from the finite mind that is Descartes himself, and from the infinite mind that is God. In sum, the source of the appearances must be a corporeal substance, a real physical thing that exists independently of Descartes' mind.

But let us stop our thinker before he takes that last step, and question him about his premiss. If he or his mind really is or would be a complete being minus the faculty of sensory and imaginational appearances, why, by his own admission, do these appearances beset him so? No doubt they fade away when he completely absorbs himself in pure mathematics or in thoughts about God and about pure finite mind, if there is such a thing as pure finite mind. But in Descartes' own experience the empirical appearances always return. So perhaps it is the nature of his mind to conjure them up for itself again and again, or to become receptive again and again to these effects caused in him by God. If, on careful reflection, one can consider this possible, Descartes is mistaken in claiming that the human

mind can attain a clear, distinct and complete idea of itself as existing free
of empirical appearances to itself. That these sometimes recede when the
mind is abstractly engaged does not prove that they are not among the
objects natural to it or naturally served up to it immediately by God. For
where is it written that all the mind's natural objects are present to it at
once? Certainly, Cartesian doubt can save Descartes from regarding these
appearances as anything more than phenomenal, but he knows from
experience that doubt cannot put an end to the phenomena as such. He
may always be saddled with them, then, even if only as appearances
recognised as such. In this sense, a sort of phenomenalist sense, the self's
body and physical environment may be as immortal as the human mind.

Thus Descartes' ideas of himself or his mind are not, I think, able to
show that the human mind is in every sense separable from body. To
show this, he must fall back on the independent attractiveness of the
thought that 'real' or 'externally existing' body is what causes the empirical appearances. This is of course an independently attractive thought to
the extent that it is unattractive to suppose that God (whom Descartes has
by now proved to exist and to be his creator) deceives or meanly frustrates
a finite mind like that of Descartes. For insofar as Descartes cannot help
taking the empirical appearances to be of independently existing bodies,
if Descartes were always mistaken in this then God would be a deceiver;
and even if Descartes can break out of the deception by means of
systematic doubt, God would be cruel in making the escape depend on
a method so hard for the human mind.

So if one is a Cartesian, the position that mind is separable from body,
not only ontologically but also phenomenally, is secured by means of two
conclusions: if there is any such thing as a really existing body, mind is not
existentially dependent on it; and: body really exists and is the separable
cause of mind's corporeal experiences.

I want now to say something about the universality of Cartesian
separability, and something about what unites the separables while they
are together. These are points on which Descartes and Plato differ
fundamentally. First, universality: in claiming that mind and body are
ontologically separable, Descartes, of course, claims much more than that
a given mind can exist apart from a given natural body. Separability is
guaranteed for him by the essence of mind in general and the essence of
body in general. From his ideas of these essences he believes he can see
that mind – any mind – can exist apart from body – any body, and *vice
versa*. This is in line with the Church's teaching, according to which every
human soul comes to the Last Judgment either stripped of body

altogether, or with a sort of supernatural body through which it can communicate and suffer, but which is not set in a natural physical environment and is not subject to the laws of physical nature.

Phenomenal separability, as I am calling it, is likewise universal for the Cartesian insofar as the Cartesian holds that mind as such is subject to corporeal appearances because and only because an associated real body causes them. It follows from this premiss that for any mind M, once the causal nexus between M and real body is broken, M is automatically separated not only from real body but also from all corporeal appearances.[2]

In sum: both ontologically and phenomenally, the possibility that a human mind is linked to corporeal things, and the possibility of its not being thus linked, flow from the nature common to all human minds; and a mind's actual linkage or non-linkage is or is based on its standing or not standing in causal nexus with something metaphysically external to itself. Its linkage or not to corporeal things is therefore not determined by any internal mental disposition of its own, still less by any internal respect in which one particular human mind may differ from another, for example in respect of strong involvement in a certain type of pursuit. Consider Descartes himself in his unusual if not unique enterprise of seeking certainty through doubt. This extraordinary practice can surely be described as a letting go of the corporeal perspective, and it leads him, or so he thinks, to the proof that mind and body are ontologically separable. But this proof applies even to minds sunk in ordinary habits of thinking, minds for which Cartesian doubt is meaningless and impossible. And this proof is not performatively given *in* the practice, but is derived from independent truths which the practice uncovers as suitable starting points. Thus what Descartes proves when he proves separation possible is a truth that would hold even if no mind ever engaged in Cartesian or similar detachment. It surely suits the doctors of orthodox theology that Descartes presents them with the discovery of a truth that is like the truths of logic and mathematics and Cartesian physics in that it holds no matter what any of us may think or feel about anything. This is by contrast with any facts or possibilities he himself might bring about through a mental activity willed by him.

Now for the question of what unites the Cartesian separables when they are together. It is not the finite mind's own agency that connects it with a body which it then feels to be its own. This could only be done by an act

---

[2] For Descartes these include memories so far as the latter depend on images grounded in the body.

of will on the part of the finite mind. But although Descartes regards his will as 'not restricted in any way' (*Meditation* IV), its unrestricted domain turns out to consist entirely of propositions to which he may choose not to assent when they fail to be clear and distinct. This unrestricted will is not a will to bring anything about except its own assertion and denial of already constituted truths and falsehoods. For this unrestricted will belongs to Descartes insofar as he is pure intellect. On its own, therefore, it cannot take as its objects things that are sensed or imagined, for according to Descartes such things can be present to the mind only when it is already united with the body. Consequently, the explanation for this union cannot be that the finite mind wants or wills to be connected with a particular body, or with some particular body or other. For without sense experience we could not have an idea, either definite or indefinite, of a particular body. And presumably any explanation in terms of the mind's wanting to be connected with body would attend to what it feels like to have a body – the mind would be assumed to have a sense of what that feels like, and to be drawn towards a corresponding existence as if it would be at home in a body. But for Descartes such feelings and the imagination of them can only arise when the mind is already embodied, so they cannot explain embodiment.

Nor can we explain it by turning to body by itself. Obviously, body by itself is powerless to connect itself with a mind. Only God, a third being of infinite power, can cause by his will a union between substances of such mutually alien natures as mind and body. Of course every arrangement of finite things depends on the will of God, but other arrangements, say of body with body, fall within a natural system and can be explained by familiar secondary causes according to the system's laws. Mind and body, however, fall within no such single system, according to Descartes; their union therefore speaks directly of a supernatural cause. On present showing, this cause is as different from finite mind as it is from finite body, since the latter are both devoid of the third thing's power to unite them. In this respect, the finite mind is as passive and inert as matter is traditionally supposed to be.

Let me now turn to Plato.

Readers of the *Phaedo* sometimes take Plato to task for confusing soul as mind or that which thinks, with soul as that which animates the body. Perhaps this is a terrible mistake. But it is not a confusion in the sense of a blunder committed *en route* to something else. For the identification of thinking soul with animating soul *is* Plato's theory in the *Phaedo*.

In trying to understand this, one might seem to discern a close analogy between thinking and animating if one identifies thinking with the exercise of intelligence and assumes, as is natural for many people, that the practical sphere is the arena for exercising intelligence. For the person of practical intelligence is switched on to the practical demands of his situation in a way not unlike the way in which a perceptually sensitive organism is switched on to signals in the environment and its own body,[3] and again not unlike the way in which the elements of a physiological system are switched on and off by chemical signals in the interest of purely biological animation. Again, someone who is irresponsive to things that interest most people may be said not to be properly alive, and even not to be properly animating his body. In saying this we need not mean that he functions below par physiologically; we may instead be regarding his body as a social presence, an instrument for action and communication, which comes to life when activated. Being alive on this level presupposes being biologically alive, and for most normal human beings, being biologically alive automatically results in life on the level of practice, except for when they are sleeping. These two modes of being alive are linked in such a way that, rather than deeming them analogous, one might, more primitively perhaps, fail to distinguish them, and thus conflate what thinks with what animates the body.

Plato's view, however, is quite different, because for him the paradigm exercise of intelligence is theoretical or at any rate not immediately practical: it deals in universals and abstractions, it is conducted at leisure from practical life, and it has no palpable effects except on the thoughts of oneself and a few interlocutors. Plato believes that the soul thinks best when dissociated from the body. He has two reasons: one is the observation that we cannot engage in the kind of thinking that for him is thinking *par excellence* when we are physically active and attending to goings on in our bodies and in our physical environment; and the other is his theory that the soul has latent within it a supremely pure and beautiful kind of knowledge which it could only have come by before birth into a body. Since the thinking soul is at its best when in full contact with the objects of this knowledge, Plato concludes that the best thing that can happen to this soul is to be separated from body upon death.

So far one might think that Plato's thinking soul cannot possibly be what animates the body; for it seems absurd to suggest that something

---

[3] Thus *phronein* (= 'to have one's wits about one') ranges in meaning from 'to be sane' to 'to be conscious'.

both animates a body and is a pure intellect that functions best away from the body. But in fact, the belief that the soul is an intellect that functions best away from body is precisely one of two assumptions that lie at the base of Plato's equation of intellect with animator. The second assumption is that this self-same intellect is also intimately connected with the body. The argument for this is mediated by the concept of the self. On the one hand it is natural for Socrates and his interlocutors in the *Phaedo* to identify themselves with their intellects. After all, if you are Socrates and I am Simmias in the *Phaedo*, then what are you and I engaged in if not paradigmatic intellection, while minimally using our bodies to exchange our thoughts? If we could think at our best without ever exchanging thoughts, or could exchange thoughts by some non-physical means, then we as intellects would not need bodies at all. On the other hand, though, each one of us knows himself to be in or intimately connected with a body. And Socrates' friends know this of Socrates, or why would they dread losing Socrates once his physical death has been decreed? So the self that is Socrates' intellect is the self bound up with his body. And the fact that in this life the soul functions best as intellect when least involved in bodily activity and sensation, together with the doctrine that the soul's intellectual activity was at its absolute best when the soul was attached to no body, now strongly points to the conclusion that intellectual activity waxes as bodily involvement wanes and vice versa. And since it is natural to think of bare biological animation as the limiting case of a soul's bodily involvement, and as the basic form which more complicated forms – the ones expressed in actions and emotions – depend on and presuppose, it is not difficult to draw the further conclusion that the soul that can function as pure intellect is the same as the soul that keeps the body alive.[4]

But now if one and the same entity, the soul, can function both as unembodied intellect and as animator of a body, what determines it to one of these functions rather than the other? And since they are alternatives, and the soul is capable of both, is neither function essential to it, any

---

[4] If bare biological animation is thought of as continuous in kind with intelligent physical activity such as playing tennis or cooking, it will seem plausible that theoretical contemplation at its fullest depends on suspension of animation, since it seems to be a fact, and not a merely contingent one, that attention used in theoretical contemplation is attention taken away from intelligent physical activity, and *vice versa*. Plato models intellection on dreaming, which the soul is free to engage in only when not governing the limbs and perceiving through the sense organs in waking life (cf. the Hippocratic treatise *On Dreams* (*Regimen* IV), 86). However, Plato then turns things round with his familiar dictum that the waking world is that of the eternal intelligibles, the dream-world that of everyday life.

more than a piece of wax is essentially the shape of a ball or essentially the shape of a cube? But if neither function is essential to the soul, we have been told nothing of the soul's nature. If, on the other hand, both are essential, what unites them?

According to the theory of the *Phaedo*, the soul becomes involved with a body because it desires to live in a way in which it only can if it has a body of suitable kind. To begin with, perhaps, the soul is not oriented to any very specific set of physical activities or pleasures, since it has no experience of any. So to begin with perhaps all that it takes to involve a soul with body is the soul's failure to understand or fully believe that its existence can be complete as a pure intellect. Not realising this, it feels incomplete, and this breeds the desire for some non-intellectual activity; and lo and behold the soul finds itself with a body, and presumably a physical environment, of a sort that would enable it to live in the way it thought would bring it completeness, but which in fact, of course, does nothing of the kind. Now it is in the body of a human being, or perhaps a human male, and if it continues to misunderstand its own original nature – which is easier now for it to do, since it has come to feel at home in an actual physical existence, and to become habituated to various kinds of embodied pleasures – then it seeks to be in a body, and always a body that would best express the way it wants to live. So on physical death, a soul in this state is reincarnated, perhaps as another human being, but also perhaps (so Plato held, to the great embarrassment of some of his admirers) as a lower animal, say a pig or wolf whose wallowing or ravening life-style fleshes out the soul's most precious previous desires.[5] Alternatively, the embodied soul may incline towards disembodiment, and achieve it or come closer to achieving it by practising its intellectuality and rejecting physical and worldly enthusiasms. This is why, in the *Phaedo*, about-to-die Socrates tries to comfort his friends by telling them that if death is the separation of soul from body, the philosopher should be glad to die, since the philosopher has lived his present life gladly practising for death by losing himself in intellectual activity.

In Plato, then, the question of separability of soul from body is not a simple one. In the first place, every embodied soul is separable from its current body, since the soul is immortal whereas any given body will wear out. Secondly, every soul is in principle separable from body altogether, since every embodied soul is in principle, or at least by virtue

---

[5] Aristotle was unfair if he meant to include Plato in his criticism of the Pythagoreans for assigning 'any chance soul to any chance body' (*On the Soul* 1.3, 407b20–4).

of its original nature, able to refine itself to the point where it wants nothing that a body can provide. However, saying this is a bit like saying: human beings by nature can live without heroin or cocaine; heroin and cocaine addicts are human beings by nature; therefore they can live without heroin or cocaine. Granted they have this capacity, they lack the power to exercise it as of now, just as human beings by contrast with bull-frogs have the capacity to speak several different languages, but someone who has never learnt a foreign language lacks the ability to exercise this human capacity. In this sense, some embodied souls cannot live separately from a body suited to their desires, while others, a minority perhaps, can.

According to this picture, the body is simply the instrument of the soul, a view that Aristotle too would endorse at one stage of his career. That is, the soul does not depend on the body except to do through it something that it wants to do. Thus it fashions and animates its body for the sake of physical action, sensation, and experience. That the soul can do this if it chooses goes along with the thought, which we find again and again in Plato, that the soul is divine or godlike. This means that in itself it has a sort of limited omnipotence. If it wills or really desires a certain kind of life for itself, its 'will is done' even if it wills what is bad for it: automatically it comes to be equipped with what is necessary. But once it is in a body, of course, what it can bring about is limited by the nature of its body and the environment.

So – to answer our earlier questions about the essence of soul – the soul for Plato is essentially a valuing power: a power to create and maintain for itself the life it truly desires and thinks good, along with that life-style's accoutrements or freedom from accoutrements. Its purely intellectual function and its body-animating function represent different bents or inclinations. If we consider soul in general and in the abstract, it is presumably contingent whether soul is embodied, and embodied this way or that, or whether it is pure intellect. What is essential and fundamental is soul's determinability, in fact self-determinability, in contrary ways. If, however, we consider an individual soul, its determinate condition – its being embodied or not, and if embodied then how – is all but fundamental for this individual. For on the one hand this condition reflects the individual's currently dearest values, and on the other hand it affects almost everything the individual does and experiences in its current life.

We may wonder how the soul is supposed to take on a body. Plato says little about this. At one point he seems to suggest that the soul 'weaves' a body for itself.[6] Certainly he does not want to imply that the soul has hands and moves a shuttle to and fro. The idea presumably is that the soul informs certain materials which in its presence grow and organise themselves into the requisite body. A previously embodied soul may start with some matter from its previous body.[7] Plato shows no sign of holding that the soul creates its body *ex nihilo*.

Some philosophers might balk at the idea that the soul has power to rearrange matter. They might, if they accepted the existence of the soul at all, feel more comfortable with the thought that the soul actually dreams its body and physical environment. Some work would then have to be done to explain whether, and if so, how, souls dreaming different physical dreams nonetheless in some sense share a world with each other. But this is not Plato's problem, for he does not strike out in the idealist direction.

It is sometimes suggested that one needs to have been bitten by the bug of external-world scepticism before one can seriously consider idealism. Certainly the bug of external-world scepticism did not get to Plato. But there is something else one should bear in mind when considering Plato's silence on these great questions of modern philosophy. The fact is that from the point of view of Platonic ethical concern, which is a point of view that pervades most of the Dialogues, it makes no difference whether the soul chooses to dream, and then becomes addicted to dreaming, its embodiment, or whether it chooses and then becomes addicted to life mediated by a real, independently existing, body in a real physical environment.[8] Whereas for Descartes this makes all the difference – one way God is a deceiver, the other way not – for Plato either way the soul in question gets what it wants, and is just as misguided in wanting it if the body turns out to be independently real as it would be if the body were its fantasy.

I have been comparing Plato's argument in the *Phaedo* with Descartes' in the *Meditations* that soul is separable from body. Let me end by comparing some of the wider purposes of those arguments. Plato offers the argument of the *Phaedo* as, *inter alia*, an instance and example of the kind of intellectual exercise that loosens the human soul's attachment to

---

[6] *Phaedo* 87b–e. The weaving idea occurs as part of a view that is rejected, but what is rejected is not the weaving, but the thought that, as with an actual weaver, the soul might cease to exist before wearing out its final coat.

[7] Cf. *Phaedo* 80c–81c.

[8] Plato can of course make this distinction even if, as I am arguing, it does not carry for him a burning question; but the word 'real' used as above would presumably not be his tool for making it, since his *realia* are immutable Forms.

its body. Since the attachment reflects the soul's misunderstanding of the true nature of happiness, the *Phaedo* argument, for those who enter into it, is an exercise in soul-saving. By contrast, what Descartes discovers when he discovers his reasons for declaring the mind separable from the body is entirely different from the intellectualisation he himself undergoes in order to reach the proof. And he cannot overtly, even if he is inclined so inwardly, claim this refinement as a sort of soul-saving without running foul of the religion of his time. For although this religion differed within itself on how much faith counts for salvation, and how much works, these were the only options considered, and Descartes' activity does not come under either. Instead, his avowed purpose in following the path of the *Meditations* from doubt to himself, and from himself to the God who is not a deceiver, is to establish 'something firm and lasting in the sciences',[9] i.e. mathematics and mathematical physics.

This is an extremely puzzling remark if it means that these sciences fail as sciences if they cannot be rendered indubitable by an argument that first doubts and then reinstates the clear and distinct ideas on which such inquiries depend. For the mathematician's performance as such is not less clear or less accurate if he lacks a proof to the effect that although the most rigorous mathematics conceivable to man can be doubted, nonetheless in the end we are theologically justified in accepting them. But surely Descartes' hope is not to make the mathematician a more successful mathematician, but rather to show the rest of us that mathematical science in its own sphere carries the same authority as divine revelation in its, since both come from the same source. Rightly understood, the practice of such abstract studies, though not a religious exercise, is not secular either, for it expresses God as reason or the natural light. Plato would surely have agreed that it is not secular, but he could not have imagined the historical context that made it so important for someone in Descartes' position to distinguish priest and mathematical scientist, in effect postulating at least two kinds of 'higher calling', one devoted to faith, the other to reason.

---

[9] *Meditation* I, first paragraph.

CHAPTER 8

Aristotle and contemporary ethics

I INTRODUCTION

In the twenty-three centuries of Western thinking since Aristotle, the subject called 'ethics' has grown to embrace many more topics than Aristotle took account of under this or any title. Many of our own central preoccupations in ethics are with questions on which, for one or another reason, Aristotle has little or nothing to say. This is worth emphasising. Because of Aristotle's pre-eminent greatness and the reach and power of his ancient authority, unwarned readers of his *Ethics* may simply take it for granted that in this or that important modern debate there is a theory of which Aristotle holds a version, or a side which he is recognisably on. Such assumptions are all the easier to slip into because so much of what he *does* have to say in his *Ethics* continues to shape our own thinking on those particular matters, and so much of it comes in direct answer to questions whose universal relevance is as obvious in our day as it would have been in his. What is more, because so much of what he has to say in his *Ethics* tends to seem to us extraordinarily sensible as well as illuminating, we can easily fail to absorb how unusual some of his presuppositions are by today's philosophical standards. In this essay I shall be bringing out some of the differences between Aristotle's concerns in ethics and contemporary concerns. However, there are parts of our Aristotelian legacy that we can wholeheartedly continue to endorse, and also parts from which we may be able to learn more than we have learned so far. Some of these too, as well as some differences, will be touched upon in this essay.

II FLOURISHING

Let us begin with a possession that it seems can hardly grow old: the great Aristotelian idea of human flourishing, or simple *flourishing* for short, since here we are setting aside the biological flourishing of plants and non-rational animals. I do not put forward 'flourishing' as the preferred translation for *eudaimonia* in general, but as excellently hitting off the narrower idea of *human eudaimonia*. For of course *eudaimonia* in itself is ascribed to the gods as well as to the best and luckiest humans. Now, the idea that gods and (some) human beings are alike subjects of *eudaimonia* is probably not an assumption we today require in order to reach ethical conclusions, even of an Aristotelian sort. But we have to allow Aristotle that assumption since it was necessary for his final argument about the content of human flourishing.[1] However, it cannot be correct to speak of god or the gods as 'flourishing'. Why not? For exactly the reason the word works so well for specifically human *eudaimonia*: what flourishes is what grows and dies and depends on an environment and can come to grief; and all this is true of humans. One does not need to believe in any god to feel the force of Aristotle's contrast, never far from the surface, between divine *eudaimonia* and the human kind which is the subject of the *Ethics*: in other words, to be constantly in mind of the universal human limitations and vulnerabilities, as well as potentialities. 'Flourishing' alludes to all that. We *are* rational beings: but mortal, implanted in an environment, at its mercy through our bodies, born in thrall to the sensations and instinctual emotions necessary for bare survival, requiring constant care and replenishment, utterly dependent for our development on somewhat more mature versions of ourselves – that is, on beings with, at best, many of the same infirmities, and wielding no more than human capacities of understanding and protection. These conditions, and the resulting needs, longings, general patterns of relationship and authority, constitute the context for realising any *eudaimonia* that might be open to humankind. Thus the concept of flourishing points both towards our highest aspirations and towards the life-form in terms of which any of our aspirations are to be achieved.

So we have from Aristotle the seed – and more than just a seed – of a truly sound and fruitful approach to the question of human well-being. According to this approach, one starts by forming a systematic conception of the most significant features of the human animal. One forges an anthropological picture, partly empirical, partly *a priori*, which may even be quite detailed while maintaining universality. Such a picture is essential for well-informed, intelligent, discussion of what is involved, at any level, in human well-being – what it consists in and how it is to be realised. In a

---

[1] *Nicomachean Ethics* x.8.

sense the picture defines human well-being and its opposite, since it shows us the plexus of respects in which human life can go well or badly. List the respects and say: human well-being – or flourishing – is or entails being well off in *these*. Such a statement is not empty: it rules out some supposed possibilities as incoherent. But it only sets the stage for discussion of substantial options. A non-question-begging anthropological picture fails to generate a unique narrowly substantial account of the human good. In particular, it fails to justify the account for which Aristotle himself eventually settles: one that (a) equates flourishing with, predominantly, the activity of virtue, 'virtue' being understood as meaning courage, moderation and the rest, and above all justice, and (b) interprets these qualities in a recognisably moralistic sense.

But there are those who 'by any ethological standard of the bright eye and the gleaming coat [are] dangerously flourishing':[2] people who are ruthless and dishonest, but intelligent, well-organised, successful, enjoying life. What about them? As contemporary ethicists we wonder how Aristotle imagines he can get away with his equation. If by a supposedly logical transition from 'living (or functioning) well (*eu*)' to 'living (or functioning) in accordance with virtue (*kat'aretên*)', then the equation rests on an equivocation between the philosopher's formulaic sense of the virtue of an *X* – that whereby an *X* is or functions as a good one – and what the ordinary person in Aristotle's culture understood by 'virtue' as applied to human beings. A hedonist would or should argue that living or functioning well is living or functioning pleasantly, with 'the (formulaic) virtue in accordance with which' understood as the capacity (or a set of capacities) for pleasure. Some hold that living well is living splendidly, which they identify perhaps with the wielding of power and the 'triumph of the will'; or with the glamour of elegance and 'cool'; the virtues, for them, correspond.

Reading Aristotle with a contemporary eye, and seeing clearly the absence of an analytic connection between 'living well' (in the sense supplied by the anthropological picture) and living a life of ethical virtue, we can be easily drawn to conclude that Aristotle attaches flourishing to ethically virtuous activity in order to give us a needed motive towards the latter. Or we may conclude that Aristotle proposes flourishing as the 'ultimate justification of morality'; that is to say: what makes it true that I ought to do what is morally right is that thereby I shall

---

[2] Bernard Williams, 1985, 46.

flourish.[3] But if doing what is right stands in need of justification, flourishing could provide this only if it is distinct from such ethically virtuous activity: whereas Aristotle all but identifies them. What is more, Aristotle knew that his equation was what we call a synthetic statement. As the style of his advocacy for it shows, he knew perfectly well that it was a contested position, and that both claim and counter-claim were logically intelligible. Aristotle of course thinks his equation well supported by reputable opinions; but an intellectually resourceful hedonist could have made a better case than Aristotle allows to appear, as could an intellectually resourceful adherent of 'living splendidly' on one of the amoralist interpretations suggested above. No doubt Aristotle can defuse their cases by arguing that what is intuitively attractive about their candidates is in some satisfactory way provided, or the longing for it taken care of, by his own. However, one cannot help wondering whether a hedonist or a splendid life-ist as clever as Aristotle might not have turned the tables by showing ways in which what is intuitively attractive about virtuous (in the ordinary sense) activity is actually to be found, in some form or other, lurking within the folds of *their* ideals. Does Aristotle push ahead simply because no such clever other voice was raised?

III ETHICAL EPISTEMOLOGY, ETHICAL REALISM

No, Aristotle pushes ahead with the equation 'flourishing is virtuous (in the ordinary sense) activity' because he is a person with a certain set of values (which he can defend up to a point, though there is no reason to believe *conclusively*), and he is addressing a likeminded audience or readership. The *Ethics* is meant for the 'well brought-up'. Only they have the right 'starting points' (*Nicomachean Ethics* 1.4, 1095b2–6). Of course, 'well brought-up' can be interpreted in exactly as many ways as 'living (or functioning) well' and as 'virtue' in the abstract philosophical sense. What it amounts to, in the context of the reception of a certain ideal of life philosophically explicated, is a pre-philosophical preparedness, developed through living and practice, to resonate to that ideal. Thus whatever their articulated ideas may have been, Aristotle's audience (the one for which he hopes) have in fact been living or trying to live as if just, courageous,

---

[3] This proposal is the definition of 'eudaimonism', according to *The Cambridge Dictionary of Philosophy* (entry by D. T. Devereux). H. A. Prichard's 'Does Moral Philosophy Rest on a Mistake?' in Prichard, 1949, 2–17, esp. 13, is the *locus classicus* for the picture of Aristotle as eudaemonist in that sense. But in that sense, Aristotle was no eudaemonist.

moderate, etc. action is an absolutely precious thing in itself, and as if any pleasure, power or splendour that could be got only by acting unjustly or in a cowardly or debauched way has no practical pull on them. The thought is not that they have been living as if those other values are of no interest (how, if so, could their culture have been one where debate about conflicting ethical ideals was such an engaging pastime?) but that when it came to a conflict they would put the morally good action first. Thus when Aristotle presents them – and himself – with his equation, he and they are immediately inclined to accept it. But the immediacy to them of its rightness or truth is an expression of their character, not of an analytic or conceptual connection between the left- and right-hand sides.

We today as philosophers may be inclined to feel that this is not a very satisfactory situation, epistemologically speaking. Or rather: we today as philosophers are divided into those who find the situation epistemologically unsatisfactory, and those who understand that dissatisfied response deeply and from within, but, by one path or another, have fought their way out of it intellectually, although they bear the scars and constantly tell the tale. In what follows, I shall largely ignore this very important difference between schools of 'us today as philosophers'. Aristotle and his audience, then, accept Aristotle's equation about flourishing as naturally and willingly as a carnivore accepts in a practical way the equation of food with flesh. (But the acceptance of the former is not, like that of the latter, mechanical or 'knee-jerk', since it is forwarded by real, though not logically conclusive, argument.) If we today are in certain personal respects like the individuals in Aristotle's audience, then we too will resonate to the equation; we may feel it a very good thing that there are people like us in this respect; and we may be resolved to bring up our children to be the same. But as philosophers we are tempted to think that we do not *know* the truth of the equation, since there is no knock-down rational basis for it: that is, no basis that would render it compelling to all alert human beings regardless of their moral formation.

Aristotle might puzzle over what it is that we as philosophers think (or know what it is like to be tempted to think) we are *lacking* here. For not to have knowledge matters only if the not-having is a privation; indeed, if knowledge is supposed to be valuable, we do not want to call something 'knowledge' unless we see the not-having as a privation. After all, none of the rival equations is analytically true either, so it is not as if in embracing ours we are missing something epistemologically better. Furthermore, it is not as if we need to be absolutely secure of our and Aristotle's equation in order to feel right about living as we do. For our living as we do, and feeling right about it, was there before we got the equation; that was what made us feel at home with it. The equation is just the ideological summary of the values we were already practising. Being able to display the equation (or thinking we can display it) as an analytic truth certainly will not make us more practical in respect of those values. But now suppose that a logically conclusive proof of the equation were produced (or, which is not completely impossible, that we have come to believe that there is, or even that we have, such a proof): then it can be shown that people with rival equations are wrong, and they can be led to see that they are wrong! But, by the above considerations, this will make no difference to their practice (cf. *NE* x.9, 1179b5–18). What is more, to the extent that their actual practice fuels an ideology, it will continue to fuel an equation contrary to ours. Thus they will be tending to affirm the latter even at the same time (according to the hypothesis) as being in a position to acknowledge that it is analytically false. And by the same token they will still be tending to reject our equation even while in a position to acknowledge that it is analytically true. This is a very curious kind of 'seeing that they are wrong'! In fact, the notion of analytic truth has been reduced to absurdity in this context. Thus Aristotle's equation lacks nothing by lacking it: its adherents can affirm in good epistemic conscience that their equation is everything it ought to be.

Most modern philosophers at this point are bound to want to say two things: (1) that adherents to rival equations can reach exactly the same position by the same steps with regard to their favoured candidate; and (2) that consequently no side is entitled to consider their own equation as knowledge, or even as true. Aristotle, I believe, operates as if it is simply not his business that the situation envisaged in (1) can arise, hence as if it is not his business to go on and consider (2). (This is all the easier in that rival equations probably represent minority opinions.[4]) That the situation envisaged in (1) can arise is not in itself going to alter our underlying practical commitments, and as long as they remain, our equation (which is the Aristotelian one, I am supposing) is in force. The modern philosopher may well want to insert a qualifier: our equation is in force *for us*. However, if it is *we* who are doing the talking here (we of the relevant practical commitments – and the modern philosopher who has just been mentioned is quite likely one of us when out of his study), 'for us' is redundant or a weakener. Aristotle is addressing his *Ethics* to us as

---

[4] They are not the moralities of 'other cultures' (the equations of which may tend, abstracted from local colouring, to coincide with Aristotle's equation): they are rivals within the same culture.

practical agents, and as practical agents we have no business to be trying to take up a standpoint in which we are no more committed to our own equation of flourishing than to any of the rivals, or to divide our individual selves into an unregenerate lower me$_1$ committed to the equation, and a higher, philosophical, me$_2$ who regards me$_1$'s commitment as just one of many possible facts about human beings.

Thus the Aristotelian equation is in force; and explication of the term on the right-hand side is quite a large philosophical programme. Aristotle's first task, as he sees it, is to get on with this.[5] Still, one can speculate on what he would have said if forced to give a general response to the fact that there might be rival equations of flourishing, each supported by a good stock of reputable opinions. He might have said that we have to argue each step of the way with each side (as indeed he does to a considerable extent in the *Ethics*), and one cannot know in advance how this would turn out. He might well have emphasised that the rivals, or anyway the plausible ones among them, in a way recognise the same values but accord them different priority. This means that the adherents on each side are not talking past each other: they have a common set of subject matters, and they cannot all be right. Finally, he would not have said that no one is closer to the truth than anyone else. Aristotle would have said that those who march under banners different from his and his audience's are not seeing things straight: they are missing the truth or are purblind to it; and the fact that they cannot be logically prevented from saying the same about us is simply not something that should disturb our confidence in our own views and our scorn for theirs, any more than we should let our picture of the world waver just because we know that paranoiacs see us as seriously out of touch with reality. (Remember, the adherents of rival equations are not persons who share 'the moral point of view' with us, but come down on the other side of some practical dilemma. They are persons who live by the belief that, in a conflict, getting pleasure or power, or maintaining 'cool', is more important than refraining from an unjust or cowardly or debauched action (or, for that matter, than discouraging it in someone else). One does not in this sense count as an adherent of a rival equation if one is simply pushing a rival equation in debate, with a view to getting, e.g., Aristotle to defend and explicate his equation more fully, in the way

---

[5] His next task, as he sees it, is to discuss the political, social, educational, etc. arrangements that would best realise what is covered by the right-hand side of his equation. When that has been done, his work in ethics will be complete (*NE* x.9, 1179a33ff.; 1181b12–15).

Glaucon and Adimantus challenge Socrates to explain the intrinsic value of justice by arguing against their own unargued (and as yet unshaken) belief that it is more than a means to an end and matters in reality, not just on the level of appearance.)

Contemporary theorists may be disappointed, or they may be put on their mettle, by the epistemological simplicity, or crudity, with which Aristotle sets up the basic proposition of his *Ethics*. In this respect, Aristotle is not, I think, a philosophical model that we in any straight-forward way can follow. In this respect, he is a reminder of lost innocence, not a leader back to it. There is, however, no shortage in the *Ethics* of philosophical refinement and dexterity once we are within the framework of Aristotle's basic proposition.

Having reached the issue of Aristotle's 'moral realism', I now cease to focus on the 'equation of flourishing', which is a universal philosophical statement, and turn instead to the question of ground-level practical judgments and feelings sparked in people by their particular situations. These include both judgments about particulars and the activations of various evaluative generalisations about persons, personal qualities, and behaviour. Aristotle, as we all know, speaks of the virtuous person, the person of practical wisdom (*phronêsis*), as the ethical 'yardstick' of the particular situations he is presented with (*NE* III.4, 1113a29–33). Aristotle is occasionally thought to mean by this that the say-so of the *phronimos* determines, in the sense of actually constituting (or 'constructing'), the truth about particular ethical questions. I do not think that this is Aristotle's view. He of course sees the *phronimos* as a good guide for the rest of us. To get the benefit of this guidance we don't (as is sometimes complained) need to be able to recognise the *phronimos* independently. To be able to do that reliably we should have to be *phronimoi* ourselves, hence in need of no external *phronimos*. To get the benefit of the guidance of a *phronimos* we only have to be lucky enough to be placed near one – one who takes an interest in us and whom we have been brought up to regard as a person to be listened to with respect. However, Aristotle, I am sure, goes along with the *phronimos*'s personal experience of forming ethical judgments, and with the experience of the less mature in getting his advice. To the *phronimos* in operation, considering how to respond in some particular situation, it seems as if he is looking for an answer which is in some sense 'there'; or if he forms the judgment instantly, the discrimination, though obvious, presents itself as what would have been correct whether or not he had realised it. He sees himself as possibly making mistakes, and no doubt as having made them in the past. And the advice he gives others doesn't consist just of prescriptions but carries explanations: he gives reasons why this is better than that, and the recipients can see the reasons once they are pointed out, and can see in the light of those reasons that the prescribed action is appropriate. By such interaction they develop their own potential as *phronimoi*. (What they have to take on trust in these sessions is that the *phronimos* has considered all relevant factors.) Thus those who accept guidance by the *phronimos*, come to the answers as right ones which were 'there', and which they might – and, on their own, would – have missed. Philosophers today have to *argue* themselves back into taking such experiences of objectivity at face value; for example: 'If we take seriously the idea that there are not *two* criteria or sets of criteria for "reality" – commonsense [or: human] criteria and philosophical criteria – but only one, then we are led naturally to the view that what demarcates "reality" is something human . . .'[6]

Aristotle, then, does not explain ethical truth as what the *phronimos* reliably apprehends: he explains the *phronimos* as reliably apprehending ethical truth. And he sometimes speaks of the apprehending as if it were a sort of perceptual access (e.g. *NE* VI.12, 1144a29–b1). A modern philosopher of not too long ago would have been impelled to ask: does this mean that Aristotle postulates a special faculty of ethical intuition, a moral sense? Well, if so, it would be a faculty developed through the right kind of habituation: but what could be the point of postulating a faculty in addition to the virtuous person's habituated qualities of character and practical intelligence? Presumably the idea of a special moral sense answers to an epistemological anxiety. Just as we justify many particular empirical claims by saying 'I saw it with my own eyes', 'I heard it with my own ears', etc., the philosopher wants us to be able to justify ethical claims analogously. But in fact we justify the ethical claims by pointing out or describing what we take to be the relevant facts in each case (often without explicitly invoking any principle of conduct). The philosophical anxiety, then, is that this sort of procedure, of which we all have an everyday understanding, is not good enough to deliver real ethical knowledge – or that its working is completely mysterious. The anxiety is bound up with the thought that if there is ethical knowledge, the properties and relations thereby known are metaphysically 'queer'.[7] How, if there are such entities in the world, could they make their impact on us *just* in

---

[6] Hilary Putnam, 'James's Theory of Perception', in Putnam, 1990, 247.
[7] Mackie, 1977, 38–42.

virtue of the fact that we have had a certain upbringing resulting in a certain kind of character?

The classic modern response to such worries has been to reject the whole idea of ethical truth: the appearance of ethical factuality is the 'projection' by us of our attitudes or feelings on to objects which in themselves are devoid of ethical qualities. In the wake of this view comes a variety of sophisticated efforts to hang on to the objectivity of ethical judgments while rejecting 'queer' entities and the mysterious faculty of ethical knowledge. There are theories allowing for objectivity without truth, and there are 'cognitive irrealist' theories allowing for truth without correspondence to realities. But how is it that Aristotle is so unperturbed by the worries which today drive us down these or similarly motivated routes? I do not mean to imply that he does not treat seriously various ancient arguments for ethical relativism (or anti-objectivism). But those arguments do not turn on the thought that there is something ontologically monstrous about, in particular, *ethical* realities (and would be even if all humans had one culture), so that our knowing *them* would be in principle mysterious: all this by comparison with some type of reality that philosophers feel to be non-'bizarre'. This is an essentially modern thought. To try to diagnose it would be to enter a huge discussion. Here I shall only tender the familiar suggestion that the thought crystallises inordinate respect for natural science. Ethical properties cannot be weighed, measured, physically analysed, etc., by science. Nor are they reliable concomitants of the properties and relations that are weighed, measured, analysed, etc., by science. Science rightly for its own purposes ignores ethical properties. But inordinate respect (an attitude of philosophers, not of scientists as such) sees science's purposes as determining what is to count as regular, normal, metaphysically unsurprising, external-to-the-observer's-mind, reality. So it comes to seem that ethical properties and ethical facts either are unreal (projections of the observer's mind) or are realities of a strange unworldly kind.

Aristotle might have commented that regarding ethical properties as unreal because natural science does not take account of them is on a par with regarding physical change and physical matter as unreal because mathematics, that paradigm of knowledge in his day, abstracts from them. Plato, after all, in some of his writings might be accused of that mistake. Moreover, although Aristotle himself has great respect for the enterprise of physical science (and notwithstanding his teleology and his mainly non-quantitative approach, he of course is just as clear as we are that the subject matter of natural science is quite other than the subject matter of moral judgments) – still, Western science at that time was still taking its first wobbling steps: it was not yet a mighty and prestigious social institution. A contemporary of his, the great rhetorician Isocrates, who was without doubt one of the most cultivated men of the classical period, had so little sense of the seriousness of the business of theorising about the universe that he dismissed all such discussions as amusements for the empty-headed.[8] There were no laboratories with state funding pouring into them, and virtually no technological spin-offs, to counteract the picture of the natural philosopher as a wild-haired eccentric. In any case, the theories themselves were so speculative. Many people – educated ones like Isocrates – would have laughed at the idea that physics puts us in touch with 'hard facts'. To an ancient Greek (and surely to most people in any period) no theoretical claim in physics or medicine could have carried the same certainty as, for example: 'Love is better than hate between close members of the same family, except under very strange circumstances – and such circumstances should be avoided like the plague.' Why, then, when we compare, on the one hand, an ethical sensibility whose exercise on particular situations (including ones that are hearsay and ones that are fictional) delivers, reinforces, and perhaps gives more precise sense to, the above generalisation, with, on the other hand, a scientific observer's (ethically) value-free focus on particulars that may confirm an hypothesis – why should we think the former less a source of respect-worthy knowledge than the latter? And if in each case the knowledge is respectable, why should we balk at admitting a known reality equally robust in each?

IV   DECIDING WHAT IS RIGHT

From the topic of Aristotle's meta-ethical stance versus various modern positions, I now pass to comparisons under the heading of 'normative ethics'. What does Aristotle's *Ethics* tell us we should do, and what does the work offer by way of guidance in making decisions? To answer this, some exegesis is necessary.

Particularly in the *Nicomachean Ethics*, Aristotle deals with human objectives at two different levels. On the one hand, and most famously,

---

[8] Like most of his contemporaries, Isocrates believed that the serious work of life was political action, and above all effective political communication. He allowed a certain value to mathematics: it was useful for sharpening young men's minds. Beyond that, while he might not have frowned upon the occasional recreational use (he was aware of the attraction), his motto would have been: 'Just say No to theoretical activity'. The character Callicles in Plato's *Gorgias* takes the same line about fundamental discussions of ethics.

there is that great objective the Good for Man, i.e. human *eudaimonia*. Aristotle sees this as the final goal of what he calls 'political' thought and action. 'Political' refers to a field where the job is to articulate and implement the best arrangements overall for life in human society. Thought and action on this level are 'architectonic' (*NE* 1.2, 1094a27). Then, on the other hand, there is what we may call 'ground-level' or 'quotidian' activity.

The fundamental step in architectonic thinking is to set out a correct substantial account of flourishing with its ramifications: this will provide a 'target' for 'political' action (*NE* 1.2, 1094a22–6). The actions and decisions to be taken in its light will be what we can loosely call 'big' ones. They will be concerned with life-shaping arrangements that are hard to reverse: those which make the context of everything else. It is distinctive of architectonic thinking that in its fundamental stage we take for granted no context other than the human condition itself. Obviously, as we move ahead to envisage implementations we have to take account of unalterable or currently unalterable features of our specific context. (For instance, geographical features, institutional features, material resources.) But the thinking preserves its universal, philosophical, and architectonic character by reflecting on and evaluating these unalterable elements in terms of their effect on flourishing as spelled out at the first stage. What mainly distinguishes architectonic practical thinking from the ground-level kind is that the latter at any given moment accepts its particular set of circumstances with no more analysis than is necessary for deciding how best to manage from within them. In the light of this distinction, which brings out a generic difference between two kinds of practical thinking, it is superficial to draw a contrast between thinking on behalf of one, or a few, and thinking on behalf of many. This is why Aristotle calls the thinking 'political' even when it is a case of individuals thinking out what path to follow in their individual lives (*NE* 1.2, 1094b7–11). It counts as 'political' because it is architectonic.

Two more points should be made. The first, which may seem too obvious to mention, is that Aristotle's architectonic thinking begins with the first line of the *Ethics*. It starts with the famous assumption that there is a 'highest good' functionally defined in terms of its endhood in relation to everything else, and it then proceeds (with arguments) to characterise this good substantially, by means of one of several logically possible equations of flourishing. Only later, a good way on, does the theme of virtuous activity moralistically conceived become central to the picture as the controlling value of the good life according to Aristotle's preferred equation. In other words, the idea of thinking with a view to deciding on right action moralistically conceived – which is the ground-level thinking of the *phronimos* – occupies a different place in Aristotle's ethical theory from the idea of architectonic thinking. The wise thinking that typifies the *phronimos* is not directed towards the architectonic goal, whether to elucidate it philosophically or to work out large-scale arrangements that would advance it; rather, it is *part of* that goal as correctly elucidated.

The second point is that Aristotle's conception of the architectonic goal does not commit him to the view that we ought to be deliberately promoting this in all our plans and decisions. Clearly it is not incumbent on human beings to be always engaging in architectonic thinking, even if it is foolish and unworthy to take no interest in it if one has the leisure to do so at all. Nor, in my view, does Aristotle see us as required at every juncture to be working to propagate realisation of the architectonic goal.[9] He sees our lives as full of different obligations, interests and commitments, and as requiring from us many immediate reactions to immediate circumstances. This by and large is the nature of a human life, and his ideal is that we live such a life well, i.e., for him, mainly in terms of the virtues moralistically conceived.[10] It would fit in with this if Aristotle holds, as he surely does, not only that we need not always be working for the architectonic goal, but also that quotidian morality constrains architectonic practice. If I could promote the flourishing of many (on his interpretation of 'flourishing'), but only by perpetrating clear acts of injustice against a few, would I be right to go ahead? There is no evidence that Aristotle, any more than common sense, thinks that I would be. What gives flourishing its status as the greatest of our ends is not the right to make absolute demands on our agency, nor the authority to justify any kind of action on its behalf.

On one level, then, Aristotle gives a full, clear, and unitary answer to the question 'What should I do?' If the question is being asked from the architectonic perspective, the answer is in terms of a goal to be achieved, a good to be brought about – whether for one, few, or many persons,

---

[9] The famous opening argument of the *NE* says that all *goods* are for the sake of the chief good, which is the architectonic goal. This does not imply that all ethically *right* actions as such are for the sake of that goal. At 1.12, 1102a2–4, he is likewise stating the relation of *eudaimonia* to the other *goods* (and the 'we' in line 3 refers, in my view, to us as engaged in architectonic practice, not as engaged in practice in general). For further discussion see chapters 9 and 10 below.

[10] It then becomes clear, but only at the end of the *Nicomachean Ethics*, that architectonic activity should include promoting the serious practice, under human conditions, of purely theoretical pursuits: this should become the distinctive quotidian activity of at least some citizens.

whether for oneself or others – and the portrait of that good is drawn in the *Ethics*. Architectonic performance, good or bad, right or wrong, must be judged against its goal, as medical performance against the goal of health. However, for the ground level of quotidian practicality, Aristotle attempts no general answer. He does not think that a useful one can be stated.[11] Apart from dividing the objects of practical interest into the advantageous, the pleasant and the admirable (noble, fine) (*NE* II.3, 1104b30–1), he does not, except in the sphere of special justice, try to elucidate principles of good action. He does not list rules of conduct, or rank them, or try to subsume some rules under others, or to reduce many rules to few or one. In short, on the quotidian level, except in the areas of distributive and corrective justice, Aristotle offers no theory at all to guide ethical decision-making. He is not a consequentialist, and in particular not a eudaemonistic one. He has commonsense deontological leanings, but shows not the slightest interest in working them up into a system. And his deontology, such as it is, involves no banging of the board against some alternative theory. Particular remarks make it clear that he does not 'found the right on the good' (not even, as we have seen, on the highest good); but he never formulates this as a general position. He is not even, it has to be said, a modern-style 'virtue-ethicist' if this means a philosopher who defines right or appropriate action as the action of the virtuous person (or the courageous or moderate or good-tempered or just, etc., depending on the case). On the contrary, Aristotle explains virtue and the virtues as dispositions for right or appropriate action and emotion (towards the appropriate people, at the appropriate moment, in the appropriate amount, etc.), but without ever being prompted to state a set of rules to which these ethical responses would generally conform. Equally mythological is the view that, for example, the courageous agent according to Aristotle acts from a rule that goes: 'Courage demands that one do so and so'.

It is true that Aristotle does give a sort of classification of appropriate response when he divides life into the spheres of the virtues; this tells us that there are as many different kinds of appropriate response as there are spheres.[12] But this is not a taxonomy of specific rules or principles, nor does it entail any.[13]

---

[11] See *NE* II.2, 1104a1–10, quoted below in section VI.
[12] Aristotle does not, however, think that there is a different kind of *phronêsis* for each sphere. *Phronêsis* is unitary.
[13] But for more on this taxonomy, or the associated idea of the ethical 'mean', see the end of the next section.

V SYSTEMATISING THE PRINCIPLES OF QUOTIDIAN CONDUCT?

That Aristotle provides no ground-level normative ethics, and is apparently quite untroubled by any lack of a system here, gives us food for thought. He so blatantly fails to produce the kind of position that it is a modern tradition to expect as a main deliverance of philosophical ethics – and he is not wringing his hands! Of course Aristotle was untouched by those historical influences that transformed philosophical ethics into, in large part, a 'jural' business of formulating and justifying rules and principles. But while not taking issue with that true observation, let us think about what goes into forming a perspective from which a philosophical ethics sans codified principles of quotidian action could seem self-sufficient. In Aristotle's case, first and foremost is the fact that he is addressing 'well brought-up' persons. Such persons should know, or be able to work out, what to do in particular situations: and these judgments they, and anyone, may well be unable to make until immersed in the situation itself.[14] Secondly, there is the fact that citizens are supposed to know the laws of their *polis*, and the laws enshrine values and principles of right and wrong: so much so that Aristotle regularly equates general injustice with disrespect for law (e.g. *NE* v.1, 1129b11ff.). However, Aristotle cannot hope for hearers or readers who are uncritically acceptant of the laws and customs of their country, and of their own upbringing; on the contrary, he must hope for ones who will think afresh about such matters in the light of his own articulated ideal of flourishing. So he assumes an intelligent, rationally responsive, audience for ethics.[15] Yet even for them he does not consider it the philosopher's job to deepen, by systematising, their understanding of the rights and wrongs of quotidian conduct. True, a system of rules may not cover every situation, and rules don't interpret themselves, but philosophers who give us systems are aware of that, and it doesn't stop them.

Aristotle's eccentricity here should perhaps make us curious to understand better the deeply entrenched modern assumption that a major, if not the central, task of philosophical ethics is to systematise the principles of ordinary personal conduct. And in thinking about the *raison* (or

---

[14] But we shall see later how they can get a bit of help from Aristotle's notion of the ethical mean.
[15] Cf. the discussion at x.9, 1180b28ff. on what sort of person is a good legislator, and especially 1181b13–14.

raisons) *d'être* of such systematics, one also naturally wonders whether Aristotelian ethics is better or worse for lacking that approach. In the present space little more can be done than advertise that question, but any discussion of it should observe two points. Firstly, the question of the value of system must be separated from that of the goodness, rightness, or adequacy of the principles themselves. Obviously there is the closest historical connection between the biblical origins of our inherited codifying approach, and the (in origin) Judaeo-Christian values thereby standardly explicated. Even so, the type of approach and any specific content it targets are distinct issues. Hence we can register our moral alienhood from classical Greece's – and Aristotle's – lack of any ethic of universal respect for persons, and failure to recognise the virtue of compassion, without taking a stand on the value or point of systematics as such. There might conceivably have been a culture where universal respect and compassion were principles, and which made its laws of the land accordingly, but whose intellectual or spiritual leaders were no more disposed to organise normative ethics than is Aristotle. Secondly, the point or value of systematisation may be (a) intrinsic to the activity itself; or it may be that (b) system makes the targeted principles more normatively effective; or (c) the value may arise through extrinsic and variable circumstances. For example, the system-building might conceivably be engaged in (a[i]) academically, just as an interesting theoretical exercise; or (a[ii]) because in doing it we are studying the unitary and harmonious will of God for man (even as the cosmologist studies a different aspect of the 'mind of God'); or (a[iii]) because we are tracing the contours of universal and eternal ethical reality. Or (b[i]) it may be thought that by reducing the principles to a very abstract few, or ideally to one, we make them more 'scientific' and epistemologically more secure: bringing out and thus reinforcing their true rational authority, so that the justifications they provide will be rationally compelling upon all rational beings as such. (Such an ambition could probably only arise in response to sceptical and sentimentalist onslaughts on the entire notion of practical reason.) More modestly (b[ii]), it may be thought that systematising the principles makes it easier to deal with hard cases and dilemmas (but could this motivation alone suffice?). Finally (c), system may be sought because of the historical circumstances: for example, things may have changed so that real-life justifications, in order to work between people, must now be allowed to depend less on trust and shared unspoken assumptions, and more on explicit endorsement of what others explicitly endorse.

These considerations (even if most of them could not have occurred to him) give us a sense of what Aristotle was not providing in not providing philosophical clarification of principles of conduct. I shall comment briefly on (b[i]), the Kantian programme, and on the example under (c). As we have seen, Aristotle is untouched by any scientism that may be animating (b[i]). There is no pressure on him to feel that what is less scientific is therefore less rational or less epistemologically secure. Neither he nor any school of thought confronted by him divines grounds for worrying that practical right reason will turn out to be somehow less authoritative than we expect of it, unless we show that rejecting its decisions, or the reasons for them, traps one in some kind of logical inconsistency. In general, nothing in Aristotle's dialectical scene makes it attractive to imagine that the authoritativeness of practical right reason depends on its formality or its abstractness or some other property with logico-aesthetic appeal. On the other hand, moral seriousness is no stranger to Aristotle. Thus he would heartily endorse some of the Kantian associations of (b[i]), in particular the thought that the virtuous agent does what is right because it is right (or because of the reasons that render it right) and not because of some ulterior desideratum, as well as the thought that the virtuous agent honours and treasures *phronêsis* and the virtues for themselves, not for external results.[16] But these positions do not depend on conceiving of practical reason as 'pure' in a rationalistic sense.

As for the case under (c): in multicultural societies, or in the context of a world-community, less can safely be left implicit, because different groups differ in many of their implicit assumptions. Fairness and mutual understanding require more formalisation, and the philosopher may be ideal for this task. But it is not a task of purification or ratification that somehow confers authority on principles which they would otherwise intrinsically lack. It is a task of equipping practical agents with what they now need for ethical intercommunication when their previous, home-grown, resources in this regard are no longer adequate for all their interactions with others. Un-talked-over principles are fine in some communal situations, like that in which Aristotle lived by comparison with modern society. On the other hand, Aristotle as a practical philosopher might well have been willing to engage in a lot more ethical codification had he lived under different historical circumstances.

[16] However, at *EE* VIII.15, 124816–17 he makes a somewhat eccentric distinction between the good and the fine-and-good agent, whereby only the latter values virtue and virtuous activities for themselves.

So Aristotle refuses to offer rules for excellent quotidian conduct, and instead he hopes to promote it indirectly by emphasising the importance of character and situational intelligence, and the role of upbringing in their formation. We may easily be left with the impression that Aristotle's philosophy holds out no practical assistance at all to the quotidian agent at the point of particular action. (Labelling the agent in that way is meant for the sake of contrast with (a) the architectonic or political agent, and (b) the excellent quotidian agent considered simply as the product of upbringing, i.e. as bearer of a set of ethical dispositions. The architectonic agent is helped by having the correct architectonic goal explained to him, and the product of upbringing will have gained from having been reared in the light of that goal.) Now, the above impression is inevitable if we assume that there is no way philosophy could be even imagined to help at the point of quotidian action otherwise than by providing philosophically burnished rules telling what to do. On that assumption, whether or not we ourselves believe in the practical usefulness of such a set of rules, we shall construe Aristotle's statement that he has none to offer as showing that he regards philosophy as completely incapable of helping quotidian practice. We might well round this conclusion off with the thought that for Aristotle this is undisturbing, since he means to be addressing only people who, on the quotidian level, would anyway find themselves knowing what to do.

However, it turns out that this is not at all Aristotle's train of thought. Here is how he states the impossibility of giving rules:

Since, then, the present undertaking is not for the sake of theory, as our others are (for we are not inquiring into what excellence is for the sake of knowing it, but for the sake of becoming good, since otherwise there would be no benefit in it at all), we need to inquire into the subjects relating to actions, i.e. to how one should act; for as we have said, our actions are also responsible for our coming to have dispositions of a certain sort. Now that one should act in accordance with the correct prescription (*kata ton orthon logon*) is a shared view – let it stand as a basic assumption; there will be a discussion about it later . . . But before that let it be agreed that everything one says about practical undertakings has to be said, not with precision, but in rough outline . . .: things in the sphere of action and things that bring advantage have nothing stable about them, any more than things that bring health. But if what one says universally is like this, what one says about particulars is even more lacking in precision; for it does not fall under any expertise or under any set of rules – the agents themselves have to consider the circumstances relating to the occasion, just as happens in medicine, too, and in navigation.

Aristotle next says:

But even though the present discussion is like this, *we must try to give some help.* (*NE* II.2, 1103b26–1104a11).[17]

And then, straight away, he propounds the idea of the ethical mean. In short, the idea of the ethical mean is something the philosopher can supply that would supposedly give some practical help in particular situations.

But how can it do that? Or how can Aristotle believe that it can: that knowing the adage that for every area of practical life there is a too much, a too little, and a right amount,[18] of some kind of feeling or action, would help one to come up with appropriate particular responses?

Presumably he thinks that bearing this constantly in mind in 'real life' disposes one to monitor one's reactions in a way that tends to refine them, ethically speaking.[19] And this is surely true. It is plausible that, in any situation, being alive to the inherent tendency of the relevant feeling or urge to action to be 'more' or 'less' than is called for, makes me better at moulding my response so that it is more as it should be. Only when the agent succeeds in determining the right response will he/she (or a bystander) be in a position to say what, in this case, 'too much' and 'too little' would have been more or less *than.* Thus the maxim to avoid 'too much' and 'too little' makes its practical contribution precisely by means of what is often called its 'emptiness' – precisely through the fact that all it says is 'avoid doing/feeling more and less than is right'! It cannot point towards what is right in the way in which a signpost does, or a commandment; but by imbuing my agency with this maxim I make it more likely that I myself become pointed towards what is right.

No doubt the general idea of the ethical mean was not exactly news to Aristotle's ancient Greek audience (although they may not have realised before following his exposition the variety of areas in which it applies, and the number of not hitherto properly noticed ethical qualities it enables one to identify). But when the idea first appears in the *Nicomachean Ethics*

---

[17] The translation is from Rowe, in Broadie and Rowe, 2002.

[18] 'Too much' and 'too little' of course do duty for a host of ways in which a response can be misplaced.

[19] Note that when he claims practical usefulness for the mean-idea, he is thinking of it as helping to elicit the responses that build good character (1104a12–b3). To the extent that the agent approximates towards fully formed virtue, the need for such monitoring lessens. The mean-idea is descriptively true of the responses of the formed virtuous agent, but no longer plays its original part in controlling them. At this point (to the extent it is reached) the virtuous agent can, and should, stop thinking of her/his responses as expressions of the right amount (etc.) of something.

it is not intended as information, or to make its full impact on the purely reflective level. Aristotle assumes, when he offers it as practical help, that the audience understands that this will be true of it only if they actively take it with them into particular practical situations. Perhaps the idea is a banality *now* (as well as 'empty'); but *then*, for those who need the help, it will pay its way. The point is worth noting if only because it shows Aristotle doing abstract philosophical ethics in a way so different from how most of us do it today.

VII   ONE NEGLECTED ARISTOTELIAN THEME

Many topics descended from Aristotle's *Ethics* continue to be explored, exploited, adapted, and creatively transformed by philosophers today. Thus a vast amount of our contemporary discussion of well-being, practical reason, the virtues, situational intelligence, the ethical role of emotion, and weakness of will, uses Aristotle as reference point, and sometimes as inspiration. But other veins too are still worth mining which do not receive the same attention. Here, I shall take just one example: the question of leisure. Aristotle's remarks about leisure are not copious, but the theme is a vitally important one for him. Most philosophers of ethics today regard as important the ethical matters that Aristotle regarded as important. Surprisingly, then, except for Josef Pieper's contribution, which is very much of the nature of a protreptic,[20] there has been practically no modern ethical discussion of leisure.[21] As can easily be verified, the topic does not appear in modern surveys and compendia of ethics.

I can think of several reasons for this. Firstly, leisure in Aristotle is associated with his notorious doctrine of the supremacy of the theoretical life, which in turn is based partly on a theological picture. And Pieper's essay, while often penetrating, ties leisure so closely to the sacred and the sacramental that there may seem not to be enough of a topic left over for non-religious philosophical reflection.[22] Secondly, *a priori* it may seem

---

[20] *Leisure the Basis of Culture* (first published as *Musse und Kult*, 1948).

[21] This is beginning to change. See the thoughtful and original discussion by Gavin Lawrence, 2006. One of his conclusions is: 'There are admittedly difficulties in elucidating the notion of free time and its proper activities. But Aristotle is correct in emphasizing its centrality' (72). For a concise relevant statement see also Dorothea Frede, 2006, 273–4. The classic study of the theme of leisure in late fifth- and early fourth-century Greek literature is Solmsen, 1964.

[22] One does not have to be a non-believer to find off-putting such assertions as: '. . . leisure . . . is not possible unless it has a durable and consequently living link with the *cultus*, with divine worship' (xiv), and: 'When separated from worship, leisure becomes toilsome and work becomes inhuman' (54). Pieper also, following Aristotle, focuses too exclusively on intellectual and contemplative

that even if there are philosophical questions about leisure, they are quite easy ones, presenting no professional challenge. Thirdly, philosophical discussion of leisure, especially in the footsteps of Aristotle and of Pieper, is sure to get on to the question of its proper uses; but to take that seriously may seem uncomfortably close to legislating how people should use their leisure-time – 'which is no one's business but their own'. In response: first, there is plenty to be said humanistically about leisure. Secondly, even if the questions are easy, one can find this out only by engaging with them. Thirdly, if for a moment we allow ourselves the phrase 'the purpose of leisure': why should that set one on the path of telling people what to do any more threateningly than a question about 'the purpose of art' or, for that matter, 'the purpose of morality'?

If we turn to existing views (the first stage of an Aristotelian investigation), Aristotle's main ones are these: leisure is in some sense the end of life; *eudaimonia* crucially depends on leisure; leisure is different from relaxation; hence leisure-activities should not be trivial amusements; leisure is the space for 'precious' (*timios*) as distinct from 'necessary' activities; thus leisure-activities, though 'serious', should be quite different in kind from the labour that goes into building up the resources for leisure; leisure-activities are valuable for their own sake; human beings need education for leisure-activities; what to do in leisure is the most fundamental question of politics; the leisure-activity *par excellence* is theoretical intellection.[23] An important modern view is that leisure is a sort of freedom. (The word comes from the Latin *licere*, which connotes having permission.)

Let us pass to the other Aristotelian initial stage of investigation: the raising of questions and problems. (a) One can point to an apparent contradiction between the Aristotelian emphasis on seriousness, which is restrictive, and the idea of leisure as 'freedom'. (b) How is leisure-freedom related to other senses of freedom studied by philosophers? It is not freedom from coercion, nor is it freedom from servitude to one's passions. More than anything, it is freedom from requirements, duties, and obligations. (c) Here one touches on a question discussed by contemporary philosophers: are we ever thus free? (d) Leisure-freedom consists in the possibility of being active without any particular reference to circumstances

---

leisure-activities. A concept of leisure that leaves no room for sport is defective, to put it mildly. One-sided too is Pieper's tendency to characterise leisure as *a state of mind*: a kind of serenity and receptiveness.

[23] *Politics* VII.14; VIII.3; *NE* x.6–8.

or requirements, or with reference to ones chosen or already laid down by oneself, and from which one can disengage at will. So 'self-expression' is a key concept. Then can something be a good leisure-activity if it necessarily involves doing something with others? (e) If the answer is 'Yes', as it surely must be, does that suggest that the self being expressed is in some way corporate – and what can that mean? (f) Is there any sound basis for an argument that the self to be expressed in leisure-activity is in some way 'higher' than the self of ordinary work? (g) And if so, might there be any interesting analogy or other connection between this and that other possible 'higher self', the subject of moral duty and practical reason? (h) In what way do leisure and leisure-activities contribute to individuality? (i) What about the activities themselves: should we take Aristotelian theorising as emblematic of the whole class, and if so, which are its essential aspects? (j) Should the activities be worthwhile (or be thought so) because of their specific content or objects, or should it be because they are free in the way sketched under (d) above? (k) If because of the specific contents, do those of different kinds of leisure-activities have anything interesting in common? (l) Leisure seems to be the ideal opportunity for being perfectionist, and for being adventurous. Is it only very rarely that these values can be combined? Do they tend to pull apart? (m) In areas where professionalism is possible, is leisure-activity necessarily amateurish by comparison? (n) If we ought to look for non-trivial leisure-activities, is this because of a duty (for want of a better word) to oneself, or is it also because a leisure-activity should not make a mockery of the kind of efforts (individual, communal, even stretching back into the past) that went into building up the prosperity and other conditions needed for leisure?

Further exploration of this ground[24] might yield a worthy addition to the tribute which continues to be paid to Aristotle in the form of contemporary work – not necessarily even work that mentions him much – on what were originally Aristotelian questions.

---

[24] Which has just now sparked as many questions or groups of questions as there are books of Aristotle's *Metaphysics*.

CHAPTER 9

On the idea of the summum bonum

I

In the minds of most philosophers and historians of philosophy, the idea of the *summum bonum* (highest good) comes embedded in a question: *what* is the *summum bonum?* The idea seems entertainable to the extent that the question seems real. For the question to seem real at least two conditions must hold. First, it must seem as if some answers are objectively better than others. Secondly, it must not seem straight off obvious what the right or best answer to the question should be. But there is also, presumably, a third desideratum, namely agreement, implicit or explicit, on the second order question of what is meant by regarding X as the highest good, whatever X may be. This second order question is my subject here.

Let me approach by observing that the notion of 'the highest good' is marginal for modern ethical theories, although arguably it is the determinative concept of every ancient such system. We have all learnt to classify the antique examples in terms of the highest good according to each. Still, no surprise if after two millennia very different themes are now to the fore. But emergence of new claimants for attention does not really explain why the once supremely important notion of the highest good has pretty well dropped out of sight.

I shall begin by identifying an influence which I believe helps explain why the notion has been in eclipse, anyway during the last century and a half of ethical philosophising. This influence, I shall maintain, incorporates a modern misunderstanding of what, historically, it means to say of something that it is the highest good. I shall next consider a different broad understanding, which we find in ancient ethics. Under this general heading I shall look at some specific suggestions as to what it means to say that X is the highest good, and at some of their implications.

Where will this get us? I am not sure. I do not know whether the concept of the highest good should be reinstated as an important theme of modern ethics. If it should and could be, then no doubt at some point it *would* be, setting us a splendid example of something ancient in ethics poking its head up out of the ground to become an issue again for contemporary-minded contemporary minds. But even if the present discussion fails to yield reason for expecting just such a philosophical revival, one may still indulge two hopes: first, that the great archaic idea of the highest good will have been enjoyed and found interesting even by philosophers who do not see it as directly contributing to their own theorising; and secondly that the discussion will nevertheless generate *some* distinction or perspective that might be useful on the contemporary scene.

II

J. S. Mill begins *Utilitarianism* with these strong words:

There are few circumstances among those which make up the present condition of human knowledge, more unlike what might have been expected, or more significant for the backward state in which speculation on the most important subjects still lingers, than the little progress which has been made in the decision of the controversy respecting the criterion of right and wrong. From the dawn of philosophy, the question concerning the *summum bonum*, or, what is the same thing, concerning the foundation of morality, has been accounted the main problem in speculative thought, has occupied the most gifted intellects, and divided them into sects and schools, carrying on a vigorous warfare against one another. And after more than two thousand years the same discussions continue, philosophers are still ranged under the same contending banners, and neither thinkers nor mankind at large seem nearer to being unanimous on the subject, than when the youth Socrates listened to the old Protagoras . . .[1]

We can extract from this passage two important immediate implications: first, that the question 'What is the *summum bonum*?' is the question 'What is the foundation of morality?'; second, that the latter was the question debated by the ancient schools when each offered its own answer to 'What is the highest good?'

Although almost every thought in *Utilitarianism* has been scrutinised, criticised, defended, and criticised again, these implications have passed unchallenged. The reason seems to be that Mill is putting forward a

---

[1] Mill, 1968, 1. As well as 'the criterion of right and wrong' and 'the foundation of morality', Mill also speaks of 'one first principle, or common ground of obligation'; 'the fundamental principle of morality, and the source of obligation' (ibid., 3, 24); 'the standard of morality' (11; cf. 6, 16); 'A test of right and wrong' (4).

theory of the standard of right and wrong. So when people discuss the ethics of *Utilitarianism*, they discuss the view that rightness is to be determined by conduciveness to the utilitarian goal, however this goal be interpreted. From that point of view, it makes perfect sense to ignore the question whether earlier philosophers who talk about the highest good are talking about the standard of right and wrong. The reasonableness of ignoring it corresponds to the fact that Mill could have announced his topic simply as the question of the standard of right, without ever using the phrase '*summum bonum*' or 'highest good'. Had he done so, he would have been more accurate. However, he would then have sacrificed the connection that supports his resounding claim that *his* question's history stretches back to the ancient Greeks.

In fact, Mill does not need that claim in order to motivate interest in *his* problem and in the solution proposed in *Utilitarianism*. These are matters too obviously important in themselves to need the frame of a dubious pedigree to catch our attention. So readers rightly concentrate on what is thus framed and ignore the alleged pedigree, which they then let go unquestioned. The result is that the two implications about the highest good carried by the opening of *Utilitarianism* tend to sink into the souls of students of modern ethics simply on Mill's authority. What get thus absorbed are firstly the philosophical assumption that being the highest good is the same as, or at the very least is essentially connected with, being the standard of right and wrong; and secondly the historical assumption that our modern focus on this standard is of a piece with the ancient focus on the highest good. Anything questionable about these assumptions then fails to surface in the natural course of modern-ethical discussion, because they add nothing of substance to modern debates.[2]

Mill may have been influenced by the fact that Kant interpreted the ancient debate over the *summum bonum* as a debate over 'the determining ground of the will in the moral law' (*Critique of Practical Reason* (5:64), in Kant, 1996). According to Kant, of course, the ancients in question were utterly misguided in identifying the source of the moral law in that way. We can see Mill's approach as combining an element from Kant with an element from 'the ancients'. It is as if Mill accepts (a) Kant's account of what was at stake in the ancient debate about the *summum bonum*, along with (b) the 'ancient' (implicit) assumption that the ancient debate was a proper debate to be holding. It should be added that in the English-speaking world Mill's influence has probably been strengthened by that of G. E. Moore. Moore understood the idea of the highest good (or *the* good) to be the idea of a single specific good (such as pleasure) which (i) is supposedly the sole *per se* good, and (ii) because of this supposed uniqueness came to be misidentified (by the 'naturalistic fallacy') with the meaning of the predicate 'good' (Moore, 1903, ch. iii; on (i) see also 1912, ch. vii). Since Moore's attacks on (i) and (ii) are devastating, 'the highest good' is, by his lights, a notion bred of confusion. Anyone reluctant to join Moore in this position (for example, anyone who felt that ancient talk of the 'highest good' is more respectable than Moore can consistently allow) may have automatically opted for Mill's comparatively unmuddled interpretation instead.

This is so, I believe, regardless of the variety of interpretations which the philosophical assumption permits. One obvious variation has to do with the difference between act and rule utilitarianism.[3] Mill's 'standard of right and wrong' or 'foundation of morality' may be understood as a reference point for judging the rightness of particular actions, or for assessing entire action-kinds, practices, character-dispositions and institutions;[4] but, either way, if the notion of the highest good gets a look in at all, the influence of Mill's presentation will make it appear as connected with, above all, the standard or foundation or principle of morality. The exact nature of this connection can then itself be variously understood. For example, one may assume that being the principle of morality is really all there is to being the highest good, so that to consider whether X is, or to identify X as, the highest good is already in fact to consider whether X is, or to identify it as, that principle. Alternatively, it might seem that one can determine that X, say the greatest general happiness, is the highest good, and then, *because of* that insight or conclusion, immediately proceed to assign to X the role of principle of morality. Mill's words at the opening of *Utilitarianism* suggest the first of these possibilities, but some later passages[5] may suggest the second. However, his adherence, such as it is, even to the second possibility assumes that the sole reason why ethical thinkers should interest themselves in the identity of the highest good is so as to identify the principle of morality. And very many of Mill's readers have gone along with this, mostly accepting his lead in silence. On one side there are those who acknowledge, with him, a single sovereign consequentialist principle of morality, while entertaining no independent interest in what it is for something to be the highest good[6] – not because they deny there is such a good, but because they don't think this status invites any questions not already covered in studying the nature and meaning of the principle of *morality*. And on the other side are those who reject monism about morality but likewise pay no attention to the notion of the highest good, presumably because they do not consider

---

[3] I here use 'rule utilitarianism' to do general duty for theories that apply the utilitarian standard to patterns of behaviour rather than particular actions.

[4] Mill understands it the second way, allowing that the conscientious agent normally is and should be guided by a plurality of 'secondary principles', i.e. the principles of commonsense morality (Mill, 1968, 22–4).

[5] Mill, 1968, ch. IV, 'Of What Sort of Proof the Principle of Utility is Susceptible'.

[6] This does not, of course, mean that they ignore questions about the nature of their candidate for sovereign principle, e.g. about the nature of pleasure, happiness, welfare, etc., and the interpretation of 'for the greatest number', etc.

there is anything for the highest good to be or do apart from being, or functioning as, the to them mythological single determinant of, again: *morality.*

III

So Mill's legacy is the common assumption that being the highest good is above all something to do with morality: that is, its special status consists in its relation not (i.e. not immediately) to any other *good* or *goods*, but to the *right*. More particularly, utilitarians spell out the special status of the highest good by means of the thought that actions or patterns of action are right or wrong to the extent that they foreseeably promote or under-mine the realisation of that good. It is, moreover, only too natural in the context of utilitarianism to understand the superlative 'highest' as indicat-ing a maximum of something. It is a maximum of some kind of good which in itself can occur in greater or lesser amounts or be distributed more or less extensively; thus the highest good is, say, the greatest pleasure or the greatest well-being of the greatest number. Clearly, then, the highest good, understood in this way, is not such that it could make sense to speak of maximising *it*.

By contrast, according to the ancient perspective which is the main topic of this paper, the special status of the highest good consists in some relation or other of this good to other *goods*.[7] To take one particularly famous example: in several places in the *Nicomachean Ethics*, Aristotle exhibits what he calls 'the topmost of all achievable goods' (1095a16)[8] as terminating a hierarchy of *goods*. The thought is that we consider com-monly recognised and sought after goods, and ask what that good is which they are all for the sake of (1094a1–b7). Or in some places the thought is that we consider commonly acclaimed goods, and ask which of them is the one the others are all for the sake of (e.g. 1097a15–1097b21). ('For the sake of' here is quite a rough expression amenable to different interpret-ations.) Answers to these questions state which good is highest. The business of asking these questions is clearly quite different from that of considering actions or practices normally regarded as justified – or as obligatory – and wondering what the fundamental standard is by which

---

[7] The Stoics are excluded from this perspective insofar as they hold that there is just one human good (namely, virtue). In general, the perspective cannot apply to any beings (such as God or the gods in, say, an Aristotelian conception) whose good is single and simple.

[8] Translations from the *NE* are by Christopher Rowe in Broadie and Rowe, 2002.

such judgments are correct. Equally, it is quite different from that of assuming a single given standard of rightness and wondering whether such and such an action or practice is right or justifiable by that standard. And by contrast with the usage natural to utilitarians (and to consequentialists in general), the highest good is not a maximum of some good that can occur in more and less generous amounts and fair distributions. It is, rather, one kind of good differing from the others in the way pleasure, virtue and intelligence are different kinds of goods. Like these goods, the highest good is the sort of thing it can make sense to aim to maximise.[9]

For the moment I want to consider one main implication of conceiving of the highest good (whatever substantially it is claimed to be) in what I shall call the ancient way. It is, quite simply, that the question whether an action or a kind of action is right or justified is in general to be settled independently of the question of its conduciveness to the highest good, whether for oneself or for others. For example, if hedonism is the theory that says that pleasure is the highest good, then a hedonist according to the 'ancient' fashion may coherently and with perfect intellectual clarity decide that something is wrong without ever considering whether doing it will bring anyone less pleasure or more pain.[10] One might ask: but what is it to hold that pleasure is the highest good if not to treat it as the general standard of right and wrong? The answer would go: this kind of hedonist holds (a) that a lot of actions are to be done or refrained from simply because they conform or fail to conform to some familiar principle, such as that one has a duty to keep promises or to show gratitude to benefactors, and not because they lead towards or away from a greater good of some kind; and (b) that such principles are self-sustaining, not grounded on anything else; *however*, when it is a question of bringing about some good G, considered as good, this hedonist is bound to consider (c) whether G will add to the pleasantness of the life of whoever it is supposed to benefit, since if it does not, the highest good has been missed, which would mean that pursuing G as a good was perhaps not after all worthwhile. Similarly, someone who in this fashion holds that self-improvement is the highest good, should treat conduciveness to self-improvement, whether her own or others', as a constraint on her pursuit

---

[9] Cf. Aristotle, *NE* I.I, 1094b7–10.
[10] If W. Frankena is right, this type of hedonism is not exclusively 'ancient': 'A hedonist about the good may be a deontologist about the right', he says, claiming Butler, Kant, and Sidgwick as examples (Frankena, 1963, 83–4).

of any other *good* for herself or them – but she should not treat it as a constraint on her every action nor as the justification of every practice.[11]

Consequently, there are two forms of hedonism: *R*-hedonism and *G*-hedonism, distinguished without reference to egoism, altruism, and universalism. The *R*- form says that all actions are right or practices justified insofar as they conduce to pleasure (whether one's own or another's), while the *G*- one says that pleasure is what should be principally kept in view in just the sub-set of actions specifically directed at bringing about good things. And there will be a similar pair of forms of self-improvement-ism, and so on for every candidate for the title 'highest good'. From now on we shall be considering only the *G*-version of any such theory.

IV

In presenting the ancient idea of the highest good as what stands in some relation or other to the other goods, I took as illustration the thought, famous through Aristotle, that the highest good is what the other goods *are for the sake of.* Although this is rather vague, we can see it as one possible way of identifying what that relation is that constitutes the highest good highest. I now want to consider two other ancient ways of identifying that relation. But first I want to set aside two possible modern interpretations of the ancient approach. These both involve the idea of 'intrinsic' goodness as it is often called. I mean the goodness of goods that are good *per se*, i.e. because of what they are in themselves rather than only because of the goodness of something else to which they may lead. According to the first modern interpretation, theories of the highest good treat the highest as uniquely good *per se*, so that all other goods are instrumental.[12] Any theory that does this while at the same time identify-ing the highest good with some one kind of good, say pleasure, is mistaken; for G. E. Moore was surely right to emphasise that different kinds of things are good *per se.*[13] However, it is certainly not true that all the ancient theories make this mistake, and I shall not be focusing on any that do. According to the second of the modern interpretations to be set

---

[11] This outline leaves open whether the agent has, among her various duties, a duty to pursue goods as good (when doing so does not conflict with other kinds of duty), or whether the normativity of the good is of a different kind.

[12] The first interpretation is visible in G. E. Moore, *Principia Ethica* (see note 2 above). For recent examples, see *The Cambridge Dictionary of Philosophy*, 2nd edition, 1999, entries on 'hedonism' and '*summum bonum*' (James A. Montmarquet).

[13] See note 2 above.

aside, there is a plurality of goods *per se,* and the highest good is a combination of them all. (This idea inspired an extremely influential but highly disputable twentieth-century view of what Aristotle means by '*eudaimonia*' (his label, so to speak, for the highest good), at any rate in Book I of the *Nicomachean Ethics.*) On such an account, what makes the highest good highest is that it consists of all the *per se* goods (aside from itself). It is not a good that could exist on its own without the other goods. We should also notice that, on this sort of account, the highest good depends for its value on the values (presupposed) of its constituents.

I shall now look at two ancient suggestions about the relation of the highest good to other goods. Both envisage a plurality of *per se* goods and a monistic highest good. And on both, the highest good *gives* value to the others. That, in both cases, is the relation that makes it highest.

v

What I am calling the first suggestion was employed by the mathematician-philosopher Eudoxus of Cnidus in an argument for hedonism. Eudoxus contended that pleasure is the highest good on the ground (amongst others) that pleasure added to any good thing *makes it better*: for example, just conduct and moderate conduct are made better by pleasure (Aristotle, *NE* x, 1172b23–5). It is clear that what Eudoxus meant was not that a state of affairs in which I perform in either of those ways is better still if at the same time I (e.g.) have the pleasure of feeling the spring sunshine on my skin or of hearing birdsong. Eudoxus meant that taking pleasure in performing a just or moderate action makes that action, which is already a good *per se,* into something better – indeed, he may well have meant better of its kind: thus the agent's pleasure in it makes just or moderate conduct a yet more perfect instance of *just* or *moderate conduct.*[14] Eudoxus's choice of examples – just conduct and

---

[14] Aristotle's testimony on this argument is not very clear. He moves from reporting what seems to be the argument I have described, to talking about, as if it were the same, an argument to the effect that a life with wisdom in it is more desirable if it also contains pleasure (*NE* x.2, 1172b23–30). Nor is it clear how Eudoxus stood *vis à vis* Aristotle's distinction between acting from virtue and doing what the virtuous agent does (ibid. II.4, 1105a17–b10). Did Eudoxus hold that even action-from-virtue is improved (made still more virtuous) by the agent's taking pleasure in it? If so, Aristotle's position that the (otherwise good) action fails to count as being from-virtue at all unless the agent takes pleasure in it (ibid. I, 1099a8–21) goes one better than Eudoxus, and may have been developed in response to him. In that case, we may also see in this dialectic with Eudoxus the seed of Aristotle's distinction (never drawn firmly by Plato) between conduct that is virtuous and conduct that is self-controlled (i.e. good, but in a way reluctant; ibid. VII, 1145a15–18; 1151b32–1152a1).

moderate conduct – was surely very deliberate. We can divine this from a comment by his contemporary, Aristotle, who knew him – they were both connected with Plato's Academy. Aristotle snidely hints that the quality of Eudoxus's arguments fell below that of his character:

Now Eudoxus used to think that pleasure was *the* good because . . . [there follows one of Eudoxus's arguments] . . . Eudoxus's pronouncements carried conviction more because of the excellence of his character than in themselves; for he was thought to be a person of exceptional moderation, and so it was not thought that he made them as a lover of pleasure, but that things were truly as he said (1172b9–18).[15]

We may surely gather from this that Eudoxus had great respect for just and moderate conduct, since one can hardly possess these virtues oneself without esteeming them and their manifestations in general. So as far as ethical theory goes, Eudoxus was most likely a *G*-hedonist, at least if his conduct was good by commonsense standards and his theory not in conflict with it. For the alternative theory, *R*-hedonism, like every consequentialist account of right and wrong, conflicts with parts of commonsense morality, in particular some of our intuitions about justice.

Anyway, Eudoxus's insight was that pleasure has the power to make a very, very good thing significantly better. Whatever can raise the value of *something as good as that* must be, itself, a truly pre-eminent good, a good beyond praise (cf. *NE* I, 1101b27–31), the supra-perfect source of perfection!

The most obvious objection to this way of promoting pleasure as highest good is that pleasure has just the same power to make a very, very bad thing significantly worse. In fact, it seems that, for every kind *K*, once a *K*-thing possessed by a subject or engaged in by an agent has added to it (in that same subject or agent) pleasure in the *K*-thing, the *K*-thing becomes a more forceful, vital, and emphatic example of *K*.[16] It is not surprising if some ancients thought of pleasure as a sort of divine force that makes each thing be more positively what it is,[17] but their culture did not in general take it for granted that what is divine is necessarily *good* from the human ethical point of view. It seems that the conclusion ought

---

[15] In fact, Aristotle indicates elsewhere that he thinks well of some of Eudoxus's hedonistic arguments: see *NE* 1.1, 1094a2–3 with x.2, 1172b9–15 and 35–1173a1; and 1.12, 1101b27–31.

[16] This is implied by Aristotle's account of pleasure in *NE* x.

[17] See *Philebus* 12b–c; 26b–c on pleasure as a divinity (Aphrodite). Empedocles calls one of his cosmic forces by names of Aphrodite. We may also think of the god-sent gilding of beauty and presence (the *charis*) that descends on a Homeric hero at a particularly significant or regal moment.

to be that pleasure, however much to be reckoned with, cannot be the highest good and perhaps is not any sort of good. For pleasure is bad-making no less than good-making. This suggests that pleasure in itself (whether because it is a sort of elemental principle 'beyond good and evil', or because it is an abstraction) is neither good nor bad.

From the ancient point of view there is another objection to Eudoxus's argument. Even if we grant that pleasure itself is good,[18] its being the sort of good that adds value to other kinds of good is not unique to pleasure. The most obvious other example is intelligence. If something is anyway good, it becomes better when done or handled intelligently. If, as many people do, we assume that intelligence is itself a good, then intelligence is on a par with pleasure.[19] They have equal claim to the title 'highest good'. But traditionally the title must belong uniquely. The ancient debate (for some reason) takes it for granted that there cannot be ties for this accolade.[20]

VI

The second suggestion I want to examine is that the highest good is 'the principle and cause of the goods'. These words are Aristotle's (*NE* I, 1102a3–4; cf. *Eudemian Ethics* I, 1217b5), but the idea can be glimpsed in Plato too.[21] The thought is that the highest good is the source of value to the other goods: in other words makes it true that they are goods at all.[22] It is easy to see how this works if the highest good is the sole *per se* good. For in that case all other goods will be means to the highest good, and it is straightforward that the value of something good only as a means derives from the value of the end. However, that case has been ruled out.[23] The situation is one in which we are trying to see what the relation is in which the highest good stands to the other goods even though some of the latter

---

[18] Eudoxus had independent arguments for this: see *NE* x.2, 1172b9–15; 18–23.

[19] Cf. Aristotle, *NE* x.2, 1172b28–34.

[20] Unpacked, the point is that while the title applies uniquely simply by being a superlative, the ancient choice of just such a formula expresses the substantial assumption that there can only be one pre-eminent 'good of goods' even though otherwise appealing criteria may favour more than one candidate. See section VII below.

[21] It is not clear exactly how in Aristotle this theme is related to the theme that the highest good is what all other goods are for the sake of. For Plato on wisdom as the good-making good, see *Meno* 87d–88e, *Euthydemus* 279a–281e. The Sun analogy in *Republic* VI, 506b–509b, may present The Good as good-making. In *Laws* II, 661b–d, 'justice and the whole of virtue' has this role. Cf. Aristotle, *Eudemian Ethics* VIII.3, 1248b25–34.

[22] As Kant says about the good will: see, e.g., the beginning of the *Groundwork*.

[23] Section IV.

are goods *per se*, not simply as means. How, on that assumption, does it make sense to interpret the relation as one whereby all the other goods get their value from the highest?

Think of being so committed to some kind of *per se* good *V* that when you are working to obtain or safeguard goods, you unhesitatingly reject or even simply ignore any options that might compromise *V*. These are options for the getting or preserving of goods other than *V*. You operate, in effect, as if these other goods have, as far as you are concerned, no value at all except in the context of your steady hold on *V* (or *V*'s steady hold on you). Letting them go when they threaten *V* is not a loss to you in that situation, because you have let go nothing that is of value in the situation. Similarly you reject or ignore options for avoiding evils – as they would ordinarily be called – if they might compromise *V*. You operate as if, in such a situation, these so called evils have no disvalue. All this holds whether the so called goods and evils other than *V* and its absence are what they are as means or *per se*. However, you do not in general operate as if *V* and its absence were the sole good and evil. On the contrary, you are completely willing to pursue and avoid those other goods and evils in the context of a secure hold on *V*. In that context, you treat them as if they have real value, positive or negative, so that you would be genuinely better off with, or without, them, as the case may be. (Hence you would not think it reasonable to secure your loyalty to *V* by training yourself to be uniformly indifferent to those other goods regardless of circumstances; for a variety of circumstances will include opportunities to become genuinely better off by, and only by, taking a lively interest in goods other than *V*.) In sum, you operate as if, anyway as far as you are concerned, the presence of *V* is not only necessary but also sufficient for its being worth your concerning yourself in a practical way with any other goods and their opposites.

A further point: your commitment to *V* is wholehearted. It is not simply true that your life would not be worth living to you without *V*, for this could be so if you were in some way addicted to *V* with an addiction you find hateful. The commitment I have in mind is one by which you would not want to be alive without caring about *V* as you do.[24] Thus suppose you are so placed that your commitment to *V* precludes you

---

[24] See Mimnermus, *tis de bios, ti de terpnon, ater chruseês Aphroditês; / tethnaiên hote moi ouketi tauta meloi* ('What is life, what is joyful, without golden Aphrodite?/ May I die when these things matter no more to me'. Compare Catullus LXXVI, where (about his passion) he begs the gods: *eripite hanc pestem perniciemque mihi* ('This plague, this killer, tear it out of me').

from pursuing something, *S*, which you would normally welcome as a good: you may wish you were not so placed, and you may well regret certain facts about yourself, for instance your poverty or some other pressure but for which you would not be in that situation.[25] But (if *V* to you is the highest good) the one thing you cannot regret about yourself is the force of your commitment to *V*, nor can you feel it a piece of ill luck if the seeds of that were sown in you by others when you were young, even though your commitment to *V* is in a sense as much to blame as anything else for your having to forego *S*.

All this applies whether you are acting so that the other goods are to your own benefit or to that of others whom you care about. In the latter case, *V* must be securely implanted not merely in your life but in theirs in order for it to be maximally true that you, in working to bestow the other goods on these other individuals, and to protect them from the corresponding evils, are working to their real advantage. Naturally, you will do whatever you can, if you have any influence in the matter, and if you care about these individuals, to protect and if necessary develop the existence in their lives of *V*, since from your point of view without *V* nothing genuinely good can happen to or be obtained by these people whom you care about.

We can take this further. You might, in addition, have some corresponding judgmental attitudes towards persons over whom you have no control or who are not your business. For example, someone is deeply and seriously lacking in *V*. His or her ethical heart is wholly elsewhere. As you see it, that person's life lacks, and stands no chance of acquiring, the source of value. When he succeeds in his endeavours, or when he fails, from your point of view he has not made any real gain or suffered any real loss. In fact, from this rather precise point of view of yours, he is a kind of simulacrum of a practical agent, if a practical agent is one susceptible of faring well or badly. You of course agree that he may fare well-or-badly-from-his-own-point-of-view. But your point of view, including as it does the judgmental element I am sketching, is such that, according to it, faring-well-or-badly-from-*his*-point-of-view does not entail faring well or badly, any more than being healthy-for-a-malnourished-person entails being healthy.

---

[25] There is no logical conflict in general between regret at being in the situation described (and the desire to avoid it in advance and to escape from it once in), and complete absence of regret for *passing up S in that situation*. The courageous did not welcome the danger in which presently, without regrets, they set aside their own good chance of safety.

On one way of looking at the matter, it is as if the various things standardly considered desirable or good are, except for *V*, whatever that may be, only potentially good, with a potential which is actualised only by the concurrent presence of *V*. This is apt enough for goods whose empirical natures in particular cases do not depend on the attitudes and choices of the persons who have them: for example, money, physical health, and many types of opportunity. What these are like in themselves is the same, whoever and whatever sort of person has them. But that does not hold for such important *per se* goods as pleasure and friends. If, for instance, pleasure or having fun is your *V*, the empirical nature of the friends you make and keep will be different from that of the friends of someone whose *V* is something different, say musicality. Let it be that you are a *G*-hedonist, but like most people you regard friendship as a *per se* good, not an instrumental one. Then your commitment to pleasure entails that insofar as you value friendship as a kind of *good* you will value only those friendships where pleasure is the main motif. If, conversely, friendship is your *V*, you will cultivate only friendship-friendly kinds of pleasure, and these will be different in many empirical ways from, say, music-friendly kinds. Here, commitment above all to *V* does not render good a phenomenon called 'a pleasure', or one called 'a friendship', that comes with its own antecedently determinate properties. The commitment shapes, rather, the very nature of the phenomenon in your case.

Let us suppose for the moment a *V*-ist whose *V* is something other than friendship and pleasure, so that the latter are examples of 'other' goods. Now, exactly how does it come about that, from this *V*-ist's point of view, his hold on *V* makes it the case that such ordinarily acclaimed desirables are *in fact* good, desirable, and worthy of his concrete positive practical interest? Well, we could say that whereas the bare abstractions *pleasure* and *friendship* elicit in almost everyone schematic and theoretical endorsement of them as objectives,[26] the *V*-ist's commitment to *V* determines specific interpretations such that not until interpreted thus do *pleasure* and *friendship* become (from his point of view) actually worth making concrete efforts for – in other words, become from his point of view actually good. According to a slightly different way of looking at the matter, we can greet with merely provisional acceptance the schematic truisms (or would-be truisms) that *pleasure* is good, and that *friendship* is, and then (if we are *V*-ists) we can hail the phenomena picked out by *V*-ist interpretations of

[26] But at least for pleasure this is not mandatory: see the penultimate paragraph of section v.

pleasure and *friendship* as what make those truisms true. (If as a result we treat the truisms as well established – or if we had considered them well established all along – then as *V*-ists we shall view opposed interpretations of *pleasure* and *friendship* as, in fact, mistaken. We shall say that the experiences, activities and liaisons which these would-be interpretations pick out are not really pleasures or friendships at all.)

I have been describing aspects of what it would be like to operate as if *V* (whatever this good may in fact be) is source of value for the other goods. I should not be surprised if, on the reflective level, very many moderns would simply dismiss any theory that says that one good is source of value for the other goods, on the ground that talking of value as something that can, as it were, be switched on or off through the presence or absence of some specific good, is confused or even nonsensical. Still, it might be the case that some who are theoretically dismissive nonetheless live or admire others who live as if, for some specific interpretation of *V*, *V* is source of value for other goods. And if *V* as specified is the only good that plays this role in someone's life, then that life is being lived as if *V* is *the highest* good. Moreover, if it so happens that you or I consider this life a very good one, and take it to be so precisely because it is thus structured by *V* as specified, then, I think, we ourselves in fact accept that *V* is indeed the highest good.

VII

Now for some complications of plurality. Several questions arise. Could it not be the case that, for example, two distinct goods are both sources of value in the same life? And could this not be so in either of several ways: either they are joint value-makers for all the other goods, or one has that role for some of the others, and the other for others, or each is sole value-maker for some and part of a joint value-maker for others? It is not clear that the answer has to be 'No' to any of these questions. These pluralisations certainly seem to be logical possibilities, and perhaps for many people they are more realistic than a monistic structure would be. The Greeks often seem to take the monistic structure for granted,[27] but it is not clear why. Perhaps they got stuck on this model because it is simplest, or perhaps because it appealed to their spirit of competition.[28]

---

[27] For example, Aristotle notoriously omits to show that there must be just one highest good. The *Philebus* takes off from the sheer assumption of this.

[28] On which see the next chapter.

However that may be, it seems to me that the idea of a value-making good is more interesting than the question whether it is uniquely or multiply instantiated. And when this type of good is multiply instantiated, it might still be useful to call the instances, each, a 'highest good'. This would mark the controlling status of each.

I have just considered possibilities of multiple instantiation within a given life. However, one might also consider different monistically structured lives, one with *V* as its master-value, another with *W* as *its*, and find oneself thinking that each is very good precisely because (respectively) of its *V*- or *W*-related structure. One would then in effect recognise different highest goods again, only located in different lives. This seems to be the situation Aristotle found himself in towards the end of the *Nicomachean Ethics*, where he distinguishes two kinds of superlative happiness (*eudaimonia*).[29] For earlier he equated *eudaimonia* with the highest good (1095a14–22; 1097a15–21; cf. 1176a31–2). In such a situation one might, like Aristotle, try to rank these kinds, arguing that one sort of highest good is better than the other (although of course it cannot be its good-maker). Or one might argue that they are simply different forms of a single generic highest good. But I do not see that we are bound to make either of these moves.

VIII

Two areas for probing will probably have come to mind. We ought to get a clearer picture of how, in the sort of framework I have been describing, recognition of goods relates to recognition of right and wrong. And: since so far I have treated the highest good only in formal fashion, considering what it can mean to assign a good the position of 'highest' without regard to substantial candidates, we should ask of a given formal account whether it favours some substantial candidates over others. Here, I shall ask these questions only in connection with the idea of the highest good as source of value.

Let us take the first question first. I have been assuming that our agent who operates as if *V* is the highest good[30] is, in practice at any rate, a *G*-style *V*-ist. That is to say, his or her adherence to *V* affects only those commitments for which the reason or justification consists in the pursuit

---

[29] The life that revolves round the kind he considers inferior he still calls 'second happi*est*' (*NE* x.7, 1178a8–9).

[30] For simplicity I shall now refer to it in the singular.

of good things as such. Otherwise this agent recognises all the usual duties and claims, and (I am assuming) gives them the weightings a decent person would give. But can such an agent think coherently about duties involving doing good or refraining from harm? The most obvious examples come under the general heading of what the ancients called justice. It is wrong to assault people or steal their goods or curtail their liberty. Of course, certain conditions have to be met for it to be wrong to attack people physically, or to deprive them of things they own, or to lock them up. But it is not one of these conditions that the persons in question be dedicated to some particular specification of the highest good. Thus a wronged person could fall into the category of those whom 'we' regard as strictly speaking incapable of *really* faring well or badly, for she might either recognise no highest good, or recognise one quite different from ours. Suppose that one of these possibilities holds. Then she is one of those simulacra of practical agency! Still, given certain conditions that have nothing to do with adoption of a highest good, it is as wrong to assault, steal from, or incarcerate her as anyone else.[31] That is, it is *really* wrong. But the notions of harm and loss to the victims seem to stand at the centre of any explanation we can muster for why it is wrong to do these things to people.[32] Yet how can we talk about harm and loss without implying that whoever suffers them fares badly? How can we talk about the *real* wrongfulness of (under certain circumstances) harming people and depriving them of goods without implying that what happens to them when they suffer these wrongs is *really* bad?[33]

One could, I suppose, stick to the original guns, and say: the harming is really wrong (wrong *sans phrase*) even though the victim only fares-ill-from-his-point-of-view. I think many would be quite comfortable with saying this – on one condition. The condition is that everyone in the picture fares well or ill just from their own point of view. There is no set of people whose faring well or ill is simple or absolute in any sense exclusive to them. But to say this is to have abandoned the framework

---

[31] Thus it is not the case that corrective justice lacks a task when the victim is of inferior character; cf. *NE* v.4, 1132a2–6.

[32] However, Terence Irwin raised with me the point that it is conceptually possible to hold that we have certain obligations to people, or that they have certain rights against us, regardless of whether they are benefited/harmed by our fulfilling/failing to fulfil the obligations. One might see oneself as, so to speak, 'ritually' bound to refrain from assault by an obligation that has nothing to do with the way being assaulted affects the victim. (Nor need one believe the obligation to be backed by a divine prohibition.)

[33] The paradox that the bad man cannot be unjustly deprived of (non-moral) goods appears in the *Magna Moralia* (of dubious authenticity, but part of the Aristotelian corpus), ii.3, 1199b10–18.

of the highest good as source of value. If one keeps that framework with its differentiation between real faring well or badly ('ours') and the qualified form – well, it is still possible to maintain that, and live as if, doing certain things to other people is really and without qualification wrong even in the case of those others whose welfare is limited to the qualified form. But this comes close to categorising them as inferior to us by a categorisation that we probably find unacceptable. Perhaps we want to be able to say not merely that in certain areas of life each person has a real and unqualified claim to consideration by every other, but that these reciprocal claims are based on our all, at some level, being equal or mattering equally, or mattering in the same way. And this is what the differentiating framework seems to deny.

A better move, if we want to keep the framework of the highest good as source of value, might be to restrict it from applying to whatever basics of welfare are presupposed in our ordinary concepts of harm, injury and infringement of rights. This modification might turn out to mean that the framework only comes into play with respect to *per se* goods.[34] I shall not attempt here to explore the implications of this suggestion.

Let me briefly consider the second question raised above: does the framework favour any particular substantial candidate? It surely does, if we assume an agent seriously conscientious about right conduct. But we should approach this by stages. Take first the simplest case, although it is not clear that this case is in fact logically possible. Here, the person operates just in terms of particular actions, whether deciding for or against them, or judging them in others. Moreover, it matters to her whether she or others act rightly or wrongly at any given time. But she does not think in terms of *dispositions* to behave in the various right and wrong ways. I said that she was decently conscientious, which is to ascribe a disposition. But *she* does not think of anyone in that way or any other such way. She just takes each piece of behaviour as it comes. She may note that, in a given agent, there are similarities between pieces of behaviour. But she never frames the thought, either to assert it or deny it, that the agent is *such as to* behave like that.

Here, the agent's commitment (as we would call it) to right conduct sets certain constraints on what V can be. It cannot be a good such that making it a very important part of life, let alone so important that it dominates pursuit of all other goods, would undermine the agent's right

---

[34] But if, as is natural, we count health and seeing as goods *per se*, as well as instrumentally, then basic welfare includes some *per se* goods. Cf. Plato, *Republic* II, 357c; Aristotle, *NE* I.6, 1096b17.

conduct. For example, wild and intoxicating pleasure is presumably a good in the abstract or in occasional carefully hedged doses. But for a person who cares about right conduct, it would probably be a mistake to make that sort of pleasure count as the good to which all other goods give way. Notice that this point is one which an agent who lacked the vocabulary of dispositions would not be able to formulate, since she could not represent to herself the fact that a lot of wild, intoxicating pleasure tends to erode morally good dispositions or prevent them from ever developing. However, as far as I can see, such an agent could be a hedonist (a *G*-hedonist, of course) in one or another way. Either she could hold that gentle, civilised, pleasure is the highest good, or she could hold that pleasure is the highest good while drawing upon some argument to the effect that wild, intoxicating so-called pleasure, and everything like it, does not really deserve to be called 'pleasure' at all.[35]

Let us now expand the agent's repertoire to include the conceptual vocabulary of moral dispositions. At once her conscientiousness about right conduct is going to lead her to think that dispositions for engaging in and valuing right conduct are good things. It would be incorrect of her to regard them as goods *per se*, because, as Aristotle is never tired of saying, a disposition gets its value from that of the corresponding activity. Logically, the agent ought now to see right conduct not simply as right, but also as good, since otherwise she cannot ground the new point that the disposition for it is a good. What is more, although a disposition is good only because the activity is good, it seems clear that if acting rightly is a good, then the acting rightly that is the activation of a steady disposition to do so is a better good than the acting rightly that happens once in a while or unreliably. And that this is so will be apparent to the agent once she can think in terms of dispositions. It only remains to point out that once the conscientious agent recognises virtuous dispositions, and the virtuous activities expressive of them, as goods, she will be under powerful pressure from precisely her own conscientiousness to put these latter ahead of all else, thereby identifying the *summum bonum* with virtuous activity.[36]

---

[35] See section VI above, penultimate paragraph.

[36] This result is close to, but not identical with, Aristotle's in the *Nicomachean Ethics*, where he defines the *summum bonum* as 'virtuous activity [of reason] *in a complete life*' (*NE* 1.17, 1098a18).

What should we mean by
'the highest good'?

PART I

That *the highest good* is a severely abstract notion will not be disputed by anyone. If we find it a difficult idea to get hold of we might first want to blame the abstractness for our fumbling. But there is a less obvious source of difficulty, which I believe has not been discussed very much. It is that thinkers have wanted very different things from the idea. It has served many different functions in ethical theory. Yet historic battles over the identity of the highest good have often failed to make clear what was at stake. In Plato's *Philebus*, for example, a competition for the title is staged between Knowledge and Pleasure, but it is never explained what, if any, the winner's essential commitments would be.[1] It seems not a waste of time to look at different interpretations of the theoretical role of the highest good. My inspection will be conceptual more than historical.

Let me start, however, with an historical point, one which has already been indicated. The question of the highest good comes to us from ancient Greek philosophy, and we encounter it there in the context of rival identity claims. This fact, while utterly familiar, is something to pause over – for two reasons. First, this context, the context of rival claims as to what is to count as the highest good, definitely colours and might even be said partly to characterise the problematic of the highest good; and this may strike us as a bit remarkable if we make comparison with other problematics involving unique objects.[2] In Western monotheistic theology, for example, once it is accepted on all sides that there is a supreme being many disputes still remain, but as far as I am aware no one engages in a dispute where two or more separately identifiable candidates

---

[1] Not far into the *Philebus* it is established that neither of the contestants can be the highest good, but they continue to battle for second place.

[2] By 'unique object' I mean the referent of a uniquely applicable predicate or title.

are put forward as claimants for the title of God. For some reason, there is not an issue about which of several previously encountered beings is going to turn out to be the God of metaphysical monotheism, in the way in which there has certainly seemed to be an issue about which of various more or less previously understood goods such as pleasure, knowledge, or virtue is going to turn out to be the highest good of ethics. Why is it that one discourse about a unique object does, and another does not, lend itself to a problematic of rival claims to *be* that object? This is a question for which I have no present answer.

I mentioned a second reason for staying a while with the platitude that ancient discourse about the highest good tends to involve competition for the title. It is that there are two different sorts of rivalry, philosophically speaking, and these suggest different models for the status of *winner*. Thus choice of model, which may be subconscious, will partly determine what we intend by 'the highest good'. The first sort of rivalry is exemplified by an athletic competition or a beauty contest. I shall call the winners of these 'pure winners', and the kind of rivalry from which they emerge I shall call 'pure-winner rivalry'. To be a pure winner is to be whoever turns out to have been best among the competitors according to the criteria employed for the sort of contest in question. Now, a human contest is a matter of inter-subjective interest. That this is so is true by definition so far as the contestants themselves are concerned. In addition, it is almost always true as a matter of social fact that contests are also participated in by others than the contestants: namely, by spectators. Because of this, being a pure winner implies in practice more than *just* having turned out to be the best by the relevant criteria. It implies being thereupon honoured for the victory, by defeated opponents and spectators alike. The honouring may or may not take tangible form, as in applause or the bestowal of a crown, medal, or cup; but it will always consist in singling out the victor as a uniquely special[3] object of admiration, respect, love, and even adoration.

For understanding what I am calling 'pure-winner rivalry', it helps if we consider why people are interested in staging, competing in, and following as spectators, contests of this type. The reason is surely twofold: first, our culture loves competition, *in propria persona* or vicarious – competition with its structure of striving, victory, and defeat. Secondly, we love, value, or admire the qualities which are tested by the competition

---

[3] In relation to the context in question.

and which provide the criteria for victory. Making these qualities the focus of an on-going competitive habit or culture is a way of celebrating the qualities for their own sake; and at the same time, through the competitive raising of standards, it is a way – also for those qualities' own sake – to generate in the world more perfect instances of them. Thus the type of rivalry that generates pure winners tends to be part of a larger pattern of activity which, in addition to satisfying the human desire for competition and victory, is dedicated to cultivating for their own sake the qualities in which the winners excel.[4]

Now by contrast consider the kind of rivalry exhibited where there are aspirants to some functional role with room for only one occupant, such as chief of police, prime minister, or head of a traditional family, clan, or dynasty. These examples differ in that, in the first two, superior aptitude for the responsibilities of the position is or clearly ought to be the main – perhaps even the only – criterion for preferring one aspirant over others, whereas this is not so for traditional heads of families: here, except in cases of mental incompetence and one or two other exceptional circumstances, preference is supposed automatically to track gender and primogeniture. However, this difference is not what I wish to dwell on now. What all the examples just cited have in common is the fact that our interest in the identity of the 'winner' is first and foremost an interest in who it is will be carrying out the duties and commitments implied by the position. It is not, primarily, an interest in who has emerged top from a competition, if in fact there has actually been one; nor does it, primarily, involve valuing for their own sake the qualities in which the 'victor' as such was pre-eminent. It may well be that among the qualities that qualify for prime minister there are some which it makes sense for us to value for themselves; but when someone interests us as having just won the *contest to be prime minister*, what is central for us is not that this person wonderfully exemplifies certain much prized qualities. What is central is that this is the one who will now be in the position of discharging the prime ministerial functions. Let us call this kind of figure a 'position-winner', since the corresponding form of rivalry is rivalry for a functional position.

---

[4] Obviously there is a perpetual instability here, since loving competition for its own sake may lead us to value the qualities merely as ingredients in the competition, while love of the qualities would lead us away from competition if a point were reached where competition was no longer the most effective way of enhancing them.

I have been trying to explain the ambiguity of the question 'Who or what is the highest or foremost?' – and of the claim, and even the argued conclusion, that so and so or such and such is the highest or foremost. Let us now turn back to ethics and the case of the highest good. This is the moment to recall the traditional roster of features by which the identity of the highest good is supposed to be determined: *perfection* or *completeness, self-sufficiency,* and others which are even more notoriously hard to interpret.[5] But for now we can ignore those problems of inter-pretation. We are not presently concerned with what the features them-selves actually amount to, nor with how they hold or fail to hold of different candidates for the title of 'highest good', but with the entire point or purpose of comparing candidates in these respects. Suppose the features themselves were simple and straightforward to understand, and suppose it were simple and straightforward to employ them so as to find out which candidate comes uppermost. It would still not be clear what we had found out. For depending on what we want from the idea of the highest good, we may have found out which of the various goods human beings aspire to is most perfect and self-sufficient and maximally pos-sessed of the other features, these being the qualities we prize most in things – and it may be that finding this out, and proclaiming and continuing to proclaim the answer in solemn celebratory style, is what we had principally come for. But alternatively, and certainly less repug-nantly from a modern perspective, we may have found out, by using those features as criteria (and then perhaps letting them recede from our attention), what the proper incumbent should be of a certain weighty functional position in our system of ethical thinking. We have a job to be filled, the job of the *highest good,* and we have a method for deciding between possible candidates for it. But none of this can get us anywhere in the end unless we have also determined a job specification. What work in our ethical theory, and in the end in our mundane practice, have we proposed for the successful candidate – the position-winner – to do? True, we might for a moment want to enjoy the sheer radiance as it were that invests X once it is apparent that X is the highest good, but our real business, surely, is to address ourselves briskly to *using* the knowledge that X is the highest good as a basis for ethical conclusions and ethical distinctions. And this presupposes that a job for the position-winner has been specified.

---

[5] Cf. Plato, *Philebus* 20d; Aristotle, *Nicomachean Ethics* 1.7, 1097a15–b21.

PART II

The distinction I have been trying to draw between the *pure-winner* approach and the *position-winner* approach, with illustrations from concrete kinds of human rivalry, is intended only to serve analysis by pointing to conceptual possibilities. I doubt whether, in relation to the case of the highest good, the distinction supports a taxonomy in which actual ancient treatments fall exclusively under one heading or the other. In some cases, the treatment may be consistent with either approach. Where this is so, modern readers will tend to assume that position-winning is at issue: that investigating the identity of the highest good is investigating what value should count as functionally central for ethical theory and mundane ethical practice. This assumption is taken for granted partly because the fullest, clearest, and best known treatment is the very obviously functional one of Aristotle, and partly because modern philosophy may simply be unable on its own to conceive of what it would be like – what it would mean – to adopt the pure-winner approach with regard to the highest ethical good: hence for modern philosophy this is not any sort of option. What on earth could it mean, having identified, as one thinks, the highest ethical good (having, for example, identified it as pleasure, or as excellent rational activity), then to leave the matter there – except for the very strange proviso that at this point it may be appropriate to evince towards this highest good an attitude analogous to that of honouring the victor of an athletic competition or a beauty contest? This is not a clear example of what we should nowadays call a theoretical attitude, even if it contains an element of contemplation; but it is not a clearly practical attitude either. And how would the highest good have to be conceived if sense is to be made of the idea of doing something like *honouring* whatever is found to hold the title?

Well, there may be several ways of answering this last question, but the only one I can think of points to a religious sort of conception, one charged with religiosity. Once we get over the impulse to dismiss this as an absurd stance to ascribe to anyone who is seriously engaged with philosophical ethics, we may begin to notice evidence pointing that way. Consider Plato's *Philebus*, which adumbrates no definite practical or political context for the discussion of the identity of the highest good, and leaves it quite indeterminate exactly how the winning contender, either as a goal or as an actuality, would enter into human life so as to make it better. At the same time, a pair of divinities, Aphrodite and cosmic Intelligence, show up as occasional characters in the concept-play of the *Philebus*, corresponding to and even at moments identified with the two supposedly abstract contestants, wisdom or knowledge and pleasure. What difference do the human antagonists, Socrates on the one side, and Philebus with the work done for him by Protarchus on the other, expect would be made by a victory either way? I cannot help hearing in the tone of much of the *Philebus* the suggestion that it would be a difference of honouring and glorifying one of these divinely personified principles over the other, whether by encomia like some of those on Erôs in Plato's *Symposium*, or by garlands hung on statues, or by musical and poetic celebrations. We should be reminded of the story of the judgment of Paris. It is natural for *us* to assume that any philosophical person who paid attention to the story would automatically interpret the three goddesses as mere allegories for the three abstract values, beauty, wisdom and sovereign rule. But can we be sure that an ancient Greek polytheistic philosophiser, in a cultural environment where conceptual distinctions have hardly yet been strongly drawn between ideals or values on the one hand, and actual forces at work in the human soul on the other, nor between forces at work in the human soul and forces at work in the cosmos at large, is not going to read, at least sometimes, the equation the other way round, so that instead of reducing divinities to abstracta, as those brought up in monotheism may wish and expect the ancient Greek philosophiser to do, the equation (sometimes, at least) generates a sense or a feeling that beauty, wisdom and sovereign rule are *powers*, each standing to the human individual as the awesome and potentially jealous focus of a sort of worshipful cult? (I speak of a sense or a feeling rather than a belief, because it is a matter of atmosphere rather than theory.[6])

Now, I do not wish to maintain that this kind of quasi-religious focus is all that a thinker would bring to bear upon some value *V* once philosophical debate had determined that *V* is the highest good. Even if it is not absurd to suppose that in an ancient Greek philosopher such a determination might naturally first trigger an effect akin to the hymning and honouring of *V*, it would certainly be absurd and repugnant to imagine the consequences as stopping there – as not going on to shape the major direction of soberly intellectual ethical inquiry with implications for

---

[6] The atmosphere had been famously evoked by Pericles in the funeral speech to the Athenians, when he calls upon his hearers to look upon the *polis* as their beloved (they are to become the city's *erastai*) (Thucydides, II.42). For Plato, see also *Symposium* 210a–212b, where the ultimate beloved is the Form of the Beautiful, and *Phaedrus* 254b, where the charioteer recollects the vision of Beauty standing with Self-Control 'on a sacred pedestal'. Here, the personified beings, although plural, are not in competition. Cf. *Laws* III, 698b5–6 on Modesty (*aidôs*).

secular practice. Analogously, perhaps, our holding up for all to admire the human pure winner of a contest of music or athletics can – and perhaps should – cease at some point from being primarily an act of applause and congratulation directed towards the victor, and become instead primarily an address to tyros and their mentors that highlights the victor as a model for improvement by imitation. My point is only that if I am right in suspecting that the direction of an ancient Greek sober ethical inquiry may not untypically have been heralded and accompanied by a more purely celebratory interest in 'What is the highest good?', then awareness of this adds an easily overlooked dimension to our understanding of what the question meant for those who asked it first in Western philosophy. Thus Aristotle's crisp reminders that ethical inquiry is for the sake of practice could now seem to us edged with a certain impatience at the somewhat precious atmosphere I have been trying to describe.[7]

PART III

Moving now to drier ground, I turn to the question of the highest good as a question about a *position-winner* according to the distinction made earlier. I am interested in the variety of roles or functions that the highest good might be cast for in our ethical thinking and practice. The rest of this paper will be devoted to distinguishing and describing some of these roles. These are the job-specifications. In effect they are alternative stipulations or interpretations of what it is to be the highest good. Someone may quickly wonder whether this is going to turn into another contest: a contest between meta-ethical demands on the formal notion of the highest good. But no such competition will be held here, because the valuable work will be over when we have simply put these different interpretations on view. We are to view them to see how various they are, not to decide which is 'best'. One lesson will obviously be that the variety is a potential source of confusion, even fundamental confusion. If a philosopher unconsciously moves between different conceptions of the role of the highest good, the resulting philosophy will not be fully coherent, and it may contain contradictory commitments. Again, if I read into a given

---

[7] *NE* 1.3, 1095a5–6; 11.2, 1103b26–9. Still, we must not forget that Aristotle also states that *eudaimonia*, identified by him as the highest human good, is *timion*, an object for honouring, which is the correct attitude towards the gods (*NE* 1.12, 1101b10–1102a4). Possibly he only means that to ascribe *eudaimonia* to a human individual is to honour that person. Even so, we also have Aristotle's ode to Virtue, whom he addresses as a maiden (*Complete Works*, 2463).

philosopher's writings a conception of that role which is different from the philosopher's own conception, I shall be hard pressed to make full sense of those writings. In fact, it may be a lesson of this survey that certain conceptions which we today might naturally reach for do not sit well with the ancient works on ethics.

(1) The conception which I shall first consider is familiar to us from J. S. Mill. Mill simply took it for granted (see the beginning of *Utilitarianism*) that to be the highest good is to be *the standard of right and wrong*, or (as he also put it) the foundation of morality. And for Mill this meant that for *X* to be the highest good is for acts or kinds of acts to be morally obligatory insofar as they promote *X*. Kant likewise had earlier assumed that ancient debates about the highest good were trying to establish one kind of good or another as the consequentialist source of our duties.[8] This *standard of right and wrong* interpretation can come in different forms or with different emphases. For example: (a) one might think that to be the highest good is to be *what is supremely desirable*, and then one might equate moral duty with doing everything one does for the sake of the supremely desirable. Alternatively, (b) one might think that being *the standard of right and wrong* is the grandest and holiest function anything can fulfil – even if the function is understood in consequentialist fashion – so that one is led to bestow the title of *highest good* on whatever good it is the promotion of which one has decided to equate with rightness.

On the first conception, then, the highest good has its special status on account of its relation to *right and wrong actions*. The reason, then, for calling it the highest of *goods* (i.e. highest in relation to them) presumably is that it more than any other sort of good is fit to function as the standard of right and wrong. It is assumed that the standard of right and wrong will be one good or another; the highest, then, is whichever good has the best claim to operate as that standard. On this sort of view the other goods are inferior because less qualified for the job expected from the highest good, but the nature of the job itself is spelled out by reference to *right action*, and not by direct reference to any *other goods*.[9] This is to be contrasted with a kind of view which we shall come to later on, according to which the actual job of the highest good (not merely the contest for

---

[8] For references, see chapter 9, section II.

[9] Thus from this point of view the whole weight of justifying the title 'highest good' falls on the background assumption of a contest of goods. On the other hand, the same perspective tends to make nonsense of the idea of such a rivalry: see below in the text on simple versus comprehensive or inclusive goods.

that job) is spelled out by reference to other goods which are lower than, because they are in some way dependent on, it.

So far nothing has been said about who is to have the highest good X, whatever this may be, on the sort of interpretation currently being considered. The most rational-seeming suggestion is that the standard of right and wrong, or alternatively the supremely desirable end which (on this view) it is our duty to promote in everything we do, is a state of affairs in which everyone has as much intrinsic good as possible, or as much as is consistent with fairness. This state of affairs, then, is that which, on this line of thinking, ought to be called 'the highest good'. However, the ancient dispute was not so much about who or how many should benefit, but about the nature of the good which it is assumed should be maximised, or maximised with fairness.[10] Is it virtue or is it pleasure? and so on. For the ancients, the highest good was a good of some kind, not a state of affairs where a good of some kind is maximised and distributed.

Another pertinent question to ask at this point is whether the highest good is simple; or is it a combination of simpler goods? A natural answer in the present context is that the highest good is a synthesis of different kinds of goods: we can call the synthesis 'well-being'. This is a natural thought because, intuitively, it is quite implausible to suggest that maximal realisation of a single simple good such as wisdom or pleasure, with no attention to any other sort of intrinsic good, is the single standard of right and wrong, or is the most desirable end for the sake of which we ought to do everything we do; whereas it is less implausible to suggest this concerning the maximal realisation of well-being. Or, to take another example of a complex good composed of different sorts of intrinsic good: it is surely completely obvious that the combination in the same individual of happiness (in the modern sense) and rectitude is more desirable than either of the constituents alone; hence each of these falls short of ranking as the highest good if to be the highest good is to be whatever is most desirable (or the maximisation of whatever is most desirable). Here we have an interesting example of the way in which a given interpretation of what it is to be the highest good affects one's choice of candidate for the role. A job specification such as those just mentioned favours candidates that are complex or comprehensive rather than simple.

(However, since complex goods are combinations of different kinds of simple ones, any notion of *rivalry* for the position of 'highest' between

---

[10] If desired, add 'with fairness' wherever relevant.

different kinds of intrinsic goods loses most of its purchase. For the most suitable incumbent will be one that actually includes many simple intrinsic goods. Being inside it, they are not in a position to run against it. The only rationale now for calling 'highest good' the end which is the standard of right, or the one which we ought to promote in everything we do, is quantitative or universalistic. This end consists in maximal or universal well-being, and the rivals which it has beaten to the post can only be such lesser or partial ends as *my well-being* or *the well-being of Europeans*.)

(2) Some of the points just made hold also for what I shall introduce as the second interpretation of the role of the highest good. According to this, to be the highest good is to be the good that it makes most sense to maximise (or to maximise with fairness). Under this conception too we shall almost certainly want to plug in a complex candidate. And here too the relation to other goods that constitutes the highest one highest is that of being a better candidate for the role than any of them; it is not a relation to them that is inherent in the role itself. However, there is a major difference between this second interpretation and its predecessor. According to the second one, maximising the highest good does not hold sway over all our actions, determining for all of them which is right and which is wrong; it holds sway only over actions designed to produce or to further the goods. It leaves room for many other principles of action – I mean moral principles of action. All that it says in saying that X is the highest good is this: even if I am a deontologist about keeping promises and speaking the truth, still, if in addition I recognise it as a duty to act sometimes so as to maximise goods, then X more than any of the others alone is what I should be maximising on those (possibly infrequent) occasions when maximising goods is indeed what I ought to be doing.

(3) Among the points common to the first two interpretations of what it is to be the highest good, there is also this: both allow for intrinsic goods other than the one that we ought to maximise, and both allow these to count as goods in their own right: they are simply lesser, less valuable, goods than the highest one. This feature is erased in the interpretation I introduce third, for according to it the job of the good called 'highest' is to be the source of value for all goods other than itself. This is the role of good-maker, or condition in the absence of which nothing else is worthwhile. Here at last we have an approach that spells out the role itself – not merely competitive success in filling the role – by reference to goods other than the one deemed highest.[11]

---

[11] For ancient references see chapter 9, section VI.

The conception has the striking, almost tragic, implication that if striving and effort are not an end in itself but are for the sake of some distinct good (as the ancient philosophers tend to take for granted), then striving and effort are completely pointless in the life of someone who lacks whatever is the highest good. For striving and effort have failed if they do not bring about the specific *good* towards which they were directed. But if the object towards which they are directed is worthless in the absence of the highest good, no *good* is attained by attaining it, and the striving and effort have achieved nothing of what they were meant for. The agent in such a case may be rewarded by a false sense of satisfaction at having achieved some good; but the striving was not for the sake of a sense of satisfaction at having succeeded, and certainly not for the sake of a false sense of that. Since most of our lives are spent in chasing after and trying to hang on to what we take to be various *goods* – whether for ourselves or for people for whom we are responsible – in fact, since this is the kind of creature we essentially are, namely practical beings, our entire existence and essential activity turn out to be fundamentally pointless if the highest good is missing from our projects. When that is the case, our successes leave us no better off than if they were failures, and on some forms of this view they leave us worse off. If achievement is achievement of some good, and progress is progress towards a better state, we are putting all our efforts into what is no more than a dream that we are progressing somewhere or achieving something. Again, we are not 'lucky' on account of any strokes of luck that forward our ends, because the lucky person has good luck, and good luck is luck that brings a good.[12]

On a traditional version of this view, the highest good is practical wisdom for using the other goods aright or for valuing them in the right way; and one is worse off having than lacking such things – such things as resources, power, honours – if one lacks the wisdom that makes them sources of good, not evil, for their possessor and his associates.[13] We can also reach the idea from another angle, as follows: the highest good in the eyes of an agent is the value (if such there be) concerning which he or she habitually refuses to compromise for the sake of other so called goods.

[12] If we were giving an example of good luck we would not point to a coincidence that allowed a serial killer to corner his *n*th victim. Cf. Philippa Foot on 'benefit': she speaks of our 'natural refusal' to say of 'the horrible Wests' (the serial killers of that name) that they were 'benefited' by the contribution of those whose behaviour made their actions possible (Foot, 2001, 94).

[13] Cf. Plato, *Euthydemus* 280c–281e.

This agent treats a certain good, *O*, as the good-maker in relation to the other goods by treating these others as worthless when they conflict with *O* and as good, i.e. worth taking trouble over, only when they are compatible with *O*. We might want to say: well, *treating* these other things as having worth when and only when they coexist with *O* (in the life of the agent) is not the same as its *being the case that* they have worth when and only when they coexist with *O*. This is true. But suppose that *O* is Aristotle's activity of virtue. Then the agent's habitual refusal to compromise over *O* presumably means that the agent is virtuous. We now can draw the conclusion that the relation of the other goods' worth to *O* is indeed what this agent takes it to be – or at least we can draw that conclusion if we agree with the Aristotelian axiom that in matters of ethics what the good person judges to be so is so.[14]

The highest good as good-maker gives us another example of how the job-specification sets constraints on what fills the position. For if under the 'other goods' we want to include some intrinsic so called goods, things which it is appropriate to value for their own sake, then the highest good must be less than completely comprehensive of intrinsic ones, and from a theory-building point of view it could easily be some logically simple good such as virtue or the good will or, for that matter, pleasure.

It may seem obvious that the highest good as good-maker is different from the highest good as the good that is most desirable or the one it makes most sense to maximise; for surely it is more desirable to have the good-maker plus the other goods than to have the former on its own. This thought is the basis of Kant's distinction between the *bonum supremum* (for him: the good will, the condition in the absence of which nothing else has worth) and the *bonum consummatum* (for him: the combination of the good will and happiness, which he conceives of as a non-moral condition).[15] However, we can formulate the concept of good-maker so that being the good-maker coincides with being the most desirable good. The trick is to construe 'good-maker' not dispositionally but in terms of actuality. Thus *O* is a good-maker when and only when it actually, so to speak, does confer value on the other goods – on the things that have worth only when it is present along with them. But for that to happen, these other things have to be present along with *it*. Thus the good-maker understood in this way is also what is most desirable. If we want this equation, then we shall perhaps say that the good-maker-style highest

[14] *NE* III.4, 25–33. For a somewhat fuller discussion see chapter II, section III.
[15] Kant, *Critique of Practical Reason* 5:110–11, in Kant, 1996.

good is at its very highest when actually doing some good-making, so that at its supreme moment it does need to be with the other things. However, it still has worth when on its own, so although it depends on them for a certain kind of actualisation, it does not depend on them for its value.[16]

(4) Another role for the highest good, but one less developed than those I have been examining, comes to mind if one thinks about the best and most precious kind of time (for Aristotle, this would be leisure), or about one's best energy or best moments as an agent or active being. If one could identify these independently (and this is surely feasible), then it could make sense to equate the highest good with what one deliberately dedicates this time or this energy to: what one precisely saves it for. (The idea is adumbrated in Aristotle's *Politics*: leisure is beautiful or fine by comparison with non-leisure time; therefore the activities of leisure should be more beautiful than unleisurely activities.[17]) The thought would be: to give one's finest time to such and such an activity is in effect to treat the activity as the highest good. If the idea of *dedication* (or *devotion*) *to* is lived out, as of course it can be, with quasi-religious intensity, then we have returned to something akin to our first take on the highest good.

There are many questions still to discuss. This last interpretation prompts the question whether the highest good must be the same for all; and the same might also be asked for some of the other interpretations. One might also question the assumption of uniqueness embodied in the superlative 'highest good'. But for now I shall end here.

---

[16] For a slightly fuller discussion, see chapter 11, section v.
[17] *Politics* VII.14, 1333a27–36.

CHAPTER 11

The good of practical beings: Aristotelian perspectives

I THE MAIN QUESTION

'Which among humanly practicable goods is the *summum bonum* or highest good?' is the first and central question of Aristotelian ethics.[1] As we might expect, Aristotle's answer is rather abstract. Even so, he intends it to be informative and to provide guidance for policy-making and action.[2] The present essay will focus on the account put forward in the *Nicomachean Ethics*, Book I, chapter 7, where Aristotle equates the highest human good with 'the rational soul's activity of virtue in a complete life'.[3] This compact formula sets an agenda that will explicate the highest good through detailed studies of (a) the *virtues*,[4] and (b) the two most philosophically controversial components of *a complete life*, namely *friendship*[5] and *pleasure*.[6] Fully spelled out, the compact formula yields a conceptually rich, and substantial, ideal.

This essay will take the compact formula as given, and will not comment on the reasoning by which Aristotle arrives at it. Nor is it my present purpose to look closely at any portion of the content of his ideal. The main question addressed here is a formal one: what does it mean in the context of Aristotelian ethics to regard X as the highest good, whatever X may be? In discussing this question, we shall be led to consider the chief components of Aristotle's ideal to see how their interrelation constitutes a whole that fits the formal account of the highest good.

II PERSPECTIVES ON PRACTICALITY

The claim that X is the highest good seems to imply that X is the good that we should strive above all to realise. But is that what the claim means? And who are the 'we' to whom the supposed implication applies?

[1] *Nicomachean Ethics* 1.4, 1095a15–16.   [2] *NE* 1.7, 1094a23–4; 11.2, 1103b26–8.
[3] *NE* 1.7, 1098a12–20; cf. 11, 1101a14–16; *Eudemian Ethics* 11.1, 1219a34–9.
[4] *NE* 11–VI.   [5] *NE* VIII–IX.   [6] *NE* VII, 11–14; X, 1–5.

To answer these questions we have to distinguish two levels of practical thinking. Before proceeding to that distinction, however, it is worth pausing over the obvious point that a practicable highest good cannot become an issue on any level except to rational beings with a multiplicity of needs and aspirations, and limited powers for satisfying them – practical beings, in short. The very phrase 'highest good' implies different goods, ranking one beyond the others and suggesting some kind of subordination of them to it. However, Aristotle remarks that everyone agrees in calling the highest good '*eudaimonia*' (usually translated as 'happiness', sometimes as 'flourishing'), and he himself constantly uses this appellation. The word itself does not bring us much closer to understanding what the highest good is, since people have very different notions of *eudaimonia*.[7] But use of the latter, more colloquial, Greek term gives Aristotle two advantages. It opens his topic to input from ordinary common sense (an important guide toward ethical wisdom, in his view), whereas 'the highest good' sounds a decidedly academic note. And the use of '*eudaimonia*' also brings the human ideal into relation with something more than human. For *eudaimonia* was a traditional attribute of the gods.[8] Aristotle can accept the attribution, although not because he accepts traditional portrayals of the gods. On the contrary, god, according to the Aristotelian philosopher's understanding, is a single unbroken, perfectly self-sufficient, eternal activity of reason.[9] There is no metaphysical margin here for any good except that activity itself. '*Eudaimonia*', then, a term implying no comparison between other goods and the good which it names, is a suitable word for the divine attribute.

In Aristotle's eyes it is very significant that common sense recognises the possibility of human *eudaimonia* too.[10] It surely is remarkable that the same word should be so naturally used both of the divine good, essential and unique in the divine life, and of a human good which is best among many and attainable only through the hazards of practicality.

We are already, with Aristotle, reflecting in a way that may seem out of place for the practical beings we are. From a 'purely' practical point of view, as it might be called, our practical nature goes without saying. When engaged in practical action we occupy the practical point of view, which like any perspective simply assumes its occupants as such. But Aristotle's

---

[7] *NE* 1.4, 1095a17–26.   [8] *NE* x.8, 1178b8–9.
[9] *NE* x.8, 1178b10–22; *Metaphysics* xii 7 and 9.
[10] The well-being of non-rational animals is not *eudaimonia*; see *EE* 1.7, 1217a20–9; *NE* 1.9, 1099b32–1100a1; x.8, 1178b25–8.

ethics is built on a cosmic anthropology in which distinctively human
existence is compared with other forms of life. We have just seen how the
truism that the highest good is *eudaimonia* implies a comparison between
human good and divine. The difference between human and divine
invites, in turn, the comparison of humans with non-rational animals.[11]
From the cosmic point of view it may even be cause for wonder that
beings like ourselves exist at all to puzzle over how the capacity for godlike
eudaimonia can occur interwoven with the needs of a vulnerable organism
making its way in a physical environment. (Since the human kind of
organism makes its way only by learning, and we learn only from others
of our kind, our way is essentially social,[12] which adds further dimensions
of complexity to the multiple nature of the human good.) This cosmic-
anthropological standpoint does not allow us to take human practicality
for granted.

Leaving wonder aside, however, there are also down-to-earth reasons
why our practicality is not just a topic for contemplation but for us an
object of intense *practical* concern. The contrast just drawn between a
practical perspective which takes itself wholly for granted, and the cosmo-
logical view which simply reflects upon the former, seems exhaustive only
if we ignore human nature and assume (legitimately, perhaps, for certain
theoretical purposes) that as practical beings we are all unwaveringly
committed to making good practical decisions, capable of discerning
them, and geared to carrying them out. Were the assumptions true in
practice, our practical decision-making could, of course, afford to overlook its own basis in the requisite organisation of the soul. Practicality
itself then might never have become a topic. (By the same token, when
ethical theory confines itself to a universe of discourse where all agents are
actively rational, the shift to an external perspective such as that of cosmic
anthropology will seem gratuitous for ethics.) But since it is equally plain
that the assumptions tend to be false in practice and that we need them to
be at least roughly true if only to satisfy our most obvious requirements,
the cultivation of practical rationality itself becomes a pressing concern
for the practical beings we are. The resulting reflection, along with experience, may even lead us to conclude that practical rationality, our
paramount resource for obtaining the other things which we value, is best
secured by means of the belief that in achieving it we achieve an *intrinsic*
good, whether or not this belief is independently grounded or even

---

[11] See previous note; also *NE* I.7, 1098a1–3.   [12] *NE* I.7, 1097b6–11; IX.9, 1169b18–19.

meaningful. Inevitably, efforts to sustain and teach this conviction will sometimes be displaced by philosophical misgivings. How is it consistent with our *general* rationality to nurture our practical reason on a possibly irrational belief? In this way, a realistic practical point of view naturally opens into a perspective every bit as external to practicality itself as the perspective of cosmic anthropology.

Whether we take good practice to be simply a resource for achieving other goods or an end in itself, it poses a special kind of practical problem because of the special way in which its reality is contingent and within our power. It is not in our power as an external good is, when close enough for us to lay hands on it or when we have the legal right to use it. Possessing good practical agency essentially depends on the would-be possessor's commitment[13] to being a certain sort of person. Where others are concerned, we can create conditions favouring such commitment, but cannot inject the commitment itself. And since commitment is not an external precondition but the core of good practical agency, the latter's reality is contingent in a peculiar way. It is self-developing and self-sustaining to the extent that commitment is present, and this fact, considered by itself, seems to place good agency in the class of things which belong necessarily to their subjects given that they belong at all. To the extent that commitment to it is lacking, good agency cannot install itself any more than it can be installed from outside: which seems to place it in the corresponding class of impossibilities. However, according to Aristotle we begin neither as clear-cut haves nor as clear-cut have-nots in this respect, but can develop in either direction.[14] Hence the initial stages are critical, taking us further and further away from alternative possibilities.[15] And since individuals develop by absorbing the values of those around them, and will pass them on in the same way, the self-propagating structure of good and bad practice is found at the collective level too, in families and communities.

There is plenty in these distinctively human facts to interest the cosmic anthropologist, but in the *Nicomachean Ethics* Aristotle's interest is practical: he lays out the facts so as to educate moral educators in the fundamentals of their task. Perhaps as moralist and educator Aristotle could not afford to pause in puzzlement at the phenomena of human imperfection; but the anthropologist should surely wonder at some of

---

[13] Thus, ancient Greek commonly uses *spoudaios* (literally: 'serious') of persons to mean 'ethically good'.

[14] *NE* II.1, 1103a18–26.   [15] *NE* III.5, 1114a12–18.

them, especially an anthropologist who, like Aristotle in his scientific studies, operates under the assumption that 'nature does nothing in vain'.[16] For instance, if we are essentially practical rational beings, how is it that sometimes we fling ourselves into irrationality with such welcoming gusto even in the teeth of its destructiveness? The Greek poets speak of Erôs and Atê sent by the gods, but experience knows that transports of lust or rage do not always swoop upon us as if from outside. Often it is as if *we* wilfully release such forces, fuelling them from within as though we find our true selves in being consumed. Afterwards we say: 'I was not myself'; but is it true? According to the Bible, 'the imagination of man's heart is evil from his youth';[17] psychoanalysis has its own explanations; common sense talks of immaturity while acknowledging the need for an occasional vacation from responsibility. A suggestion that paves the way to an Aristotelian response would be that what we seek when we kick over the traces of practical rationality is the taste of a fantasy highest good: a state of pure abandonment in the immunity of knowing that nothing else matters or even exists beyond some immediate enthralling object, whatever it may be.

We meet this human propensity with efforts to repress, contain, sublimate. By themselves, though, such responses fail to come to terms with the fantasy highest good's claim to *be* our highest good. The claim has power because it seems to ring true. Hence, various attempts have been made to take it seriously. In each case, the claim is acknowledged to represent an ideal of perfect fulfilment, and some form of approximation is recommended. One type of approach, emphasising satisfaction rather than ecstasy, looks to raise the ratio of the individual's fulfilled to unfulfilled desires. This can be done either by keeping desires constant and finding surer ways of implementation, or by leaving the facts as they are and adjusting desires to whatever is at hand.

But an Aristotelian response would not follow either of these routes. Instead, it would begin by figuring out what sort of being one would have to be to live in perfect fulfilment. It would see that one would have to be independent of the mercy of circumstance. No needs could distract one, so one's only need (if so it can be called) would be for the fulfilling activity. One would not be beholden to a physical or social environment but would constitute one's own company, one's own sustenance and instrumentation. One would be immortal, because one's activity could

---

[16] See, e.g., *Generation of Animals* v.8, 788b21.   [17] Genesis 8:21.

not fail unless the very love of life were to fail from within, which seems incompatible with perfect fulfilment. Fulfilment for such a being must consist in an activity suitable to its nature: an activity, therefore, that is endlessly interesting and perfectly self-contained. What has just been described is the life of a god, according to Aristotle's understanding.

Thus, if humans need sometimes to escape from practicality, not in order to fall asleep but because we crave positive engagement free from practical constraints, we have a model for the kind of activity in which it makes sense to seek liberation. The model is divine activity: free, sufficient, untouched by anything external. It hardly seems to matter for this argument whether we suppose this paradigm to be something real or only conceptual. Either way, Aristotle takes it seriously in practice when he fashions his famous defence of human theoretic thinking, arguing that we are at our most godlike in this purely intellectual activity, which shapes itself from within and seeks no satisfaction beyond itself.[18] Against those who caution mortals not to aspire beyond their mortal level, Aristotle encourages us to 'act immortal' so far as our lives permit.[19] In this, he – and we, if we resonate to these intimations – have gone some way toward acknowledging the claim of what above was termed 'the fantasy highest good'.

We are thereby led to recognise intellectual, or spiritual, or imaginative, activity for its own sake as *a* fundamental human good. A much more careful argument would be needed to support the position that such activity should be accorded the status of *highest* human good. In any case, this essay has yet to consider what a claim of this stronger form would mean. But the weaker conclusion is not necessarily less significant for anthropology and for education.

In the light of what has emerged so far, Aristotle's contribution to ethics can be seen as a double corrective for ethical theorising that centres on the concerns of what was earlier labelled the 'purely' practical point of view. Such an approach takes for granted our established reality as practical beings, and our commitment to whatever is to count as practical success. It considers what principles a rational decider should use; how they should be applied; how they can be justified; whether they can be defended as objectively valid or binding on everyone; whether principles of morality take precedence over other kinds of principle, and if so, why they do. These, along with questions about the principles of justice, are

---

[18] *NE* x, 6–8; *Metaphysics* I, 1–2; *Protrepticus* B 23–8.   [19] *NE* x.7, 1177b19–34.

still frequently assumed to be definitive of the field of philosophical ethics. Yet in Aristotle's ethical thinking these problems are not in the forefront. On the contrary, *his* two great problems reflect fundamental limitations of the purely practical perspective. The latter depends for its existence, just as studies which assume it depend for their ethical relevance, on a supply – which nature, as a matter of fact, does *not* automatically guarantee – of good practical agents: hence the problem of moral education. Nor can the practical perspective, or studies that assume it, begin to confront, as a question for ethics, the problem of what we should do with ourselves when not called upon to be practical.

III   WHAT IS IT FOR *X* TO BE THE HIGHEST GOOD?

It is often assumed, I think, that in assigning to *X* the status of highest good one is claiming that *X* is that which we should seek above all to realise.[20] To examine this assumption in the context of Aristotle's *Nicomachean Ethics*, we must distinguish two levels of practical thinking: (1) that of the 'statesman'[21] (*politikos*), whose chief task is to set and preserve values and principles, and shape accordingly the lives of those for whom he or she is responsible; and (2) that of the 'individual' whose life is so shaped. It is a difference of roles, not persons. A statesman is an individual simultaneously, and in political constitutions where offices rotate, leaders revert to being mere individuals. For Aristotle, the paradigmatic statesman is of course the political leader, but the obligation to engage in the kind of thinking (*politikê*) that typifies the statesman is not confined to those who occupy or expect to occupy political office. The thinking in question may be described as 'fundamental policy-making'. It involves not only ethical reflection but planning in accordance with the values endorsed. Thus, the head of a family is or should be a 'statesman' in relation to those under his or her responsibility, and every free adult should keep a statesmanly eye on his or her own life. The 'individual', by contrast, is the person regarded as actually living out the detail of the life thus planned.

So does Aristotle conceive of the highest good as *that which one should above all strive to realise*? When the question is posed with reference to the *statesman*, the answer turns out to be 'Yes and no'. If the question is

---

[20] For more discussion see chapters 9 and 10 above.

[21] This word and its clumsy adjectives are high-flown and sexist, but less misleading than the alternative, 'politician' and cognates.

whether it is a conceptual truth for Aristotle that the statesman should above all strive to realise the highest good (whatever it may be), the answer is 'Yes'. For Aristotle, if one is a statesman, or acting in one's capacity as statesman, one should make every decision with a view to realising the highest good. This is because, as is clear from *Nicomachean Ethics* I,[22] realising the highest good is the definitive goal of statecraft as such. If, however, the question is whether, according to Aristotle, for X to be the highest good just is for X to be what the statesman should above all strive to realise, the answer, I think, is 'No'. Instead: if it is the case that X is that good which the statesman should above all strive to realise, this is *because* X is the highest good. That the statesman should be dedicated above all to promoting X is not the reason why X is the highest good, but is, rather, the consequence of X's having that status among the goods.

Thus at this point consideration of the statesman leaves us without an explanation of what it is for something to be the highest good. Let us, however, shelve that inquiry for a moment, and turn to apply our current question to the *individual*: does Aristotle conceive of the highest good as that which the individual should above all strive to realise? This time the answer is 'No' on both fronts. Aristotle does not hold that the individual should do everything with a view to realising the highest good. Nor therefore does Aristotle hold that for X to be the highest good is for X to be that for the sake of which the individual makes every decision he makes.

We can support the first point, that for Aristotle it is not the case that the individual should do everything with a view to realising the highest good, by considering that the denial of this would tend to elide the distinction between the statesman and the individual;[23] and also by noticing the many passages that show Aristotle's virtuous individual in action, yet not acting with an eye on realising the highest good or *eudaimonia*. Promoting conditions for *eudaimonia*, for oneself and those around one, is obviously one very important concern for the virtue of practical wisdom; but when, for example, the virtuous and wise individual exercises justice, he or she acts from reasons of fairness as determined by reference to desert and proportionality: furthering *eudaimonia* or happiness is not, as such, a mark of just action.[24] The courageous individual

---

[22] 1–2 (1094a26–b11); cf. 13, 1102a5–25.

[23] This distinction is also discussed in chapter 8, section IV.

[24] *NE* V, 3–5. Note that far from portraying happiness as the wise individual's one goal, generating a single rule for life, Aristotle warns us not to expect absolutely firm rules of practice: *NE* II.2, 1104a1–10.

faces necessary danger in battle simply because it is his duty and the fine thing to do (i.e., anything else would be shameful).[25]

It is of course the case that, in exercising justice or courage, virtuous individuals may very well in themselves be actually *instantiating eudaimonia*, given that this is defined by Aristotle as 'the rational soul's activity of virtue in a complete life'. For the conditions indicated by 'in a complete life' may be fulfilled. We shall come to them.

So what is it for *X* to be the highest good, according to Aristotle? On the reading to be explored in the rest of this essay, it is for *X* to be 'the principle and the cause of the [other] goods'.[26] This is not to be taken as implying that the highest good, whatever it is, causes the existence of goods such as health and wealth and friendly connections, thereby doing duty for the ordinary causes of these things, such as exercise, prudent management of resources, and willingness to co-operate. The meaning, rather, is that the relation to the other goods which constitutes *X* highest is that of rendering them good and worth having, and therefore worthy of efforts to obtain and to preserve.

Asked 'What is the highest good?' a person might answer: 'Pleasure' or: 'Love and friendship'. It would be one kind of mistake to maintain this seriously, without qualification; some pleasures, some kinds of love and friendship, are destructive, degrading, corrupting, etc. Faced with plausible examples, the respondent might agree. In that case his or her natural next move would be to modify the original claim to (for example): 'The highest good is *worthwhile* love and friendship.' But a philosopher would see this reply as inadequate too, since it shows no grasp of what is at issue in claiming so-and-so to be the highest good. Perhaps the respondent means: 'It is what everyone should value most.' It might even be correct to say this of worthwhile love and friendship. But even if so, worthwhile love and friendship cannot be the highest good according to the philosopher's understanding. If some forms of love and friendship are worthwhile, it is because of something about them over and above the features that bring them under a general definition of love and friendship. This something else is what makes good love and friendship good; they, as it were, do not make themselves so. According to Aristotle, the 'good-making' factor is virtuous activity: the truly good and desirable friendship

---

[25] *NE* III.7, 1115b11–13; 8, 1116b2–3.

[26] *NE* I.12, 1102a2–4; cf. 4, 1095a26–8 (reporting a position which Aristotle does not reject, although he rejects the Platonist interpretation of it); cf. *EE* I.7, 1218b7–14.

is that of actively virtuous friends.[27] This argument can be generalised to show that the highest good (conceived of as 'good-maker') cannot, whatever it is, be a good form of something of which bad forms are also possible. Activity of virtue in a complete life (i.e., Aristotelian happiness) fits this last condition, and so does activity of virtue *tout court*. For the moment I shall focus on the latter.

The idea, then, is that activity of virtue in relation to the other elements of a complete life, whether severally or together, is what makes those so called advantages worth having. I say 'so called', because, although we all want them (and want them also for our loved ones, and perhaps for a yet wider circle), and act and feel about them as if they are worth having and would contribute to happiness, outside the context of actual or assured activity of virtue they are, at most, conditional promises of advantage. Activity of virtue, actual or assured, discharges the condition. It provides, as it were, a field – we could call it the 'eudaimonic field' – in which those items take on the substantiality of goodness and function as ingredients of genuine happiness.[28]

But why on earth should one accept this strange picture according to which standard desiderata such as health and freedom are not in themselves actually good and worth pursuing by anyone who wants them, but somehow depend for their goodness and true desirableness on being embedded in a context of virtuous activity? This essay contains no attempt to argue that the strange picture should be accepted. It confines itself to laying out the basis of an Aristotelian acceptance of it.

The basis is to be found in a certain Aristotelian axiom: 'The good person [i.e. the person of virtue] is the measuring rod in matters of value.'[29] Now consider the virtuous person in process of contemplating the activities of someone corrupt or vile. To virtuous eyes, the other's life is not desirable. The contemplator not only could not, but would not live that way on any terms. Now suppose the contemplated corrupt agent is seen as achieving some of the usual desiderata or as possessing them perhaps to an exceptional degree, or as operating through or about them to his or her pleasure or satisfaction. We ask the person of virtue: 'Is that life now any more desirable because of the prosperity which has just appeared in it?' The predictable answer is: 'Not to me.' The virtuous

---

[27] *NE* VIII, 4.
[28] Cf. *EE* VIII.3, 1248b26ff.: 'The good person is one for whom the natural goods are good.' Cf. *NE* V.I, 1129b1–6. For a fuller development of the theme, see Plato, *Euthydemus*, 280b–282e.
[29] *NE* III.4, 1113a25–33.

person no more wishes he were leading the contemplated life when prosperity is part of it than when it is not. So according to the virtuous person, who by Aristotle's axiom is a true measure, the usual desiderata add no value to an ethically worthless life. It follows (for anyone who accepts Aristotle's axiom) that the usual desiderata add no value to an ethically worthless life.

But does the negative judgment passed by the virtuous person somehow make it the case that the other life and the goods in it are worthless? Does the virtuous person rule this fact into being? One can see how Aristotle would reply to this, even though it is not easy for us to see how we could get back to the point – if we even wanted to – from which it would also be our own considered reply as philosophers. Aristotle would say: 'The virtuous person judges as he does because of what he sees about the other's life. He sees confusion of values: means being prized as if they were ends, ends precious in themselves exploited as means. He sees opportunities for good being missed through failure to understand the kind of good they are opportunities for – hence, in relation to this agent, they were never really opportunities. Since an opportunity for good is itself, as such, a category of good,[30] here we have an example of how the agent's personality cancels the value (so far as he himself is concerned) of a good which is present in his life. The virtuous person sees all this in the activities of the agent contemplated. *What* he sees is what leads him to form his judgment, and what he sees makes that judgment true. Thus, the so called good things in the contemplated life are not worthless because the virtuous person thinks so. They are made worthless by the activity – its character and limitations – of the agent concerned. By contrast, an agent of opposite character makes worthwhile the goods in his life by acting about them in appropriate ways.'

Obviously there can be no ground for congratulating a person on reaching some desired objective, or on a piece of good fortune, if he or she is in fact no better off. The same applies to self-congratulation or disappointment when someone fares badly. If each is the final judge of his own ethical worth, then the truth in these matters is as each sees it; getting what one wants is success and brings one closer to happiness. But if we can have ethical failings and be blind to them, then one who is blind in this way, yet cares about having the things which everyone finds desirable, lives in a dream. In reality, according to this metaphysic

---

[30] *NE* 1.6, 1096a23–7.

of morals, there is for this agent no practical difference between failure and success in obtaining or keeping those things. I cannot lose an advantage the gaining of which could have brought no benefit to the person living *my* life. Disappointment and satisfaction at how things go for me presuppose my worth, actually or probably expressing itself in virtuous activity. For beings such as we, essentially practical, it is a chilling possibility that instead of its mattering how things turn out for us, we operate in a dark where, unknown to ourselves, success and failure add up to the same – the state of our*selves* being what renders our efforts pointless at source, before we even make them. Nor, for such beings, could there be any more pressing necessity than that of ensuring the truth, more or less, of the practical assumption of our own worth which all our projects imply.

On this account, the highest good, so far as it consists in activity of virtue, is not primarily a good whose conditions we ought to act in order to secure. To the extent that it is true that we ought to act in order to secure it (different extents for individual and statesman), this truth follows from the more fundamental fact that the highest good, so far as it consists in activity of virtue, is the *sine qua non* of its mattering whether we secure anything else at all.

IV IS THE HIGHEST GOOD NO MORE THAN ACTIVITY OF VIRTUE?

In using the expression 'the highest good, so far as it consists in activity of virtue', we seem on the brink of treating virtuous activity as identical with Aristotle's highest good. It is true that virtuous activity becomes happiness in the presence of the other elements (the ones making up a complete life), while they in turn, if sufficiently provided, become happiness in the presence of *it*. But these contributions to happiness are not symmetrical. Virtuous activity contributes by being already, from its own nature, unconditionally good. That is why it can make the otherwise valueless other ones good, rendering them constituents of a way of being which is properly called 'happiness'.

Virtuous activity, then, is a good that is prior to happiness and more fundamental. In view of this priority, as well as the fact that virtuous activity plays the principal role in the constitution of happiness (it figures as the metaphysical agent of good in relation to the 'passive' other elements), one may be tempted to conclude that the highest good is activity of virtue *tout court*. This conclusion seems reinforced by the fact that Aristotle would certainly not want to say that goods which support virtuous activity even when there is no hope of its becoming happiness (through lack of some important component of the complete life) are therefore not worth having. Virtuous activity as such is good-making, and makes good the resources needed to support it, whatever the other circumstances may be. Is *it*, then, rather than happiness, the highest good? Or is virtuous activity in fact identical with happiness? Neither alternative represents Aristotle's view. He not only repeatedly refers to the highest good as 'happiness', but rejects any general identification of happiness with virtuous activity.[31] A happy individual, he says,[32] is not easily dislodged from happiness except by major misfortune: but it can happen, and unless the person is killed or disabled, he or she continues in virtuous activities, making the best of harsh circumstances.

But even if the lesson of that particular text is clear, the general issue is not completely straightforward. Two points bring this out. First, Aristotle's ultimate paradigm of happiness is god. It might seem out of place to speak of the divine activity as 'virtuous' as if to exclude an alternative. But, at any rate, since this activity is perfectly self-sufficient, the activity alone suffices for a 'complete life'. Hence happiness and the supremely good activity necessarily coincide in this limiting case. (If, therefore, we wish to say that the divine activity is the highest good, this ought to mean that it is the highest in the universe, or something like that: but not that it is highest in relation to other goods in the divine life.) Secondly, on the human level there is no sharp break between merely virtuous activity and happy activity, since the former, even at its most austere, depends on some measure of the other goods. One cannot exercise virtues such as temperance and justice except in relation to goods such as food and fellow-citizens.[33] And one must have the necessities of life to act at all. (Hence, there are, presumably, degrees of happiness. A person might lack one of the important elements of a complete life – for example, if he were blind – yet still count as happy rather than not.[34]) Now, the two points may pull in opposite directions if either is made a ground for identifying human happiness with human virtuous activity *tout court*. The comparison with god could be drawn so as to suggest that humans are happiest when their virtuous activity involves the minimum

---

[31] This seems clear notwithstanding Richard Kraut's arguments to the contrary in Kraut, 1989.
[32] *NE* I.10, 1100b22–1101a11.
[33] *NE* x.8, 1178a28–b3.   [34] The example is from Lawrence, 1997.

of other goods.[35] (But what if the virtuous poor would *welcome* more of the other goods? If so, their dissatisfaction with the *status quo* would have to be interpreted as failure to recognise or fully appreciate their happiness.) On the other hand, the second point suggests the argument: mere virtuous activity differs from conspicuous happiness only by degrees; so the former is happiness too, but to a lesser degree. However, since the degrees increase with the amount or number of other goods present (up to the point of superfluity), this argument indicates that human happiness is greater the more it differs from divine happiness in respect of dependence on factors other than virtuous activity.

The main difficulty of equating the highest good with activity of virtue *tout court* is that, on these terms, no one can reasonably want a good whose absence does not hamper his or her virtuous activity, but whose presence would make it easier, say, or more enjoyable. For if the presence of the thing is superfluous so far as the subject's actual engagement in virtuous activity is concerned, the thing is not part of his or her happiness, and should count as not worth having. Some philosophers have defended the equation, even accepting the paradoxical conclusion just drawn, but Aristotle is not among them. Again, it would be strange to argue (if anyone has) that a person actively virtuous but living in poverty should welcome improved circumstances not because prosperity contributes to one's happiness, but because it makes one more satisfied with the happiness one already exemplifies! If contentment is necessary for happiness, the argument falls short of showing that even the pauper's virtuous activity is to be counted as happiness; and if contentment is *not* necessary for happiness, it is not clear that the virtuous pauper has any business seeking to become less needy. He should, perhaps, be contented with discontentment! But according to Aristotle, if in fact such a pauper wishes for, hopes for, tries for, welcomes, an improvement in her condition, these attitudes are entirely appropriate as attitudes of *this* person toward *this* person's situation and prospects, for (as before) in matters of value 'the good person is the measuring rod'. Before, we saw this 'measure' principle illustrated by the ordinary good person's refusal to be impressed by the life-style of a bad one even when the latter is laden with presumed desirables such as wealth, fame, privilege, etc. We now see the principle

---

[35] Compare *EE* vii.12, 1244b5–12 and 1245b13–19, where Aristotle puts forward and then defeats the paradoxical thesis that since happiness involves self-sufficiency, the happy person should not need friends, the point being illustrated by the case of god, who is too self-sufficient to need a friend and therefore will not have any.

upholding an ordinary judgment about happiness even when it diverges from some philosophical theory[36] to the effect that virtuous activity alone is, for humans, happiness under all circumstances.

Obviously, difficult circumstances can make virtuous activity harder for the subject. But being harder does not necessarily render it shorter or less frequent. Hardship stimulates greater activity of virtue in those who can rise to the challenge. Should they then prize the hardship, on the ground that the resultant heroic activity more closely approximates to happiness? One can hardly say 'Yes', since this concession implies that one who looks back on an episode in which he rightly (as he believed then and still believes) refused under torture to betray his country's secret, should, if he has proper values, treasure the event as an episode of something like *happiness* (and should still wish something like happiness for those he loves?). Alternatively, it might be argued that the actively virtuous person has reason to welcome better circumstances (as we normally call them) in that now she can be actively virtuous in more contexts or bring more virtues into play. Certainly, this may be one's reason (and if so, surely a good one) for preferring to be free of hardship or privation. It is not the only reason, however. Over and above that sort of reason for looking forward to having his sight again, the cataract patient looks forward to the pleasure of seeing well, of fully exercising the faculty of vision. This natural faculty is not a virtue in the sense relevant for Aristotle's ethics. The activity of vision is desirable *per se* as well as for facilitating other activities, including those of virtue.[37] But it is not desirable *per se* because it itself is an activity of virtue. How do we know that it is desirable *per se*? From the fact that the good person, like everyone else, values it for what it is.

All practical activities aim to produce an ulterior result, but there is an important distinction which Aristotle might have said more to emphasise. In one sort of case, we aim to produce a result mainly as a basis for further activity of the same kind – for instance, farming, which is a way of life. In the other kind of case, the desired result will displace the circumstances which made the original activity necessary or possible – for instance, fighting a war for the sake of peace with security. In times of peace, gentler virtues should come into play, upstaging those that show themselves most in times of crisis and austerity. No doubt peace-time offers more choices, but it would be difficult to make the case that the

---

[36] Cf. *NE* I.5, 1095b33–1096a2.   [37] *NE* I.6, 1096b17–19; cf. *Metaphysics* I.1, 980a20–8.

virtuous activities of peace are necessarily more numerous or open to more individuals, or show greater or more various virtue, than their wartime counterparts. The rational desire for peace on the right terms is not grounded on the prospect of more, or more virtuous, virtuous activity, but on the distinct prospect of a happier way of life. The difference is made by such factors as freedom from fear, and from stress, privation, and hardship. Activity of virtue carried on under such conditions is more desirable than activity of virtue carried on in their absence – because of the character of the conditions themselves, not because they add to the sum of excellent activity. That they add to it is, as a general claim, much less obvious than that a decent peace is preferable to war. It is preferable because of the independent natures of war and peace themselves. These independent natures do not, of course, make peace unconditionally more desirable than war. It still remains true that in the absence of suitable activities of virtue, peace will not have been worth fighting for.

V IN CONCLUSION

Finally, two reflections, one practical, one metaphysical.

(1) It is a particularly important task of statesmanship, in changing times, to prepare individuals to switch into newly appropriate modes of excellent activity. The point about war and peace is good in itself, but Aristotle also brings it forward as an analogy for business and leisure.[38] Our natural desire for leisure will turn out to have been for something pointless to attain unless we are morally and intellectually equipped to employ it in suitable activities of virtue. Suitable activity, Aristotle argues, would be the kind it makes most sense to ascribe to divine beings who are beyond the need of those special material and social conditions that make leisure a human possibility. So for humans at leisure Aristotle recommends the godlike 'theoretic' use of the mind, and he recommends this precisely because it is godlike[39] (even more so, he thinks, than beneficent statesmanship on a grand scale). But such a recommendation for human leisure need not depend on theological assumptions, nor on Aristotle's conception of divinity, nor on any narrowly specific understanding of 'theoretic' thinking. Unencumbered by these we can see sense in the idea that leisure is a time for laying aside the kinds of activity needed to procure it, and for doing something of quite a different character.

---

[38] *NE* x.7, 1177b4–12; *Politics* vii.14, 1333a30–b11; viii.3, 1337b29–1338a13.
[39] *NE* x.8, 1178b8–23. For an extensive discussion, see Broadie, 1991, chapter vii.

In leisure, we act as if the infra-structure has nothing to do with us. It is not unreasonable, then, to recommend leisure-activities approximating the activities of absolutely free beings, whether or not such beings exist or are properly reckoned divine. In any case, worthwhile leisure-activity is one way of instantiating the highest human good. Engaged in it, we make the other goods worth having: both leisure itself, and the economic and social resources on which it depends.[40]

(2) It remains to respond to the metaphysical impulse that identifies the highest good with virtuous activity *tout court* on the ground that virtuous activity plays the leading part in the constitution of happiness. One response gives in to the impulse, respects Aristotle's equation of the highest good with happiness, and consequently identifies happiness with virtuous activity of excellence. We have seen the difficulties of that. Another response would be to give in to the impulse, distinguish happiness and virtuous activity, and conclude *pace* Aristotle that happiness is not the Aristotelian highest good. But the impulse is not well founded. The unconditional good which is virtuous activity is prior to the good which is happiness. Because of this priority, virtuous activity *can* give worth to other things generally desired, and *would* give worth to them if they were available. But the prior good is not, because prior, the highest good, if the highest good is that which *gives* worth to any of the usual desiderata, including those not necessary for the unadorned activity of virtue. Activity of virtue needs more than its status as prior (indeed, primary) good if it is actually to *make* the other things worth having and getting. The additional condition is that they, too, *be at hand*. If they are on the scene or in the wings, and if virtuous activity is present or assured, we either have or are set to have all the elements of happiness together: the bonific activity, and the items on which it can 'act'. This sounds like Aristotle's compact formula: 'rational activity of virtue in a complete life'. The formula expresses a combination consisting of a bonific element and elements capable of being made good by it. This combination is the highest good for human beings. When the combination is realised, the highest good is realised; and when the combination is realised – the

---

[40] The choice of worthwhile leisure-activities would be a mark of the virtue of practical wisdom (*phronêsis*). But the excellence exercised in good theorising is *sophia*, which Aristotle carefully distinguishes from *phronêsis* in *NE* vi. It is very revealing that Aristotle mounts an argument that *sophia* is a human virtue in the same generic sense in which courage, justice, etc. are (*NE* i.13, 1103a8–10). If we accept the point, which many find counter-intuitive (as would many in Aristotle's original audience), then we should recognise as virtues in the same sense any cultivated qualities by which human beings excel in whatever leisure-activities we regard as worthwhile.

combination of good-making agent with its suitable patients – the patient-elements are thereby made good. We may want to identify the good-making highest good with the active agent of this axiological transaction, i.e. with virtuous activity actually bonificent in the presence of the other elements; or, more inclusively, we may want to identify the good-making highest good with all the factors whose compresence is sufficient and necessary to result in the being made good of the patient-elements among them. But this would seem to be a distinction without an ethical difference.

CHAPTER 12

Taking stock of leisure

I chose 'leisure' as the theme for this occasion[1] partly because it's a topic which everyone – anyway, everyone present this afternoon – knows quite a lot about informally from their own experience. I chose it also because philosophy is supposed to be concerned with, among other things, human life and human nature in general, and reflecting about leisure is largely a matter of reflecting about its place in human life as a whole. It is not easy to say what is essential to human beings, because the attributes that seem deeply characteristic of us form such a long list, whereas stating the essence of something is traditionally supposed to be a matter of giving a single pithy fundamental formula. If, however, one is allowed to point to the essential by simply listing typifying characteristics, then the capacity to appreciate leisure and distinguish it from non-leisure must surely count as essential to human beings.

This is not to claim, of course, that the concept of *leisure* is universal to all cultures, nor that if a certain culture lacked this notion it might not all the same get along as well on the whole as we do, who have it. For conceivably that culture might recognise and realise some equally important human capacity whose object figures not at all in our own reflections and deliberate arrangements. We can be quite liberal in forming our list of essentially human capacities as long as we allow that there may be whole peoples, and long stretches of history, in which one or another essentially human capacity goes systematically unrecognised and largely or completely unrealised. But if this has ever been true of the capacity to appreciate leisure, it will not remain so if the ideals enshrined in the UN Universal Declaration of Human Rights ever take hold on a worldwide scale. For Article 24 of the Declaration says: 'Everyone has the right

[1] Inaugural lecture at the University of St Andrews, 30 April 2003.

to rest and leisure, including reasonable limitation of working hours and periodic holidays with pay.'

By coupling the terms 'rest' and 'leisure', this statement seems to sit on the fence about their relation. Although both rest and leisure are contrasted with work ('working hours'), and no doubt both are needed periodically, they are obviously not the same. We rest when sleeping, but time for sleeping is not on that account leisure time. A life contains no leisure that is divided entirely between labour and the rest needed for renewed labour. Rest is inactivity, whereas leisure is the opportunity for some kind of desirable activity. Beasts experience rest, and no doubt ought to be allowed it at due intervals where this depends on us, but it can hardly be said that they experience or are capable of leisure. We need rest as organisms, whereas we need leisure as persons and individuals.

Let us assemble intuitions about leisure. To call them intuitions is not an automatic endorsement. Even the best of them may not hold true for every single case of leisure, and some may be inaccurate from the start. For example, people at the top of the social and economic scale used to be called the 'leisured classes'. We might therefore think, since those who do the physically heaviest, most laborious, work tend to be at the other extreme of that scale, that the true opposite of leisure is toil. But then if opposites stand and fall together, it would follow that making the work less toilsome and intrinsically unrewarding would remove or lessen the need for leisure. Yet that is surely not so. Something sets up the need for leisure, but it is not necessarily or not only toil or drudgery. Again one may wonder whether leisure necessarily answers to something which stands to it as its opposite, and also whether leisure is a good such that the more of it the better. I think if in heaven there are 'perpetual Sabbaths' it would be a misnomer to call this state of things 'perpetual leisure', unless perhaps it necessarily incorporated an occasional contrastive look back to weekday life in this world. Certainly in this world one can have too much leisure, and be at leisure though one would have preferred not to be. And where a reasonable person cannot find it welcome, it answers to no need, and so can hardly be considered a good. On the other hand, one might maintain that we understand leisure as something essentially good and desirable, so that undesirable leisure – for example, enforced leisure – does not really deserve the name, just as a joke that's not funny is not a joke, and a friend one would be better off without is not a real friend.

I shall assume that leisure is something desirable, being a kind of freedom: freedom to *do what one feels like*. The word itself says this, coming as it does via French from the Latin '*licere*', to be permitted. When some philosophers talk in a very general and abstract way about desires and pro-attitudes they seem to overlook the huge difference between *doing something because one must,* and *doing something because one feels like it.* These philosophers are usually expounding a theory of action and motivation in which the fundamental contrast is between on the one hand beliefs, which can be true or false, and on the other hand every kind of directedness towards action, from wayward impulses to deep laid plans. Kantians and others recognise the difference I am talking about when they speak of the clash between duty and inclination, or between reason and impulse – although they would be mistaken if their way of making the contrast commits them to holding that impulse and undeliberated inclination cannot be expressions of reason.

Without question, doing something because one must involves subordination of a kind – perhaps of several kinds. But it is a mistake to think, as the classic contrasts between duty and inclination, between reason and impulse, might possibly encourage one to do, that doing something because one must, as distinct from because one feels like it, necessarily involves going against some impulse present at the time. One can quite wholeheartedly do something because one must; yet even then it feels, and is, quite different from doing something simply because one feels like it. The difference is what I shall now be talking about. The distinctions and contrasts I shall draw will be analytical in nature. That is to say, very many, perhaps most, concrete human activities cannot be cleanly placed just on one side or the other. Does one prepare or listen to a lecture of philosophy because one must or because one feels like it?

Let us first consider what it is to do a thing because one must. Clearly, it is consistent with the action's being voluntary and in some sense chosen. The person is not being physically forced, or playing out instructions absorbed under hypnosis, or literally incapable of holding back. If someone goes off to work because he must in the sense we are considering, he can still choose not to complete the journey if confronted with some very good unexpected reason not to. This is by contrast with an addict who enters a pub or gambling place literally because he has to: he cannot be deflected by any intervention short of physical disablement. The necessity involved in doing something because one must is conditioned on the agent's prior objectives, commitments and needs. I am not here going to discuss the reasons or justification there might be for thinking of an action as something one must do. I am only concerned with what it is and what it is like to act in this mode. As I have said, it certainly need not involve going against some contrary inclination. Many of the things we must do, we do quite automatically, without at the time being stirred by any occurrent feeling, and without dwelling on what would be involved in not acting. However, sometimes we do act from or partly from an occurrent feeling, and I believe that on this it is possible to generalise and say that over a large range of typical cases the feeling is a negative one of aversion to, fear of, or anxiety about acting or facing the consequences of acting otherwise. And even when one actually experiences no feeling, still when explaining one's action one will say 'I was averse to taking such and such a risk', 'I was afraid of losing such and such', 'I was averse to telling a lie [or: to telling that lie]'. Even when the action is the doing of something positive, rather than avoidance of something – for instance, when it is an act of charity – to see it as something one must do is to see not doing it as wrong or as having unacceptable consequences. My point, then, is that to do something because one must is to do it because otherwise one does or incurs an evil of some kind. This is by contrast with doing something because one feels like it, where the action itself is appealing because of its own nature.

What one must do imposes itself because of the gravity of the alternative: gravity that reflects the depth of our commitment to the projects and principles for the sake of which what must be done must be done. Along with the metaphors of gravity and weight go the metaphors of constraint and shaping. What one must do is shaped by whatever wider requirement it is that makes the action something one must do. Not only must I do *at least* what is required, but very often I manage much better if I do *only* that: I manage better if I act efficiently. I probably ought not to take any interest in the nitty-gritty or texture of the doing of the action itself, except so far as this is necessary to get it done in accordance with the requirement. Thus often when we do what must be done, what we do is whittled, honed, and simplified so that it is all and only what it needs to be, in order to fit into the wider practical framework.

Up to now, the shaping forces I have had in mind are the agent's own commitments and principles. But we also have to bring in the conditions of action. Most of our action is in response to external conditions, and a great many of these conditions one would not have chosen. This is not to say that action under and in response to such conditions is necessarily uncomfortable. Of course it is not. Often one has adjusted, and the adjustment is often desirable and not at all degrading. And clearly action under and in response to conditions one has not and would not have chosen is not on that account to be deemed not free. Of course we can be and normally are autonomous when we act under such conditions. Since human beings most of the time are acting under such conditions, it had better be the case that this does not in itself remove their autonomy – or human autonomy would be in very short supply. But even so, our thoughts about freedom also include the idea of acting entirely from oneself, and in a way this ideal cannot but seem more desirable than acting under adjustment to external conditions. One might put this by saying that a being who was completely unconstrained by external conditions would never choose to take on for its own sake such a constrained form of existence. Such a choice of constraints on the part of an initially unconstrained being would only make sense if it were made for the sake of some kind of ulterior benefit which could not be had without the constraints. This is not to say that we ourselves, as we are here and now, ought to desire or yearn to be absolutely free spirits unconstrained by external conditions; nor that we ought to regret that any benefits attached to being under those conditions cannot be had by us independently. Some ancient philosophers – Plato and Plotinus come to mind – may think us defective for not being filled with such yearnings; if so, this is because they believe that we are in some sense meant to be such absolutely free spirits – perhaps they believe that once we were, but fell from that blessed state through some terrible error or sin which even now keeps us on the whole slavishly satisfied with being the more limited creatures we have turned into. But we can resist this line of thought by observing that even if we cannot help sometimes feeling that *A* is a better or – to use a word not often heard in contemporary philosophy – a nobler state than *B*, we may do so without necessarily holding that *A* is better *for us* than *B*. Maybe *we* are beings who essentially flourish only within an external limiting environment, so that if *we* were to survive after taking leave of all such environments we should be utterly deprived and frustrated: unable to adjust to having nothing to adjust to, like the shade of Achilles in the underworld or the poor little soul in the poem attributed to the Emperor Hadrian, destined for an existence in which there will be no battles, no statecraft, and no fun. But even if all this is true about us, it is also true that we do have a sort of dream of perfect freedom, a dream which deeply charms us even when we are not the slightest bit inclined to embrace the kind of religious or metaphysical story which has to be told by anyone wishing seriously to claim that the dream shows *us* in our ideal state. Perhaps we have the dream of perfect freedom because, as well as being practical rational animals, we are also fundamentally leisure-needing animals. As well as choice there is choice squared. As was said before, the actions we do because we must are chosen by us. But the actions we revel in are chosen by us *for occasions or within frameworks chosen by us.* And these self-chosen occasions and frameworks are designed not to deliver up their contents as required by some wider controlling scheme, but to protect and encourage the specific actions and activities which unfold within them. This superior order of chosen-ness, chosen-ness taken to a power of more than one, is characteristic of what we do in leisure.

But although *what we must do* may be less chosen in the way I have just tried to explain, what we must do has priority. We can negotiate through postponement, converting it into *what we must do by some future deadline.* But as the deadline looms, the action becomes *what I must do now.* In a straightforward clash with something I would do not because I must but because I feel like it, what I must necessarily wins the rational preference. In this way, for disciplined agents, doing something because one feels like it gets crowded out of a busy life. That is to say, such choices get crowded out if forced into direct competition with practical necessities. Thus they need to be protected from any such contest. Special time should be set aside for them. Such options *only then* get to compete: they are chosen always within or from the point of view of their own proper time and they compete, of course, only with each other.

In a very clear sense, then, the actions or activities of leisure are or should be treated as incommensurable with the intrinsically far more powerful tribe of practical necessities. This is not to say that the former are immeasurably to be preferred, in the sense of being assigned practical priority. That would be even more absurd than giving to practical necessities unrestricted practical priority. After all, practical necessities sometimes do have to be granted priority across the board; sometimes, through no one's fault or failing, there is no time for leisure. Or to put the point in an overtly modal fashion: sometimes it is a practical necessity that our waking time be completely occupied by practical necessities. But when it is practically possible that our waking time not be completely occupied by practical necessities, our well-being demands that we treat leisure as a practical necessity. That is: for a sensible person the practical possibility of leisure entails its practical necessity.

Here, then, is an important difference between leisure itself and the actions or activities which go on in it. For the whole point so far is that these actions and activities are *not* necessary: they are not what one does or maintains because one must. Let us now explore the positive effect of their segregation from the necessary. The main point is that choice under segregation is allowed to be governed by aspects that are hardly permitted to obtrude when we are doing what we must. We may now be swayed and absorbed by the immediate specificity of what we are doing; by what doing it physically, sensually, or intellectually feels like; by the intrinsic and intimate texture of the action or activity; and by these aspects of its instruments, its materials, any objects it refers to, and its modes of presenting such objects. Thus our interest is guided by elements we were meant to relegate to the cognitive margins when implementing some principle or purpose beyond the action. We are free to concentrate ourselves into just being here-and-now doers of what we are doing; and free also to be caught by and to explore unexpected ways in which our activity or what we are active about resembles and relates to quite other things: references sternly ignored by the disciplined practical focus.

I shall continue to contrast doing what one must do with doing what one feels like doing, but it should be pointed out that the word 'do' or 'doing' has different resonances (if not meanings) in the two phrases. When I do a thing because I must, I am concerned to get it done, and so while I am doing it I am concerned to get on with it, i.e. get closer to the point where it has been satisfactorily done. By contrast, if I am doing something because I feel like doing it – and here let me emphasise 'feel like *doing* it' – I logically cannot be bent on getting it done, and on just getting on with it. I am not carrying out an action so much as engaging in an activity.

A moment ago I was speaking of how differently our attention is disposed when doing what we must and when doing what we feel like. I now want to look at another epistemic or cognitive difference, and at some differences in modes of value and evaluation. As we go along it will turn out that 'doing what one feels like' is, as many of you may have suspected from the start, a bit of a misnomer: the phrase has been a simplification to get the discussion going. For the category of doing what one feels like can involve necessity in ways of its own. And when we examine the form of this necessity, the idea of what counts as 'one', as the self, comes under pressure.

Now a crucial point in much of what follows is that, typically, what I must do is apparent to me before I carry it out, and the principle or project which renders it necessary is also clear in advance. This is not to say that I necessarily gave thought to these things before acting, or that I had them consciously in mind, or that I deliberated about them. The point is no more than this: it is not in and through the action itself that I find out what I must do, and why. So if you ask me what I am going to do and why, I can tell you. By the same token, if I try but fail, or am prevented from acting, I can tell you what I was trying for, or what I would have done if not prevented. When, however, we do deliberate because we don't already know straight off what is the right thing to do in a given situation (whether it's a question of moral rightness or some other kind, need not detain us), the constraints imposed by projects and principles figure in our actual temporally prior calculations. But where there are no actual temporally prior calculations, there is still a fact that makes it true that I knew beforehand what I must do: this is the fact that I could have explained beforehand what it was, and no doubt would have if someone had asked me, whether the someone was somebody else or myself.

Obviously what I am leading up to is the observation that leisure characteristically offers safe haven to activities where only through doing do we find out what is the right move to make, and therefore only by actually making it do we see how it fits into its context, and thereby see that all along the context was calling for, demanding, or necessitating that move. (It might be a move just in one's head, or it might be the arranging of something next to something else, whether sounds or shapes or colours.) All this happens by aesthetic intuition or something analogous to aesthetic intuition. The fact that seeing the rightness of the move essentially depends on actually making it, means that the making of the move was not governed by a previously articulable intention to make it. Thus if before the last moment the person had been distracted, he or she might well never have known what the move would have been that didn't get executed. So what did govern it if not the maker's prior intention? For plainly the move was governed and shaped by something, perhaps by the context itself to which it answers so well. However, now we may be in a territory where we cannot say firmly what was generated before what. Perhaps what I have been calling the context was already publicly there and laid down before the particular agent or practitioner involved ever entered the scene. But there are cases where the right move is right because it beautifully fits a context itself authored by that self-same practitioner. It is the right move within some evolving poem or piece of music or something of that sort. And now there may well be no way of telling whether the move is made because it is right for its pre-existing context, or the context was generated because it would be right for the move, or both context and move were generated by a single process that designed them for each other from the very beginning.

It is rather natural, in discussing the phenomenon I am talking about, to ascribe what is going on to a process 'within' the creative person, rather than to the person him- or herself in the straightforward way we ascribe to people the making and keeping of promises, the formation and carrying out of plans. It is as if the individual, the self, is not sufficiently in charge of what happens for it to be ascribed to him or her. And yet something is very much in charge of what happens, since the development or what comes out of it is far from random. Here the idea of inspiration gets its purchase: an idea which can be indulged in more and less seriously. It is worth noting that our discussion so far suggests that if the idea of inspiration does take hold, it does so because we are assuming that *human selves are essentially practical agents*: loci of decision; beings who choose to do this rather than that because of what is apparent about the options in advance; beings who plan beforehand, and judge later by reference to prior requirements whether the action went well or was successful; beings who have to know what they propose, and why, because actually deciding to do it often crucially depends on obtaining, through advance presentations, the prior advice or approval of others, or on their own judgment that they could justify the action to others if challenged. But equally our discussion so far might be taken to show that *human selves are essentially much more than practical*. It is, of course, inevitable that the practical, moral, and social side comes foremost to our attention. To survive, human beings have to deal with practical necessities first, and so the corresponding aspect of the self must always have first claim on their consideration.

I have just been dwelling on the epistemic or cognitive difference between knowing the right move beforehand and discovering it only through enactment. I now turn to a set of qualities which in universities are particularly esteemed in connection with knowledge and cognition, but which have their application in many parts of human life. These are such qualities as precision, exactness, rigour, and in general perfection. It is simply a fact that a huge number of the subject matters, materials and human capacities with which and in respect of which we operate in doing what we must do, are capable of being developed to a depth and reach and degree of refinement which go way beyond whatever is needed for practical purposes and which can actually interfere with timely and efficient practical execution. It is also a fact that human beings want to respond to these possibilities: where there is freedom for alternatives, human beings are simply not satisfied with the rough and readiness of the practical. Think of what human food would be like, and the conditions for consuming it, if basic biological requirements were the sole determinants of what we ate and how. Think of practical knowledge, its inherent patchiness, its superficiality, its reliance on unstated assumptions, its elements of guesswork, its readiness to plump for one side or other of a question because there is no time to wait for adequate reasons to appear, and one is held responsible for what one lets happen as well as for what one enacts. Going with the flow of an activity or a subject matter itself, letting it emerge and ramify in its own patterns, letting it suggest its own standards of excellence and its own agenda of questions and challenges: this is what leisure lets us do, thereby unleashing the giant force of human perfectionism, and delivering countless improvements to the quality of life which then take their place as recognised parts of human welfare, and generate about themselves new industries and practical concerns.

Can conclusions be drawn about what sorts of activities are suitable for leisure? I do not think the philosopher should try to go much beyond obvious generalisations, such as that leisure-activities should not be destructive of the conditions for obtaining and preserving the practical necessities, including leisure itself. One can also say that it is a misuse of leisure to fill it with ordinary work when there is no practical necessity to do so. This is not to imply that laws or sanctions should be passed against workaholics, but habitual workaholic behaviour shows a sad failure to value one kind – perhaps the most exquisite even if not the most vital kind – of freedom. Again speaking generally one can say that the leisure-activities encouraged by a society ought to include, and advertise as central, ones that are not trivial pastimes but challenge and develop people rather than just entertain them. The reason for this is not just that our self-realisation is a good, nor just this plus the fact that the more challenging activities tend to generate all sorts of useful and pleasant inventions and so forth, which raise the quality of life for everyone. The reason, I believe, includes the desirability of a sort of evaluative balance between, on the one hand, the enormous effort of toil and practical intelligence expended, going back generations, in order to produce and safeguard the necessities of life, leisure itself among them, and, on the other hand, the excellence of what is done by those who are (when they are) free from the yoke of necessity. This thought is, and must remain, rough. The thought is that unless some of the things principally done or aimed for in the haven of leisure are or have to do with what is beautiful or sublime or deeply interesting or eye-openingly adventurous, or unless in some way they represent extraordinary human or philanthropic achievement, society is somehow failing properly to recognise the worth of all that those other poor devils have done which has helped to make leisure possible.

If we ask further what leisure activities should be like, the ever-present contrast with doing what one must can guide us to a broad twofold distinction. There will be activities that *turn their backs on* the everyday practical world: such as the study of the stars, pure mathematics, the abstract branches of philosophy and science, certain kinds of art, certain kinds of music, the creation and exploration of exotic fantasies. Then there will be activities that *target* – take as their subject matter, comment on, re-enact, celebrate, or otherwise thematise – aspects of the practical world, whether in literature, historiography, dance, drama, sport or countless other activities.

I have not tried to locate religious activities in this classification, and I do not think I can get far by trying to generalise about their possible connections with leisure. Where, as presumably happens in all religions, time is set aside for ritual or worship, this sacred time is not strictly speaking leisure, since it would be false, not just an over-simplification, to call it time for doing what one feels like ('*licere*', the root of 'leisure', again). Even so, it is impossible to leave this subject without touching on the rich and complicated topic of the Sabbath, since this very ancient idea of a divinely commanded weekly day of rest, embedded as it was in a set of ethical expectations which Christianity later made universal, has been the historical seed from which eventually sprang Article 24 of the Universal Declaration of Human Rights. The Sabbath prescribed in the Decalogue is a not a day of leisure – that idea was not in play, I believe. As the Hebrew word indicates, the Sabbath is a day of rest from work. But this is not the rest of a resting weary animal (even though Sabbath rest is ordained for domestic beasts as well as their owners). For the Israelites were *commanded* to rest as a way of sanctifying the day in question, and in this manner to celebrate their covenant with God. To rest because you are divinely commanded to, rather than just because you physically need to or feel like it, makes this a *sui generis* form of rest. The commandment, I suppose, expresses the presumption that left to ourselves we shall tend to work and make each other work on and on, whether out of greed or anxiety or because we can easily tend to become physical and spiritual drudges without aspirations. The commanded rest resembles leisure in that both are forms of freedom from the 'tyranny of the practical'. But whereas leisure as I have discussed it is freedom for human self-realisation, in itself a non-religious idea, the Sabbath rest is a prophylactic against secularisation of the self. On the other hand, it is not just a matter of putting the everyday self on hold for one day a week on pain of otherwise breaking a sacred commandment. Things are more positive than that. For the Jewish people, the Sabbath has always been an occasion of joy and self-celebration; thus, as Heine wrote, the evening when the work-week ends and the Sabbath begins is when every Jewish man becomes a prince.

It would be a pity to move on without a glance at the Biblical reason for the original identification of the Sabbath with the seventh day, and at some of the theological questions raised thereby. The reason is: God created the world in six days, and on the seventh he rested from his completed work of creation; God blessed and sanctified the seventh because it was the day of his own rest. (Before turning to theology, we can parenthetically seize why, given this account of the origin of the Sabbath, mapping the idea of leisure on to that of the Sabbath is not a straightforward operation. The Israelites were commanded to rest from work on the seventh day because on that day God had rested from his work of creation. If, however, human leisure is, as the discussion so far has shown, time for human creative activity, then if the Sabbath were identified as a time of leisure, it would seem to follow that humans best keep the Sabbath by somehow, on that day, imitating God in his moments of creative work rather than in his moment of rest and disengagement from creation; in other words, by imitating the opposite of the state of rest which God entered on the original seventh day.)

The author of the book of Genesis seems not to have worried that once the world was created complete in all its parts, it might still need to be upheld in existence by God lest it take the plunge into non-being. On the contrary, the God of Genesis is shown unproblematically resting after his work. But by the time of Augustine, if not earlier, professional philosophers and Bible exegetes had started their probing. Surely God had no need of rest to relieve weariness from work, since God's work is necessarily effortless. Surely the universe cannot have been let go by God in the way a human maker lets go of his or her finished product. For even once created, the universe cannot exist on its own. It continues to exist not merely at God's good pleasure, but in the closest possible dependence on God's power, which only by constant re-creative exercise 'makes every creature abide'.[2] As Descartes was to argue more than twelve centuries later, no less divine power is needed to conserve the world from instant to instant than was needed to create it new. Any other view would imply that the world has, of itself, the power, once created, to continue in existence independently of God, or at least the power to make a contribution independent of God's to its own continued existence. Either of these possibilities renders it less likely that God was needed for the world to exist at all in the first place, or less likely that, as the Scottish version of Psalm 100 unforgettably puts it, 'without our aid thou didst us make'.

---

[2] Augustine, *The Literal Meaning of Genesis*, iv. ch. 12.

So Augustine in his 12-book commentary on Genesis makes it clear that God's rest on the seventh day cannot mean that God ceased to maintain the world in being. What then was the difference between the six days of creation, and the day which followed, given that in both these epochs God is equally making it the case that the world exists? Well, according to Augustine it is the difference between making something new according to a finite set of stages corresponding to the six days of creation, and maintaining the completed thing in being; these are two aspects of the world's dependence on God. But Augustine still must explain why the seventh day, when God still actively kept the world in being, is singled out as the day on which 'God rested'. Augustine's response to this problem in the 12-book commentary seems to develop as he goes along, but his final view there is that God's rest from creating the world signifies that God has no need of creatures. That is to say: not only does God not need to make creatures in order to use them for some purpose which God could not accomplish without them, but God does not even need to create out of simple creativity. God does not need creatures in the way we might say Beethoven needed his symphonies: Beethoven could not be himself and complete without creating works of music. Hence even though Beethoven obviously did not need his own works of music as a craftsman needs tools and materials, i.e. in order to be able to compose them in the first place, still Beethoven needed to create those works, and therefore it was needful for him that the works should come to be. This, as I understand it, is what Augustine denies concerning God and the world. God has, and would have had, a completely fulfilled life without creatures and without engaging in the creation of them. (This very strong claim of divine transcendence could never have been guessed from a simple reading of Genesis, where the story of God, like the story of the world, begins with God's creation of the world.) Thus God's rest on the seventh day signifies the divine self-sufficiency: a self-sufficiency which perhaps had to be specially declared *after* the work of creation, thus leaving us in no doubt that God was also truly self-sufficient beforehand. And the fact that this one day in the seven was the one God wished to sanctify shows, according to Augustine, that God in self-sufficient mode is more sublime than God in mode of creator.[3]

Turning away from the Sabbath, and its consequent theology, and back to our topic of leisure and leisure activities, we may by contrast note more

---

[3] Ibid., iv. chs. 14–16.

keenly some of the ancient pagan influences which have shaped this humanistic concept. On the potentially vast subject of leisure in classical antiquity I must be brief, for soon I shall reach the limits of my time, and soon (though I hope not sooner) the limits of my knowledge. Pagan humanism about leisure is often shot through with religiosity, only of course not that of the Bible. The slants we get tend to be those of poets and philosophers: that is, tribes which need leisure in order to engage in their characteristic activities, and which can be expected to sing or meditate some of the time about these very activities themselves and the leisure enshrining them. They are sometimes defensive and self-promoting in ways that point up the fact that their leisure does *not* command society's automatic respect – a problem which could not arise in connection with Sabbaths ordained by a god who is God of the whole people. Many of Plato's and Aristotle's educated contemporaries thought abstract theoretical studies a pretty good waste of time by comparison with a career as a politician or a general. Plato superbly responded that under just one condition would the best minds be spending time wrongly if they spent it in pure mathematics and philosophy: this was the highly unlikely situation in which the community is truly ready and willing to accept the rule of philosophers. Aristotle on his side insisted on the superior godliness of theoretical philosophy, his reason being that the gods in their self-sufficiency must be conceived as beyond practice and politics, living an eternal life of the mind in an eternal bubble of leisure.

Again, just as there have been philosophers who saw earlier thought as half blindly groping or zigzagging towards consummation in their own philosophy, so poets and perhaps sometimes philosophers have seen leisure and the material superfluity which underwrites it as somehow naturally ordained for support of their own activities. What are princely courts and princely courtliness *for* if not celebration of life in poetry when the practical day is done, or its analysis in philosophy? Great deeds by gods or men lack the full complement of achievement so long as they lack their glorification in song. In similar fashion, philosophers have maintained that the universe ultimately exists in order to become cognisant of itself through them. Occasionally one can almost hear old poets and historians suggesting that the great events might as well never have happened at all if no one comes after to tell of them and hear tell. This, we may think, is pushing it. And is it tactful for poets to send patrons the message: your bounty exists just so that we may make it and you meaningful through poetry? Or for a philosopher in similar position to imply: your bounty exists just so that I through my philosophy may show what a minute speck you are *sub specie aeternitatis*? But often enough, I believe, and fortunately for posterity, these messages must have been *exactly* what the patrons already in a sense accepted or were ready to be persuaded of, even if such an attitude in them existed side by side with proud eagerness to demonstrate to the circle of their peers their involvement, albeit vicarious, in what their poet or philosopher (or their composer or artist) was doing. These patrons, often enough, believed in the superiority of that work because the practitioners themselves ardently believed in it and made their belief show up true again and again by producing artefacts and mentifacts of exquisite, inspired, quality. This was the quintessential fruit of leisure; it came into being not because it matched a requirement, but because it was a new thing to love: which seems a good note on which to end an inaugural talk.

References

Alexander of Aphrodisias, 1983. *Alexander of Aphrodisias on Fate*, translation and commentary by R. W. Sharples, London.

Aristotle, 1984. *Complete Works, The Revised Oxford Translation*, ed. J. Barnes, Princeton.

Audi, R., ed., 1999. *The Cambridge Dictionary of Philosophy*, 2nd edition, Cambridge.

Augustine, 1982. *The Literal Meaning of Genesis*, translated and annotated by John Hammond Taylor, SJ, New York/Ramsey, N. J.

Ayer, A. J., 1956. *The Problem of Knowledge*, London.

Belnap, N., Perloff, M. and Xu, M., 2001. *Facing the Future*, Oxford.

Black, M., 1956. 'Why Cannot an Effect Precede Its Cause?', *Analysis* 16, 49–58.

Bobzien, S., 1998. *Determinism and Freedom in Stoic Philosophy*, Oxford.

Broad, C. D., 1938. *An Examination of McTaggart's Philosophy*, Cambridge.

Broadie, S., 1991. *Ethics with Aristotle*, Oxford.

Broadie, S. and Rowe, C., 2002. *Aristotle, Nicomachean Ethics, translation, introduction, and commentary*, Oxford.

Chisholm, R. M. and Taylor, R., 1960. 'Making Things to Have Happened', *Analysis* 20, 73–8.

Coope, U., 2005. *Time for Aristotle*: Physics *IV. 10–14*, Oxford.

Cooper, J. M., 2004. *Knowledge, Nature, and the Good*, Princeton.

Descartes, R., 1985. *The philosophical writings of Descartes*, translated by J. Cottingham, R. Stoothoff and D. Murdoch, Cambridge.

Dray, W., 1960. 'Taylor and Chisholm on Making Things to Have Happened', *Analysis* 20, 79–82.

Dummett, M. A. E., 1954. 'Can an Effect Precede Its Cause?', *Proceedings of the Aristotelian Society Supplement* 28, 27–44.

1964. 'Bringing About the Past', *Philosophical Review* 73, 338–59 (reprinted in Le Poidevin and MacBeath, 1993, 117–33).

Fischer, J. M., 2002. 'Frankfurt-style Examples, Responsibility and Semi-Compatibilism', in *Free Will*, ed. R. Kane, Oxford, 95–110.

Flew, A., 1954. 'Can an Effect Precede Its Cause?', *Proceedings of the Aristotelian Society Supplement* 28, 45–62.

1956. 'Effects Before Their Causes? Addenda and Corrigenda', *Analysis* 16, 104–10.

1957. 'Causal Disorder Again', *Analysis* 17, 81–6.

Foot, P., 2001. *Natural Goodness*, Oxford.

Frankena, W., 1963. *Ethics*, 2nd edition, Englewood Cliffs.

Frankfurt, H., 1969. 'Alternate Possibilities and Moral Responsibility', *Journal of Philosophy* 66, 829–39.

Frede, D., 2006. 'Pleasure and Pain in Aristotle's Ethics', in *The Blackwell's Guide to Aristotle's* Nicomachean Ethics, ed. R. Kraut, Oxford, 255–75.

Gale, R. M., 1965. 'Why a Cause Cannot Be Later than Its Effect', *Review of Metaphysics* 19, 209–34.

1968. *The Language of Time*, London.

Gorovitz, S., 1964. 'Leaving the Past Alone', *Philosophical Review* 73, 360–71.

Gotthelf, A., 1976. 'Aristotle's Conception of Final Causality', *Review of Metaphysics* 30, 226–54.

Hippocrates, 1931. *Hippocrates, with English translation by W. H. S. Jones*, London/New York.

Hume, D., 1955. *A Treatise of Human Nature*, ed. L. A. Selby-Bigge, Oxford.

Jackson, F., ed., 1991. *Conditionals*, Oxford.

Kant, I., 1996. *Immanuel Kant, Practical Philosophy*, translated by Mary J. Gregor, Cambridge.

Kenny, A., 1963. *Action, Emotion and Will*, London.

Kraut, R., 1989. *Aristotle on the Human Good*, Princeton.

Lawrence, G., 1997. 'Nonaggregatability, Inclusiveness, and the Theory of Focal Value: *Nicomachean Ethics* 1.7. 1097b16–20', *Phronesis* 42, 32–76.

2006. 'Human Good and Human Function', in *The Blackwell Guide to Aristotle's* Nicomachean Ethics, ed. R. Kraut, Oxford, 37–75.

Le Poidevin, R. and MacBeath, M., eds., 1993. *The Philosophy of Time*, Oxford.

Lewis, D., 1986. 'Counterfactual Dependence and Time's Arrow', *Philosophical Papers* vol. II, Oxford, 32–66; reprinted in Jackson, 1991.

Long, A. A. and Sedley, D. N., 1987. *The Hellenistic Philosophers*, Cambridge.

Mackie, J. L., 1966. 'The Direction of Causation', *Philosophical Review* 75, 441–56.

1974. *The Cement of the Universe*, Oxford.

1977. *Ethics: Inventing Right and Wrong*, Harmondsworth.

McTaggart, J. M. E., 1908. 'The Unreality of Time', *Mind* 17 n.s., 457–74.

1927. *The Nature of Existence*, Cambridge.

Mill, J. S., 1968. *Utilitarianism* etc., Everyman's Library, London/New York.

Moore, G. E., 1903. *Principia Ethica*, Cambridge.

1912. *Ethics*, London.

Pears, D. F., 1950–1. 'Time, Truth, and Inference', *Proceedings of the Aristotelian Society* 51, 1–24.

1957. 'The Priority of Causes', *Analysis* 17, 54–63.

Pieper, J., 1998. *Leisure the Basis of Culture*, translated by Gerald Malsbary, with an introduction by Roger Scruton, South Bend.

Plato, 1997. *Complete Works*, ed. J. M. Cooper, Indianapolis.

Prichard, H. A., 1949. *Moral Obligation*, Oxford.

Putnam, H., 1990. *Realism with a Human Face*, Cambridge, Mass.

Schofield, M. and Nussbaum, M., eds., 1982. *Language and Logos*, Cambridge.

Scriven, M., 1957. 'Randomness and the Causal Order', *Analysis* 17, 5–9.

Solmsen, F., 1968. 'Leisure and Play in Aristotle's Ideal State', *Rheinisches Museum für Philologie* CVII, 1964, 193–220, reprinted in vol. II of Solmsen, *Kleine Schriften*, Hildesheim.

Sorabji, R., 1983. *Time, Creation and the Continuum*, Ithaca.

Swinburne, R., 1968. *Space and Time*, London.

Thalberg, I., 1972. *Enigmas of Agency*, London.

Thucydides, 1919. *History of the Peloponnesian War*, translated by C. Foster Smith, London/New York.

Waterlow [Broadie], S., 1982, 1988. *Nature, Change, and Agency in Aristotle's Physics, a Philosophical Study*, Oxford.

Williams, B. A. O., 1985. *Ethics and the Limits of Philosophy*, Cambridge, Mass.

Wright, G. H. von, 1971. *Explanation and Understanding*, London.

Index of names

Achilles, 188
Alexander of Aphrodisias, 35–6
'Aristotelian' determinism, 38, 46, 48–9
Aristotle, 42, 159, 197
  on decision-making, 123–6, 130–2, 172–4
  and ethical epistemology, 116–23
  on *eudaimonia* (happiness, flourishing)
    human and divine, 113–15, 167–8, 178–9
  and 'eudaemonism', 115–16
  on the good person as 'measuring rod', 120–1,
    164, 175–6
  on the highest good, 124–5, 139, 141,
    149, 157, 166, 172ff.
  on the highest good as 'good-maker', 124–5,
    144–5, 174–7, 182–3
  and the Lazy Argument, 36
  on leisure, 132–4, 165, 181–2
  on moral development, 169
  on the now, 72, 78–84
  on perfect fulfilment, 170–1
  on place, 79–80, 81
  and the practical view-point, 171–2
  on *sophia* as a virtue, 182
  on the soul, 101, 109, 110
  and system in ethics, 127–9
  and teleology, 46–8, 85–100
    (= ch. 6 passim)
  on virtuous activity and happiness/
    the highest good, 115–16, 164,
    177–81, 182
Augustine, 195, 196
Ayer, A. J., 18

Beethoven, L. von, 196
Belnap, N., Perloff, M. and Xu, M., 57
Black, M., 18
Bobzien, S., 33
Broad, C. D., 77
Broadie, S., 181
Butler, J., 140

Callicles, 123
Catullus, 145
Chisholm, R. M. and Taylor, R., 18
Christianity, 194
Chrysippus, 33, 34–5, 36; *see also* Stoics, and
  determinism
Cicero, 33–4
Coope, U., 81
Cooper, J. M., 88–90, 91

Democritus, 101
Descartes, R., 111–12, 195
  as dualist, 76, 101–6
Devereux, D. T., 116
Dray, W., 18
Dummett, M. A. E., 18

Empedocles, 143
Eudoxus, 142–4

Flew, A., 18
Foot, P., 163
Frankena, W., 140
Frankfurt, H., 50
Frede, D., 132

Gale, R. M., 18
Gassendi, P., 101
Genesis, book of, 170, 195, 196
Glaucon and Adimantus, 120
God, 55, 64, 128, 153–4, 194, 197
  in theology of the 'seventh day', 195–6
Gorovitz, S., 18
Gotthelf, A., 88
Gundersen, L., 54

Hadrian, 188
Heine, H., 194
Hippocratic writings, 108
Hume, D., 9, 41